IAN MACLEAY has been a Chelsea fan ever since he saw them play one Christmas morning in the late 50s and Jimmy Greaves scored four times. He went on to start the widely respected cult fanzine *Cockney Rebel* and has co-authored two acclaimed books with the club's former chairman Brian Mears: *Chelsea: A Hundred Year History* and Chelsea: *Football Under the Blue Flag*. He also wrote *The Working Man's Ballet* with Chelsea legend Alan Hudson, which is now regarded as a classic of the genre. He lives in Surrey.

Joe Cole

HE'S HERE, HE'S THERE,
HE'S EVERY !@#$ING WHERE

IAN MACLEAY
FOREWORD BY TERRY VENABLES

JOHN BLAKE

Dedicated to the memory of Carol Milne,
a dear friend and a tremendous fighter.

Published by John Blake Publishing Ltd,
3 Bramber Court, 2 Bramber Road,
London W14 9PB, England

www.johnblakepublishing.co.uk

First published in paperback in 2009

ISBN 978 1 84454 732 6

British Library Cataloguing-in-Publication Data:

A catalogue record for this book is available from the British Library.

Design by www.envydesign.co.uk

Printed in Great Britain by CPI Bookmarque, Croydon CRO 4TD

1 3 5 7 9 10 8 6 4 2

Photographs courtesy of Clevamedia, Empics, Action Images,
Rex Features, and Getty Images.

Papers used by John Blake Publishing are natural, recyclable products
made from wood grown in sustainable forests. The manufacturing processes
conform to the environmental regulations of the country of origin.

Every attempt has been made to contact the relevant copyright-holders,
but some were unobtainable. We would be grateful if the appropriate people
could contact us.

Contents

Acknowledgements

Special thanks to Terry Venables for the foreword, and the help and encouragement he has extended to me over the years. Greatness makes great demands. To John Blake for his belief in the project and continuing determination to innovate. To Stuart Robertson who reminded me of the principles of sports writing. To my own little team: Patrick Hagglund for his exhaustive internet research and Ravi Mistry for his IT expertise. Also thanks to my lawyer and chum Peter Harris. Greg Kimberley was of wonderful assistance in researching Joe's career in Claret and Blue. The Layden brothers, Paul and Mark, for their help with Chelsea matters. To loyal friends and supporters Steven Hill and Dave Ayling, who helped me see Joe strut his stuff so many times. Special mention also to Brian Mears and Mark Bosnich.

Lastly, to my family for their support. My wife Marie, daughter Jacalyn, Aidrian and brother Ken; I couldn't have done it without them.

Foreword

When Joe Cole smashed in his excellent goal against Sweden in the World Cup Group B game it was for many fans the high spot of the tournament – a moment when an English player could rightfully take his place on the podium with a flash of inspiration on a par with anything a Henry or Zidane could conjure.

For me it was another rung of the ladder that Joe has climbed in his long ascent to the very top of the game he so desperately loves.

I have followed the career of Joe since he was a youngster, earning the kind of press few players could survive – let alone a teenager. But Joe Cole is an example to any youngster because he adapted to the inhuman amount of pressure and expectation heaped on his young shoulders. Joe was portrayed by the media as the artful dodger, hailed as one of the most technically gifted players London ever produced.

So few talents grow in the hothouse of fame but the Joe Cole of 2006 is now the most seasoned of professionals, with back-to-back Premiership medals in his collection. To arrive at that point Joe has taken on the necessity of combining into his play the athleticism and hard work needed for the modern game. His great thirst for improvement made him part of the team ethic demanded at the top of his profession.

Joe embodies many of the diverse elements of Chelsea Football Club both old and new; the style, swagger and efficiency of the Abramovich era combined with the generosity of spirit, virility and magnetism from the fabulous Cup-winning '70s side.

I was lucky enough to wear the number 10 shirt in the Chelsea blue of another glamorous era. Since then it has been worn with distinction by such luminous talents as Bobby Tambling, Alan Hudson and Gianfranco Zola. Jimmy Greaves still casts a giant shadow over any Chelsea forward. The present incumbent is a worthy successor to the heritage of the number and encompasses all the best qualities of the sport in the 21st century.

Joe Cole is now a major figure in the Premiership, and his story best mirrors the definitive impact that the Abramovich billions have had on the English game and is about to have on the European and World competitions.

Terry Venables
Summer 2006

Introduction

O N FRIDAY, 20 January 2006, the London *Evening Standard*'s headline introduced a story of a northern bottle-nosed whale that had swum up the Thames and past the Houses of Parliament. Other headlines concerned the police watchdog's report on the shooting of the 27-year-old Brazilian Jean Charles de Menezes at Stockwell Tube station the previous July. There was also a report about the comeback of Michael Barrymore in the *Celebrity Big Brother* TV show.

In the 'News in Brief' column, there was an item featuring Chelsea footballer Joe Cole. 'Cole has received a string of death threats. The messages were allegedly sent to the midfielder at the club's training ground in Cobham this week. Two letters are said to warn that Cole, 24, would have his throat cut. A third contained a drawing of a blood-splattered footballer. Each was addressed to the England star who was said to be "badly shaken" by the threats. They come less than two weeks after he was beaten in a row over model Keeley Hazell.'

Encapsulated in these few lines was a plot structure for a *Desperate Footballers' Housewives Special*; it summed up the beautiful game in the 21st century – celebrity, money, sex, crime and violence. Yet the player involved was no yob caught up in another cycle of despicable behaviour. Instead, he was an individual enveloped by the vortex of fame, at the point where simple adulation becomes complex adoration. Joe Cole was one of the purest talents of his generation now playing for the richest club in the world. His story is the story of the modern game and of the far-reaching changes that Russian money has had on it, but to understand the implications fully, we have to go back to north London in 1981.

1
Blowing Bubbles...
But Not For Ever

'He's the sort of talent that you can
build teams around.'
Matthew Le Tissier, November 2002

JOSEPH JASON COLE was born in Camden Town on
8 November 1981, under the star sign of Scorpio. An astrologer
would tell you Scorpios have a laid-back nature, but beware the
sting in their tail.

Little Joe was a Chelsea fan and a frequent visitor to
Stamford Bridge. At the time he went, the worst of the
hooliganism which blighted the name of the club for so long
was over. Their future superstar could sit in the Shed safely
and it was from there he watched his idols wearing the blue
shirt. England centre-forward Kerry Dixon was one of his
early heroes. Joe joked that he could do Dixon's signature
because he would get his autograph from him every week. In
his prime, Kerry was a huge favourite with the crowd and one
of the deadliest strikers of that era. With his blonde hair and
strong physique, he looked like he had stepped out of the *Roy*

of the Rovers comic strip. Kerry finished up as Chelsea's second-highest ever scorer.

Another of Joe's favourite players was the Chelsea captain Dennis Wise. Perhaps the young Joe should have taken heed of Flaubert's advice – you should never meet your idols because you'll come away with gilt on your hands. Joe clashed with the volatile Wise early in his career at West Ham and was upset by his volatile, abrasive nature. Wise, whose small stature belied a ferocious, win-at-all-costs attitude, was an intimidating character. Wise's career was about to go into freefall and, after a successful spell at Chelsea, he was to endure less successful times at Leicester, Millwall and Newcastle. The problem was, as Brian Mears, whose family created Chelsea, so memorably said, 'If Wise is the best player in your team, then your team has a problem.'

Joe was a ball boy at Chelsea for three seasons in 1993/94 and '95. They needed them more in those days before the stadium was remodelled. The instruction to the lads was to throw the ball back at the players as quickly as possible with the minimum of fuss. Young master Joe had other ideas though and would flick it up, juggle it before volleying back to Andy Townsend and co. Later Joe had a season and would sit on the infamous 'benches' area situated in front of the West Stand. This was an enclosure where the Chelsea members sat on primitive wooden benches exposed to the English climate. More often than not he would be huddled with his mates in the teeming rain watching Vinnie Jones giving master classes in the art of midfield play.

Joe was adopted, and his foster parents provided him with a

stable, happy home. Joe's mother was Susan and he had a brother Nicky and sister Charly. His adoptive father was called George Cole (no connection with the star of the classic *Minder* television series). The family had a bulldog called Binnie which led Joe to develop a life-long love for dogs. His late grandparents were a huge help to him and before each game he plays he spends time thinking of them. He made the most of an environment in which he could work on his God-given talent. To this day he remains respectful, very approachable, polite and fully aware of his role-model status. He grew up well adjusted and modest; these attributes were to act as a buffer against the pressures that have been exerted on him as his profile developed within the game and the public consciousness.

The importance of family to Joe was shown when, in March 2005 with his career going ballistic, he purchased a building in Arlington Road, Camden, for over £700,000 to relocate the family business 'Meter Cabs' from Kentish Town. Celeb clients have included Cherie Blair, Jude Law and Kate Winslet.

In 1981, when Joe was born, the world news was dominated by the same theme as a quarter-of-a-century later – global unrest and terrorism. Following the US-Iran agreement, 52 hostages held in Tehran since 1979 were released; Pope John Paul II was wounded by a gunman, as was President Reagan; and Egyptian President Anwar Sadat was assassinated by Islamic extremists. The winter of 1981–82 saw The Human League taking the Christmas Number One with 'Don't You Want Me?', and Soft Cell's classic 'Tainted Love' and Ultravox's 'Vienna' were other huge hits of the day. In sport, John McEnroe beat Borg to win Wimbledon.

JOE COLE

A few days before the birth of Joe, Chelsea Football Club had lost a Division Two away fixture to Rotherham 6-0, watched by a crowd of 10,145. The Chelsea team included Mickey Droy, John Bumpstead and the splendidly named Peter Rhodes Brown.

Joe's first school was St Mary's Primary School in Camden. He stayed there till he was seven, and loved every minute of it. When the family moved he went to St Aloysius RC College in Hornsey Lane, Highgate. Most of the pupils came from the London Borough of Islington, which despite its now trendy image, had higher levels of economic and social disadvantage than the national average at the time. The school was founded in 1879 by the Jesuits, and it was the alma mater of the famous actor Peter Sellars. Another famous old boy is Radio London presenter Danny Kelly. Joe's favourite teacher there was a Mr Simons, with whom he keeps in touch and gives tickets to for him and pupils to watch Joe in action.

Joseph Jason Cole grew up playing football; everywhere he went, he would take a ball with him. The tricks came to him naturally; he practised them hour after hour, perfecting each discipline. A technician as brilliant as Joe can bend the new lightweight balls in the air as skilfully as the great Brazilian winger Garrincha. Juggling was another of his strengths and he spent hour after hour practising with a tennis ball, beach ball or even a golf ball. In the modern game, less and less emphasis seems to be placed on ball skills but Joe was a throwback to an earlier generation of ball artists.

It may be hard to believe now, but 40 years ago Scotland had in their ranks some of the greatest footballers in the world.

BLOWING BUBBLES... BUT NOT FOR EVER

There were whirlwind wingers like Jimmy Johnstone, Charlie Cooke and Willie Henderson; midfield greats like the inspirational 'Slim Jim' Baxter, renowned for his passing ability. The common denominator among all these heroes was that they were all great ball players, footballers who liked nothing better than dribbling with the ball at their feet, beating opponents at will, and executing tricks that would make the crowd gasp in awe.

The basis from which this talent derived was from the hundreds of hours they would spend controlling a small India rubber ball. These could be purchased in those days for six old pence or, to give its nickname, a 'tanner', giving rise to the 'tanner ball players', that group of footballers who had honed their talents in this way. They rehearsed their arts in the streets, when there were fewer cars. It took an enormous amount of dedication and willpower to devote hours and hours to the honing of these ball skills, and this was often done alone, without the benefit of the supportive camaraderie of friends or team-mates.

Another factor that gave these maestros of ball control an edge was the uneven surfaces of the paved or cobbled streets, which would cause the ball to bounce at different heights and angles, lending practice sessions an unpredictability that stood players in good stead for the uneven surfaces they would encounter throughout their careers.

One of Joe's greatest skills was his mastery of the 'wedge trap'. It was a neat way of controlling a falling ball by turning the body slightly sideways to the oncoming ball. Joe could then trap the ball between the inside of the foot and ankle and the ground. His timing and execution of the manoeuvre put him in a class of his own.

Joe told *Esquire* magazine: 'Coming from a council estate there was football being played constantly and we had a lot of good players. But I had this: if someone could do something with a ball when I was eight or nine that I couldn't do, I wouldn't go to sleep that night until I could. I'd just stay there till it was pitch-black, just doing it and doing it.'

Soon the scouts from the big clubs were flocking to see the youngster. It was routine for them to cover thousands of matches, most of them involving prospects as young as eight. 'You never win anything with kids,' was the famous quote by Alan Hansen, but he could not have been more wrong. Clubs looked for the 'four corners' in a youngster: technical, physical, mental and social. Joe ticked all these boxes. Nobody had more tricks and natural ability. What stood out also was his uncanny eye for a pass. Physically he was just a dot, but he was never frail and was very tough. Mentally he was also strong and tremendously focused. Apart from his Chelsea heroes he was a huge fan of Paul Gascoigne. When he watched Gazza strutting his stuff in the 1990 World Cup, nine-year-old Joe was already telling his family that one day he would be playing in the World Cup himself. That sense of belief never left him.

The social side of Joe's early years was very strong; he had a good support network with his parents and Uncle Brian. Even as a small child Joe never had to carry anything and was excused most household chores to help him conserve his health for football. At an early age he was dining on his favourite meal of roast and mashed potatoes, green beans and chicken, washed down with his favourite tipple Lucozade.

Joe's childhood activities were 90 per cent football-related. He liked a little bit of carp fishing, a hobby that he has rekindled an interest in in recent years. The Cole TV was watched when he flopped down after a hard day on the football pitch. Being a London boy he could identify with the character played by David Jason in his favourite show *Only Fools and Horses*. Joe also enjoyed watching videos and DVDs; amongst his all time favourites are *Rambo*, *Armageddon* and *Independence Day*. Young master Cole was also a great fight fan and so the Rocky films were also favourites. Ricky Hatton is his favourite boxer.

But his main interest was football, football, and more football. As his reputation spread, he spent more and more time playing the beautiful game. He raced through the age groups and soon was playing with the big boys in the sixth form. George Cole was concerned that Joe was over-doing things and ordered him to rest. Sometimes Joe would mention he had 'detention', but really he was avoiding punishment of a different sort from the clattering tackles and rough challenges in the playground, accrued as he dribbled around his seniors time after time. All his friends were chosen from the lads that played football with him. Although his real best friend was the ball, he had a little gang of friends who had all attended Haverstock school – Ossie, Al, Paul and Jason. When Jason recently ran in the London Marathon, his old mate Joe was standing in the rain shouting him on. Joe later attended the post-marathon party and spent ages signing autographs and chatting about his life and times.

Jimmy Neighbour was the person credited with talking Joe into signing for West Ham. Jimmy played 96 games for West Ham himself, scoring six goals. A pacy winger, Jimmy had previously played for Norwich and Tottenham. He won a FA Cup Winners medal in the 1980 Hammers side alongside Frank Lampard Snr and Billy Bonds before becoming involved in the youth set-up. That is where he first saw Joe playing for the district side. The youth sides he was in were virtually unbeatable, crushing all opposition and running up record scores.

Joe joined West Ham at the age of ten as a schoolboy. With virtually every top club, including Manchester United and Arsenal, marvelling at his skill and chasing his signature, it was surprising that he opted to go to Upton Park to lay the foundations of his career. West Ham on their day were the best footballing team in London – their wonderful performance in the 2006 FA Cup Final was testimony of how they kept the tradition alive – but economics always dictated that they had to sell their best players to richer clubs.

West Ham could not afford to compete with the top sides to buy big names – their only option at the time was to produce their own talent. They had a wonderful network of scouts and many links to clubs and schools all over London, and were known as a nursery side for other teams. The players they have produced over the years reads like a *Who's Who* of the game's top names.

Tony Carr was the head of the West Ham youth set-up. A

former apprentice, he cleaned the boots of Bobby Moore before injury forced him to quit the game at the age of 21. He became the youth academy director in 1973. His first memory of Joe was in the 1995 South East Counties League Cup Final played against Chelsea at Stamford Bridge. Frank Lampard scored the winning penalty in the shoot out, and Rio Ferdinand scored two goals in the actual match. But it was Joe who stole the show. As Tony told the *Times,* 'He blew my mind, the tricks, fantastic dribbles and outrageous back heels, that weren't circus tricks but would create a goal.'

Carr created a wonderful atmosphere for the young hopefuls. He made it enjoyable for them and, consequently, Joe had no fear. He had lots of touches of the ball and was always trying out new tricks. Carr noticed that even at that age he appeared driven and had a real desire to make the grade.

West Ham were founded ten years earlier than Chelsea, being formed in 1895 as a works side of the Thames Ironworks and Shipbuilding Co Ltd, from which they got their original nickname of the 'Irons'. In recent years, this has been discarded by all but the most diehard fans. In Cockney rhyming slang, an 'iron' was a homosexual and opposing fans were quick to latch on to this. The name was changed to West Ham in 1900.

After a spell at Plaistow, they moved to a pitch in the Upton Park area originally known as the Castle, which is the symbol still shown on the badge that Joe used to kiss. The badge came from the Castle Mail Packet Company. Their works team were known as the Old Castle Swifts and a neighbour of the Thames Iron Works Shipping Company both firms being situated on the east bank of Bow Creek. In 1895 the Old Castle Swifts team folded and Arnold Hills, the owner of the Thames Iron Works, purchased their lease for the ground at Hermit Road and merged the teams. Hills was an interesting character, a Victorian temperance advocate who made his money through business tycoonery. Hills adopted the crossed rivet 'Hammers'and 'Castle' in recognition of this union.

West Ham have never won the league; the supreme moment in their colourful career was on 30 July 1966, when England won the World Cup by defeating West Germany 4-2. Three of England's greatest heroes that day – Bobby Moore, Geoff Hurst and Martin Peters – were all home-grown West Ham players, having graduated from what was known as 'The Academy of Football'. The *Daily Express* can take credit for coining the phrase in the mid-1960s.

In the World Cup Final, Geoff Hurst became the only player so far to score a hat-trick. Zinedine Zidane of France and Ronaldo of Brazil have both scored twice in more recent finals, but his proud record remains intact. Martin Peters scored England's other goal and Moore, England's captain, was voted the Player of the Tournament.

Joe grew up in the shadow of the legend of Bobby Moore. He was the youngster's favourite player, and still is. One of the reasons Joe chose to join West Ham was because of his hero and the strong family values the club stood for. Moore tragically died of cancer and one of Joe's favourite charities is the Bobby Moore Fund for Cancer Research.

Just as some actors become identified with one great film role in their careers – Marlon Brando in *On the Waterfront*, or

Jack Nicholson in *Chinatown* – so footballers can become identified with one great performance in a game. Best against Benfica in 1965; Matthews in the 1955 FA Cup Final; and Ricky Villa in the 1981 FA Cup Final replay spring to mind. Perhaps the most famous definitive performance, though, was Geoff Hurst in the 1966 World Cup Finals.

So young Joe had a great tradition to try to live up to – football played in a romantic and cavalier fashion. In the 1960s, Hammers fans used to crow that 'West Ham won the World Cup'. The essence of their attacking football was a freewheeling, high-tempo passing game. Huge emphasis at that time was placed on individual technique, while the quality of the pass today is measured by the ease with which the receiver can control it; more often than not, the ball is laid off immediately. In the 1960s, the quality of the pass at West Ham was judged by the way it was struck. Their players always looked so good on the ball.

Joe's style had a great many of the strengths so respected in that era. His passing boasted a seemingly endless variety of permutations – long and short, high and low. He could curl a pass or deliver it dead straight. The youngster's footwork was so neat he could play the ball with the inside or the outside of the foot. Nothing excites a crowd more than a ball hit with the outside of the foot; it contained an arrogance all of its own. The Cole songbook also contained tricks with the instep, heel or even the toes and, to this day, he has not lost the infectious enthusiasm he had as a boy.

Full credit must go to Jimmy Hampson and Tony Carr at West Ham for the way they monitored and shaped Joe's career.

Another huge influence on his career was the ex-Chelsea and England winger Peter Brabrook, who worked as a coach at Upton Park. Brabrook, a recognised winger with the skill of an Arjen Robben, started his career at Stamford Bridge, making his debut in the 1955 Championship-winning side. After 57 goals in 271 games, Peter joined West Ham in 1962 for a fee that smashed the Football League record for a winger.

Peter's pop star appearance and affable nature made him one of the biggest names of the day. The prime function of his game was to collect the ball, move it forward by beating opponents and delivering telling crosses. As the emphasis in the 1960s gradually swung towards teamwork and possession, work-rate became the buzzword. Players like Brabrook were seen as a luxury item, almost unaffordable.

Brabrook first met Joe when he was ten and they are still friends; Joe has never forgotten the debt he owes him. The winger soon saw in Joe a player with the rare value of close control and the almost lost art of dribbling. Having worked with Frank Lampard Jr and Rio Ferdinand, Frank was of the view that Joe was the best young player he had ever worked with.

Brabrook was given the coaching job by the then manager Harry Redknapp, another huge influence on the career of Joe Cole. Joe was Redknapp's biggest success at West Ham; never had a young player possessed such outlandish gifts and been such a crowd-puller. As he rose through the ranks at West Ham, there was something of an unknown quantity about him, but everybody at Upton Park felt that he had the potential to reach the very top. The conjuror's tricks he could perform with a ball were breathtaking, and almost Brazilian in spirit. The fans loved him, he entertained, and he always seemed prepared to put on a show.

Like Brabrook, Harry was a winger, playing 149 games in an 11-year career which started in 1964. Never a household name, nevertheless he was a real Cockney character and one of the most popular players in the club's history. This was the club's 'golden' era; their standing was never higher in the game, although they never reached the rarefied pinnacle of league glory. Harry played in the same team as Moore, Hurst and Peters around the time Roman Abramovich was riding his first tricycle. Harry rejoined West Ham in 1992 as an assistant to another legend, Billy Bonds. Billy had made the most appearances for any West Ham player, having notched up a staggering 793 games.

Throughout his time at West Ham, Harry's man-management skills were sometimes overlooked, but the part he played in bringing Joe Cole into the top flight cannot be underestimated. The problem facing Harry was a perennial one for managers of middle-ranking clubs, and particularly for a team and fans who had a history of nurturing and developing great players – how could he build a team that would include talents like those of a Cole, and retain them in the face of cash inducements from other bigger, higher-profile clubs?

Joe went to the FA School at Lilleshall when he was fourteen and his burgeoning talent had him marked out as a future superstar. Joe's academic career had stalled slightly at 13; he had taken his SATS and was getting 'A' grades but all his energies went into football. He lacked application and had no interest in things like computers. Video games were an obsession with him at that time, though. There was one game in particular that he would play for hours – *James Bond-007* on Nintendo 64. He gambled with mates 50p a game – a significant amount of money for a schoolboy. Often the games at Lilleshall would last throughout the night until 6 or 7 in the morning as Joe and his chums played the 4-player game. Francis Jeffers, an ex-Everton and Arsenal player, and a future Chelsea team mate Scott Parker were famous names around the place at that time. Lilleshall was good for Joe as he started mixing with kids from all over the country, some of them highly educated, which helped him rapidly develop his social skills.

Like all educational establishments, Lilleshall had its iniation ceremonies. Joe's was to score a goal with an overhead kick in his uniform. No problem – Joe could scissorkick with the best of them; but the problem was that he was required to do it on a muddy pitch resembling a First World War battlefield. Susan Cole had a lot of washing to do that week.

Harry Redknapp was always asking Tony Carr who he had coming through on the conveyor belt of talent that the Academy produced. If any youngster showed exceptional promise he was invited by the manager to train with the first team for a couple of days. Joe soon became the talk of the club as he unveiled his unique range of skills. His mentor at Lilleshall was the much-missed DT Jones who took great interest in the development of the young Londoner. DT was a huge influence on Michael Owen's career and was largely responsible for bringing him through to the big time. Young master Cole was himself now on the threshold of breaking through. He was becoming more vocal on the pitch. Verbal abuse of officials and diving did not exist at the Academy level. Critics of such systems insisted that the football played was too nice and antiseptic.

Joe made his initial impact in the 1998/99 season, playing just eight games. He made his debut against Swansea in a Third Round FA Cup tie at Upton Park on 2 January 1999. He came on as sub for Berkovic after 65 minutes, with the game ending in a 1-1 draw, with the Hammers losing the replay.

Joe's first Premiership appearance was against Manchester United at Old Trafford, and it could not have been much more of a baptism of fire. Joe replaced Trevor Sinclair after 46 minutes. The Claret-and-Blues lost 4-1, with Lampard scoring for Hammers.

At the end of January, Joe picked up his first Man of the Match award for his performance against Wimbledon in a 0-0 draw. It was his first start and he was only on the field for 70 minutes, but did enough to impress everyone there. Coincidentally, the man who replaced him, Paolo Di Canio, was another player new to the set-up, who would, like Joe, go on to become another West Ham legend.

That season, West Ham won the FA Youth Cup for the third time in their history. The high spot of the run to the final was a 4-0 thrashing of the highly rated Arsenal youth side in a sixth round replay. Joe was the star of the night making two goals, one of them a cracking drive from Carrick, and delighting the crowd with his technical gifts. Winning the cup was a record-breaking affair because the 9-0 aggregate score was the highest ever recorded in a final in that competition. Their opponents were Coventry City, who were trounced 3-0 at Highfield Road and then 6-0 in the second leg at Upton Park. The hapless goalkeeper was Chris Kirkland, who later joined Liverpool for a huge fee.

Joe was the undoubted star of the final, partnered by Michael Carrick in midfield. The Geordie-born midfielder was to follow Joe's footsteps into the full international team and he'd also enjoy a big money move across London.

A huge crowd of over 20,000 watched the young Hammers collect the trophy. It was the platform that first launched Joe to national recognition by giving him a showcase for his unique talent. It was in that game that the crowd had their first glimpse of the 'showboat' tricks that were to dazzle fans – and opponents – in the years to come.

Redknapp sensibly kept Joe out of the limelight as much as he could. Brabrook may well have been a very significant influence on Harry at this time, recommending that Joe should be handled with a great deal of care, and introduced gradually to the physical and media pressures of the first team.

Brabrook recalled a story about a young prospect at Chelsea in the 1950s called David Cliss. The guy was like a Martian, his talents were simply out of this world. Cliss was hailed as the golden boy of his generation, a ball-juggling prodigy who was going to take the world by storm. His reputation as a schoolboy made him the hottest property in the game.

Chelsea beat off a host of clubs, including West Ham, to land Cliss. Jimmy Greaves had just signed for Chelsea himself but was unsure if he had done the right thing. As far as he was concerned, he could not see himself making any progress with a player of Cliss's ability in front of him. That is how good Cliss was but, for a variety of reasons, he only played 24 games for the West London side before drifting out of the game.

Brabrook was amazed that Cliss had not made the big time, but always recalled the burden of expectation he had to carry from a young age. And all of this was in an era without the blaze of the media spotlight that we have today.

As far as Joe was concerned, things had been moving steadily in the right direction. Redknapp saw Joe as the replacement for Eyal Berkovic. A cultured midfielder with a hard edge, Berkovic was very popular with the crowd. He had become another of West Ham's great characters, and was once described by Rio Ferdinand as being the worst-dressed player at the club.

Joe always had a sharp eye for fashion and was of the opinon that the East Europeans were terrible dressers and claimed that he had not seen one that dressed well. At that time he was going through a Paul Weller/Mod phase, wearing retro suits and Ben Sherman shirts. In his column in the *Sun*, Chris Waddle awarded Joe 'The worst haircut in football' award, which seemed a bit harsh.

Joe's star continued to rise and the Upton Park faithful were wowed by a string of mature performances. His profound football intelligence shone through, his game had urgency and speed without panic. He still had two-and-a-half years on his contract, which was rumoured to be worth £5,000 a week, but Redknapp was already linking him with a contract worth £7,500 a week.

The day after his eighteenth birthday, Joe was called up to

the England Under-21 squad. Already, he was being seen as the long-term solution to the problem left flank position in the national side.

In November, he scored his first goal for the club, a last-gasp winner against Birmingham to put the Hammers into the quarter-finals of the Worthington Cup. The game took place at St Andrews and the home side twice took the lead. The West Ham skipper Steve Lomas and substitute Paul Kitson both grabbed equalisers before Joe settled it.

The goal was simple, scored from close range after Lomas had set it up. For Joe it was a glorious moment. He had arrived in the big time. West Ham had a hard core support which always followed them regardless of where they were playing. Actor Ray Winstone, in his wonderful exposé of modern football, *All in the Game*, described the Worthington competiton as the 'Worthless' cup, but to Joe and the Hammers fans who made the trip up to Birmingham in mid-week it was an exhilarating moment.

Joe was soon an adopted 'East Ender'. Every young man born in that part of London wanted to be Joe Cole. Ray Winstone said that his dream job would be playing up front for the Hammers. Unlike the 1960s, when footballers all aspired to be film stars – notably Bobby Moore modelling himself on Steve McQueen – it seemed at the time that Premiership footballers' image, profile and riches were what everyone wanted to be part of.

Kevin Keegan, then the England manager, told the media at the time that, if Joe maintained his good form, he could make the squad for the European Championships in 2000.

BLOWING BUBBLES... BUT NOT FOR EVER

In a match against Villa at the end of January 2000, Joe set up a chance for the gangly Paulo Wanchope with a cleverly flicked header. A surprised Wanchope found himself in front of an open goal, but blasted over from an impossibly close range. It was one of the worse misses ever seen in the Premiership and was constantly re-shown on Sky.

The first goal Joe ever scored in the Premiership was against Bradford City. It came in an amazing nine-goal thriller that West Ham won 5-4. That amazing game was remembered most for Di Canio's incredible antics after he demanded the ball from Lampard who was about to take a penalty.

It was a game that would live in the memory of everyone who was lucky enough to witness it. Bradford went ahead through Dean Windass after half an hour but goals from Trevor Sinclair and John Moncur put the Hammers in front. On the stroke of half-time Peter Beagrie levelled for Bradford from the spot after a penalty kick had been awarded, and Bradford raced to a 4-2 lead when Jamie Lawrence scored twice in the first six minutes of the second half. Paolo Di Canio had been taking severe punishment from the Bradford defence and when he had the second claim for a penalty turned down he began to lose the plot. He implored Redkapp to sub him, but Harry refused. Joe was taking a similar buffeting from the Bradford rearguard, but was still running at them. Di Canio returned to the fray and shortly afterwards West Ham were awarded a penalty almost as unclear as Beagrie's, when Kitson went down in the box. Lampard, son of the assistant manager and nephew of the manager, was the regular penalty taker. Yet to show his true potential, Frank was still a huge influence in the club and commanded respect. Di Canio tore the ball from his hands, desperate to score himself. He brushed Frank's protests aside and still in a state of extreme anxiety and anger smashed the ball home.

Joe made it 4-4 when he went round two defenders and lashed the ball home. It was his first goal at Upton Park in the big time, and the start of a new millennium - what else could he do but crowd surf in the Bobby Moore stand? John Moncur followed him, together with a possee of stewards. The East End had not seen such a knees-up since Trevor Brooking had won the Cup. The only person who did not join in the celebrations was Di Canio who retrieved the ball from the back of the net and raced up-field, anxious to re-start the game and win it. Which was exactly what he did, beating three defenders to set up the chance for Lampard to thunder home the winner.

Joe's hopes of joining the Euro 2000 squad ended on 4 April when he was injured against Derby County. It transpired that the injury, at first thought to be bruising, was, in fact, a broken leg and, with that, Joe encountered his first real setback.

In 1999/2000, Joe played 22 games and scored once in the Premiership. West Ham finished ninth, which represented a pretty successful season. The following season, Joe was fit and looking forward to linking up with new signing Davor Suker, the ex-Real Madrid striker. Around that time, another young prospect was making a breakthrough into the squad – Michael Carrick. Along with Rio Ferdinand and Frank Lampard Jr, the quartet were seen by many as being the nucleus for the future England squad.

BLOWING BUBBLES... BUT NOT FOR EVER

Things did not go quite so well for Joe that season, despite playing 30 games and hitting the back of the net five times. Joe spent the season fluctuating between bewitching and bewildering a demanding West Ham crowd. Joe started brightly and, in early autumn, he had a mini purple patch scoring neat goals against Coventry and Bradford in successive weeks. Spurs knocked the Hammers out of the FA Cup and Sheffield Wednesday dumped them out of the Worthington Cup.

The team's home form was not as good as the previous year. Towards the end of the season, Joe was dropped to the bench for a game at Villa Park. Redknapp was openly admitting to the media that he was still not sure of Joe's most effective position. This was one of the problems in the formative years of Joe's career. He was such a good player that he could literally play anywhere. Equally at home on either flank, he could also operate through the middle or drop deeper back in midfield. Consequently, his burgeoning talent was spread too thinly. For the sake of his team, more often than not he would play in a position not best suited to his talents, but in a role that probably no other player could comfortably adapt to.

Joe always hinted at another dimension to his game, and there was a significant element of dissatisfaction that bubbled just below the surface; he'd do his job for West Ham, but there was always the feeling that, given a consistent role, he could deliver so much more. It was also occurring to Joe that if his ambitions – and supreme talent – were to be realised, then he might have to consider moving from West Ham. There was so much that he wanted to achieve – particularly European football, the Champions League and selection for the national

21

team – that he had to consider his options, and whether staying at West Ham would be beneficial to his career in the long term. At 18 years old, Joe Cole was unclear as to how exactly he could conquer the world that was waiting for him. Soon though, he would be offered a golden opportunity to further his career at the highest level.

In March 2001, Chelsea came to Upton Park for a Premiership clash. Joe missed a good chance early on to put the home side ahead, hitting the woodwork from close range. Stuart Pearce was playing at the back for the Hammers and, at the time, was approaching the age of 39 but was busy imparting his knowledge to youngsters like Cole. Pearce took an early knock and went off, and with him went any chance of the home side winning. Though not a great reader, Joe was fond of a good book, particularly when travelling to a European game. His favourite book was Stuart Pearce's autobiography, appropriately named *Psycho*.

Chelsea won the match 2-0 with goals from their powerful strike force of Jimmy Floyd Hasselbaink and Eidur Gudjohnsen. Their coach, Claudio Ranieri, was impressed with Joe's performance that evening and was already compiling a dossier on him. Chelsea were in grave financial problems at that time and many of their fans were very concerned for the future of the club. Joe looked to be another luxury item to them – coveted but unattainable.

Redknapp had constantly changed Joe's role within the West Ham set-up as he searched for the most effective formation to allow Joe's talent to be fully realised. The beleaguered manager was always a loyal supporter of his young star, and would publicly endorse his qualities whenever the opportunity arose: 'No one thinks more of Joe than me and I have no doubt he is going to be a great player.' Di Canio was also a great fan of Joe's, and one of his earliest memories of his time at Upton Park was a tiny Joe putting the ball through his legs in training. At that time, he called him a 'scaled-down Zidane'. Di Canio was full of praise of Joe in his autobiography: 'I see him do certain things with the ball and have no clue how he does them. The way he spins off tackles, the way he dances through traffic. His movements are natural, feline; he's like a young tiger. He shows you the ball and then makes it disappear like an illusionist. At the same time he has the grace and control of a ballet dancer, no muscle is out of place in his body.'

Di Canio's volatile temper and on-field antics would come to dominate his prolific career, but he showed a great deal of maturity and sensitivity towards his younger team-mate once Joe had broken into the squad, and he helped to smooth the way for the young footballer with his lavish praise and pleas for the media to go easy on him. He said, 'Joe has been massacred in the press recently. People seem to forget he is a 19-year-old. They expect him to deliver a goal every game. You need to be patient with him. Let him run free. I see a lot of myself in him and I like to think of myself as an older brother to him.' The tabloids were quick to turn on Joe. An obscene amount of press had made him a famous name before he appeared in the Hammers first team. Joe admitted later that it had not helped his progress. The press were now hinting that he might be a prancing circus pony rather than a raging bull. The same thing is happening to today's up-and-coming players. A few weeks before the 2006 World Cup, Arsenal prodigy Theo Walcott was included in the squad before he had even made his debut in the Premiership, unleasing a huge amount of hysterical press coverage on the 17 year old – and in the event, the precocious player didn't even feature on the pitch in the competition.

At the age of 19 Joe was becoming one of the most marked men in the Premiership – David Batty of Leeds was given his marching orders for a particularly bad two-footed challenge on him. Batty was famous for the punch-up he had with his own team mate Graham Le Saux in a Champions league match in Russia. Joe was picking up niggling injuries and knocks as his reputation grew and opponents became more aggressive and physical towards him.

Joe recovered his form towards the end of the season and scored a fine goal against Coventry to confirm this fact but, despite the best efforts of the team, West Ham finally finished a disappointing 15th in the table. In November, Rio Ferdinand had been sold to Leeds for a then British transfer record of £19 million. The West Ham fans were devastated because they saw Ferdinand as being the future of the club. It was the start of the destruction of one of the greatest collections of young players that football had ever seen. Manchester United had the 'Busby Babes' so tragically decimated by the Munich air disaster. Harry Redknapp had been an Arsenal fan as a kid, and saw the Busby Babes' last game away at Highbury. The match ended 5-4 to United, and the memory of those brilliant youngsters haunted him throughout his career. Harry's dream was to build a side of young players blessed with similar talent, and perhaps, for a short while, he can claim to have done so.

In more recent times, the Old Trafford youth system has produced the Beckham, Scholes, Butt and Neville brothers combination that formed the nucleus of their 1999 treble-winning side. Similarly, Chelsea in the 1960s had their brilliant 'Diamonds' side of London talent including Terry Venables and Bobby Tambling.

West Ham fans were concerned for the future, naturally, and while they could still admire the undeniable skill on the pitch, they wanted more. Joe's progress had been slow, and he was far from the finished article.

Upheaval hit the Hammers when Redknapp, after years of frenetic transfer-dealing, left the club in the summer. The manager had allegedly fallen out with the chairman over exactly how much was available for transfer fees.

The period of change and unease continued, as the West Stand was demolished for work to begin on the new Doc Marten's stand. Another of the casualties was Harry's assistant, Frank Lampard Snr. This had a knock-on effect, and soon Frank Lampard Jr was sold to Chelsea in the summer for £11 million. At the time, it was a fee that stunned the football world, and the consensus of opinion was that Chelsea had paid far too much for an underperforming midfielder. Lampard had scored 39 goals in 186 appearances in claret-and-blue. The jury was still out on him for many reasons. After the move, Lampard levelled criticism at his former club, claiming they had stifled his natural attacking game in his last season at Upton Park, and that he'd been given a raw deal having been forced into a more defensive role. 'I was restricted... we had

Paulo Di Canio going forward all the time, and Joe Cole who is virtually a forward. His strength is in attack and he is not so good at that defensive side.'

Years later, he would tell the media how he never had a relationship with the West Ham fans, something that Joe Cole managed to preserve over the years. Ferdinand always speaks glowingly and shows gratitude for his time at West Ham and always receives a warm reception at Upton Park.

Ranieri must take full credit for the growth of Lampard as a midfield force. He was most keen to see his big-money signing get amongst the goals, something that was achieved prior to Mourinho's arrival.

Woodford-born Glenn Roeder, youth team manager, was appointed as Harry's replacement in July 2001, and he immediately endorsed the view that Joe Cole was integral to his plans for the team, saying, 'As everyone knows, Joe is such an exciting talent. Like Michael Carrick, a player of his young age will improve every season. They've already got themselves into the full England squad, which is amazing when you consider how young they are. I'm really looking forward to working with both of them this year.'

Glenn was best remembered for his playing career as a skilful defender for QPR and Newcastle. Glenn's only managerial experience was during unsuccessful stints with Gillingham and Watford, though he had been part of Glen Hoddle's England coaching team.

Roeder took West Ham to a highly credible 7th in his first season in charge, an achievement that was all the more admirable after a difficult start, when the fans were calling for him to be sacked. At this point, the future looked bright for the club with its fine crop of youngsters. Sadly, though, the momentum was not to last. Under the Chairman Terry Brown, a decision was made not to make a significant investment in the squad, and that was to have fatal consequences.

For Joe, 2001/02 was a highly successful season and, at the end of it, he was on the plane to Japan and South Korea with the England World Cup squad. He also finished runner-up in the PFA Young Player of the Year award to Stephen Gerrard of Liverpool.

Joe had played in 30 Premiership games but failed to score a goal. Despite displaying prodigious talent at times, he found it difficult to make a match-winning contribution. Joe's solitary strike came in January 2002 in an FA Cup game against Macclesfield Town of the Third Division. Some critics suggested that it was his lack of goals that slightly hindered his final breakthrough into the international set-up. Joe recalled that time when he was interviewed by Chelsea fan Tim Lovejoy in *Esquire* magazine: '[When] I came into the side at 17 people expected me to be a messiah. I think that was always the case with me – I was a very good player at West Ham, but because I wasn't Wayne Rooney, at that standard at that time, people were quick to write me off – experienced people in the game as well. People did really write me off.'

Roeder's hopes of a Cup run were ended by Chelsea in a Fourth Round replay at Upton Park. A few weeks earlier, Chelsea had thrashed them 5-1 at Stamford Bridge in a Premiership match. Their nemesis, Hasselbaink, scored twice. Joe was the Hammers' most effective player as he tried to counteract the Chelsea onslaught. To complete a bad day for West Ham, the tempestuous Di Canio was sent off after 70 minutes after an ugly clash with Jody Morris.

Freddie Kanoute's goal forced a replay when he scored at Stamford Bridge in the FA Cup clash the following week, and Joe played an inspired game. All his efforts were in vain, though, as Chelsea won the replay 3-2, after West Ham had twice taken the lead. Another of the West Ham fame academy, Jermaine Defoe, scored that night and looked a real prospect. Fortunately for Chelsea, John Terry headed a last-minute winner, after earlier conceding an own goal.

Joe was appointed club captain in what turned out to be his final season at West Ham. At the start of the season, he gave his first indication that he might consider leaving Upton Park, citing that this would help him fulfil his potential, saying 'I agree with people who say I should compete at the highest level.' Roeder's award of the captaincy to Joe was probably a sweetner to try and get him to secure his future at the club. West Ham had many fine captains in their history, Bobby Moore being the best example, but Billy Bonds was another marvellous leader by example and drove his men on in the style of Tony Adams. Trevor Brooking had a different style but was a great inspiration. Joe was delighted to take his place among them. The previous season had been awkward for him but as Don Hutchinson, the Hammers' £5 million signing from Sunderland, wrote in a programme: 'Joe was unfairly criticised and I think he's responded in a magnificent fashion, leading the Hammers up the table.'

Joe was determined to increase his goal tally and, in the first home game of the season against Arsenal, he opened the scoring with a finely struck, left-footed effort. West Ham raced to a 2-0 lead but defensive errors meant that the game was drawn 2-2. Thiery Henry capitalising on one to score one of his classics.

Few players in the Premiership were capable of matching Joe's magical skills, or the way he loved running at people and beating defenders, but his efforts were channelled into more of a team ethic as West Ham struggled to keep pace with the competition. As the season progressed, the team's form and confidence took a nosedive. They were unable to win a home game until January – a 2-1 win over Blackburn – and their fate was sealed. West Ham's ten-year run in the top flight was at an end.

Roeder came under huge pressure. The fans attacked his home in Essex and, after a heart problem, he left West Ham, to be replaced in the interim by Trevor Brooking as caretaker manager. Brooking was another West Ham legend who had racked up nearly as many appearances (635) as Bonds. Brooking had a cultured, elegant style and, when Joe first broke through, obvious comparisons were made with Brooking's unrivalled finesse. Brooking was seen as a sort of elder statesman and represented all the good values of the game – an undeniable idol in the eyes of West Ham fans, and there could be few better mentors for the younger players than him.

West Ham, surprisingly, did the double over Chelsea in the 2002/03 season. In September, they beat them 3-2 at Stamford Bridge with the talismanic Di Canio scoring twice. Chelsea were unbeaten at the time and it was the Hammers' first win.

Joe said that he hoped that it would be a turning point for them. It wasn't to be, though, for by the time the teams met again in May, the Hammers were down and almost out.

Chelsea, haemorrhaging cash, desperately needed the points themselves to qualify for the Champions League. Joe drove West Ham on throughout the game and won the midfield battle against his former colleague Lampard. Di Canio was Chelsea's scourge that season, coming on as a sub for Les Ferdinand after 56 minutes. The script was written for him – 15 minutes later, he scored the only goal of the game from close range.

It was too little, too late, though. The following week, West Ham crashed out of the Premiership after losing to Birmingham, whose fans taunted the West Ham faithful with a rendition of their theme song 'Keep Right on to the End of the Road'.

Having done all he could to keep his team in the Premiership, it was the end of the road for Joe, too. The time had now come to hang up his West Ham shirt with the 26 squad number and the Doc Marten's logo. He had performed heroically to keep his side up but, ultimately, even his skill was not enough. At the highest level, critics observed that his game lacked depth and maturity. The stats showed that he had been a key man in the Hammers' fight for survival. His ratio of tackles was only bettered by a few household names like Patrick Vieira and Dietmar Hamann. Along the way, he had managed to accumulate nine yellow cards. Naturally, he was voted Hammer of the Year.

West Ham were resigned to offloading Joe; they did not

want to lose him but, facing financial meltdown, they had no option. In all, 13 players left the club that summer, including Trevor Sinclair, Freddie Kanoute and the dream-maker Di Canio. It should have panned out so much better for them all.

The West Ham board would have preferred to sell Joe abroad and had alerted Celta Vigo and Deportivo la Coruña. Barcelona, one of the most powerful clubs in the world, had expressed interest in him, but no firm deal emerged. When push came to shove, Chelsea were the only club in Europe to have the purchasing power to clinch the deal.

With the advent of Russian billionaire Roman Abramovich, and his bottomless pit of riches, Chelsea suddenly became the most attractive option for many of the world's superstars. The Chelsea fans were amazed and thrilled at the procession of world-class names migrating to west London. In 1991, their hopes for silverware had rested on the shoulders of new signing Joe Allon from Hartlepool, who cost a massive £300,000. Now, they had a plethora of stars to admire, with total transfer fees amounting to over £110 million. One of these was the eagerly anticipated Joe Cole, who had promised so much in the claret-and-blue, and who would now have to deliver in royal blue, while rubbing shoulders with some of the world's finest players. His skills may have shone at West Ham, but fans wondered whether he'd be able to hold his own, and earn his place, in a new-look Chelsea first team comprising millionaire superstars.

Harry Redknapp, in his first term of office at Portsmouth, was alarmed at the turmoil caused by Joe's departure from Upton Park, and expressed doubts about the Hammers' ability to recover from the sale of so many good players saying, 'Getting rid of Joe Cole is the final straw. It's a sad day and a massive blow to the fans. How can they hope to get back into the Premiership?'

In the first programme of the 2003/04 Nationwide League Division One season, West Ham chairman Terence Brown wrote of Joe's departure: 'We would have sold him even had we retained our place in the Premier League. During the last 18 months, we had discussions with Joe and his father, in an attempt to persuade Joe to extend his contract beyond the summer of 2004. Had financial terms been the issue, I am sure we would have reached an agreement, but unfortunately Joe wanted to play Champions League football and felt his future lay elsewhere. His preferred route was to fight to keep us in the Premier League and then leave to join a team playing in the Champions League, ensuring his place in the England squad and delivering a large cheque for us along the way to assist with the team-building which we would have undertaken had we retained our Premiership status. His alternative route was to see out his contract and leave at the end of the current season under the Bosman rule. Under those circumstances, Joe was free to commence negotiations with foreign clubs.

'We therefore had to accept an offer during the close season. No club in the Nationwide League and few in the Premier League can invest nearly £8 million in the services of a player, no matter how talented, to play a maximum of 45 League games. I do hope nothing I have said will reflect badly on Joe. I have known him since he was 11 years old and he is a smashing lad, possibly the best all-round product of the

Academy in my time as chairman. He has a great deal of affection for the club and I would not be in the least surprised if, one day, we see him back in our claret-and-blue shirt.'

Without Joe, West Ham did survive, thanks to Alan Pardew, the eventual replacement for Roeder. After losing to Palace in the play-offs in 2003/04, they scraped back into the Premiership after narrowly beating Preston at the Millennium Stadium. But, by that time, Joe was building a reputation for himself in west London.

2

The World at His Feet

'I have been dealing with expectation since I was 17 or younger
when I got into the first team at West Ham. People expect me to
do amazing things every time I get the ball.'

Joe Cole on signing for Chelsea

IN THE SUMMER of 2003, Chelsea Football Club were on
their knees and facing financial ruin. The reports vary, but
the club was reliably reported as being in debt to the tune of
anything from £80–£100 million. The deadlines for
repayments were imminent. The then owner, Ken Bates, had
been trying to sell the club for some time, or at least manage
to attract some serious investment. The TV revenue usually
paid in August had already been mortgaged.

It was an open secret that Arsenal had been casting envious
glances at their prime assets, players like Eidur Gudjohnsen,
John Terry and William Gallas. Something fairly drastic would
have to occur to save Chelsea from bankruptcy and the break-
up of their squad. That, in turn, would affect results on the
pitch, and an unavoidable slide down the league to the
ignominy of the lesser divisions.

The story has been told many times, and it reads like a plot from a far-fetched novel. Down and nearly out, Chelsea were bought by one of the richest men in the world who was prepared to pour money into it. Chelsea were known as one of the sleeping giants of English football, although, in recent times, their sleep had turned into a coma. The last time they had won the title was almost half-a-century earlier.

Multi-billionaire Roman Abramovich had a dream – to make Chelsea the most powerful club in the world. And as results have shown over the first couple of years of his reign, he has gone a long way to achieving that dream.

Abramovich was born of Jewish origin in October 1966, a few months after England had won the World Cup. His place of birth was Saratov on the Volga River in southern Russia. Orphaned at an early age, like Joe, he had a tough start in life. His mother died when he was 18 months old and his father, a collective farm worker, was killed in a construction accident when he was four. The future oligarch was brought up by his uncle and moved to the Komi province in the Arctic Circle, 1,000 miles from Moscow, where temperatures in winter plunged to -30°C. His early years were spent in a Soviet-era tower block where the residents were too poor to maintain their own boiler room and the place smelt of urine. While the local kids were playing football, Roman was indoors, a solitary child, watching and waiting.

Abramovich eventually moved to Moscow with a second uncle and enrolled at the famous Gubkin Oil and Gas Institute. From there, he dropped out of two colleges and was then drafted into the Russian Army. Having served his time, he started his own business selling plastic ducks out of his one-room apartment, and went on to build a second-hand tyre business.

The serious money started to be made when he began to trade in oil. This enabled him to raise $200 million to buy into the privatised oil industry as Soviet communism collapsed. Roman's mentor was the original Kremlin oligarch Boris Berezovsky, who gave him the money to fund the audacious insider takeovers of the State corporations. Critics of the oligarchs were of the view that the national wealth had been sold for peanuts at a rigged auction.

In 1996, he was appointed to the board of Sibneft, which was soon to be valued at $2 billion. Three years later, he was elected as a member of the Russian Parliament. In 2001, he was elected as governor of Chukotka, a desolate, frozen wasteland of a province in the far north-east of Russia, into which Roman poured a substantial sum of money to improve the lot of the indigenous population.

During his meteoric rise to becoming the second-richest man in Russia, his companies had faced the usual allegations of fraud, money laundering, racketeering and corruption, although, by virtue of being Governor, Abramovich automatically earned immunity from prosecution. He looked for a base for his business interests in one of the European capitals. The first stage of his operation was the switching of his huge financial empire to the UK-registered, financial-industrial holding company in the name of Millhouse Capital.

Roman Abramovich was unknown when he landed in London, but in a few months he was as famous as Robbie Williams. A fiercely private man, for years no pictures of him existed. Since taking over Chelsea, he is one of the most sought-after subjects of the paparazzi. At 36, he was young and rich beyond anyone's wildest dreams, and had a shy, withdrawn manner that many found intriguing. He appeared reluctant to make eye contact with anyone who came close to him, giving him an air of detachment, someone who was much more at home in the background making private deals in quiet corners, rather than talking about them in public.

The Chelsea deal was brokered by the Israeli football agent Pini Zahavi, who had previously engineered Rio Ferdinand's move to Manchester United for £30 million. Zahavi was a former sportswriter, who was linked to Abramovich through his strong ties with Russia's Jewish business community, of which Abramovich was the leading player. Zahavi was a master wheeler-dealer, a 'Mr Fix It' whose cut of the Chelsea deal was reported in some circles as being around £14 million. Not only did he mastermind the deal, but he also was a central figure in the first wave of transfers which rocked the football world to its foundations. To this day, he is a key member of Abramovich's entourage.

A major factor in attracting Abramovich to Chelsea must have been the neighbourhood, with its King's Road cachet. While Upton Park stood in one of the most deprived areas of the East End, Stamford Bridge was located in the bijou playground of the super-rich. Spurs was another option at the time for Abramovich, but it seemed that the allure of Chelsea's set-up, geographical location and the salesmanship of its senior management team was simply too much for Abramovich to resist.

The other crucial factor was that Chelsea were in the Champions League in the forthcoming season. At the end of the previous season, Chelsea had qualified for Europe by virtue of a narrow 2-1 victory over arch-rivals Liverpool, the winning goal coming via Danish winger Jesper Gronkjaer. It was perhaps the most vital goal ever scored in the history of Chelsea Football Club, because if Chelsea had not managed to qualify, then it would hardly have been a viable proposition for the Russian.

It was widely believed that the only game of football that Abramovich had witnessed was an epic Champions League tie between Manchester United and Real Madrid, that United won 4-3, with Beckham scoring twice, although it was not enough to stop them going out on aggregate. There is no doubt that Abramovich had sound business reasons for investing huge sums of money into Chelsea, ensuring him acceptance into the UK and European corporate arena. But he was fast becoming a huge fan of the game as well, and his undeniable enthusiasm – and growing love for the cut and thrust of a Premiership season – went far beyond a cold business venture, and endeared him even more to Chelsea's rapidly growing army of fans.

Without Abramovich, Chelsea would have sunk without trace. At first, the press expressed doubts that the huge sums being bandied about as potential investments in the club would never materialise – they were proved so wrong. Nobody in the history of the game had ever put so much of their own money where their mouth was.

It has been said that the deal that saved Chelsea was done in the Dorchester Hotel, those present being Ken Bates; the self-deprecating tycoon Abramovich; Trevor Birch, the financial expert; Eugene Tenenbaum, Abramovich's financial adviser and director of Millhouse Capital; and Richard Kreitzman.

Once Abramovich had been granted access to the toy shop, he started spending. What happened in the next few days was unprecedented, as he embarked on the biggest spending spree in football, although the reasons for the sudden spulrge were unclear. Claudio Ranieri, the manager at the time, seems to have had little say in the matter. The agents appeared to have the casting vote, and even England coach Sven-Goran Eriksson had been identified as a potential target; interestingly, many of the players who arrived at Stamford Bridge were particularly favoured by the England manager.

Chelsea went to Joe Cole's current club, West Ham, for the first acquisition. The player was his team-mate, 18-year-old Glen Johnson, a full-back who had only made 14 appearances (including two substitutions) in the claret-and-blue. Glenn Roeder had given him his premiership début, and it was even suggested that the south London-born Johnson may have ended up staying at Upton Park on a year's loan.

Gianfranco Zola, voted in a recent website poll to have been the greatest player to ever to don a Chelsea shirt, had returned to Sardinia to play for Serie B side Cagliari. Abramovich tried to buy him back, but Gianfranco, one of the game's gentlemen, had already given his word and remained loyal to the Italian club.

Joe Cole was purchased for £6.6 million on 5 August 2003. Zahavi was understood to have carried out all the negotiations with West Ham on the deal. Claudio Ranieri hailed the signing of Joe as 'the new Zola' and, in so doing, raised everyone's expectations to new levels. 'He is fantastic one-on-one with an opponent... he's very clever and passes the ball very well.' The Italian went on to compare him to the recently departed Italian genius. 'Cole is clever, strong and an Englishman. When I arrived, I said I wanted a blend of English players and some experienced ones. Without Gianfranco, I need a player who can dribble and run with the ball and beat an opponent. I think Cole is this type of player.'

The signing of Cole took the frantic spending spree to nearly £60 million. He was the fifth player to join Abramovich's all stars, claiming at the time, 'It was a difficult decision, but I feel now is the time to make a break from West Ham.' A spokesman for the West Ham Supporters Trust bemoaned the fact that he would be linking up at Chelsea with Frank Lampard, despite the fact that Abramovich's money for Johnson and Cole had certainly helped West Ham avoid administration. To show the depth of feeling for Joe, at one of West Ham's home matches, some fans hoisted a banner emblazoned with the slogan 'Say it ain't so, Joe'.

Aware that the fans might feel betrayed by their team captain – and the fact that he had crossed London to one of their bitterest rivals – Joe tried to smooth over the difficult situation by hinting that he would consider finishing his career at West Ham. 'I would like to think that I could return here some time in the future.'

Chelsea's swoop for the young West Ham captain fuelled rumours that they would not be pursuing their interest in Manchester United midfielder Juan Sebastian Veron. However,

Ranieri was given authorisation to purchase him as well, and he was signed for £15 million within hours of the Champions League deadline.

At the time, Sir Alex Ferguson had tracked the career progress of Joe Cole since his début for the Hammers, and if he had not signed for Chelsea, then United may well have splashed some of the Veron cash on Joe. Another northern Premiership club, believed to be either Liverpool or Newcastle, had also enquired about Joe's availability.

In addition to the West Ham duo, Chelsea had by then purchased Damien Duff (£17 million from Blackburn), Geremi (£7 million from Real Madrid) and Wayne Bridge (£7 million from Southampton, with Graham Le Saux being part of the deal). The new wage bill was estimated at being in the region of more than £70 million.

In an interview with BBC Radio 5 Live's Pat Murphy, the late Brian Clough was not reluctant to voice his opinion about the state of play at Stamford Bridge. 'You've got to hand it to Chelsea and their mysterious Russian owner with the deep pockets... They've brought something fresh into our domestic game. No one has a clue where all the new players are going to find themselves on the park, and I reckon they'll still be introducing themselves to each other when the clocks change.

'Their manager has brought the Christmas Stocking Formation to the team. When you dug deep into the stocking as a kid, you never knew what would come out first – the sweets, the toy or the three-penny piece. At Chelsea, they haven't got a clue what's in the stocking and what will be pulled out first. Who's going to play where?

'I'd love to know who's going to do all the fetching and carrying for all these glamorous, over-priced internationals who love to bomb forward yet can't tackle their dinner, never mind a ball. Veron, Cole, Duff won't get their hands dirty doing the donkey work.'

Abramovich's spending was still far from over – almost in deference to Clough, Claude Makelele. Described as the best midfield spoiler in the world, he was signed from Real Madrid for £15 million. It was a wonderful signing – Makelele was highly effective at breaking up opposition possession, and could turn defence into blistering attack.

Cole's signing was greeted with a mixed reception in the press. Ron Atkinson wondered what his best position was. Comparisons were being made with Zola, but Big Ron's view was that Zola could play off the front and still get goals. He doubted whether Joe would be able to score enough goals, citing the fact that he had only scored 13 goals in his entire West Ham career.

Lampard was delighted that he was linking up with Cole again, rating Joe as 'a great player, very skilful'. Veron, too, was looking forward to lining up alongside Joe in the Chelsea midfield. He was telling the media that Joe was the best player in England. Rio Ferdinand, Cole's former West Ham team-mate, had briefed Veron about Joe's vast potential. At that time, the partnership looked mouth watering. The showboating on the training ground must have been a joy to behold.

The first senior match Joe played for Chelsea was the away Champions League qualifier against SK Zilina of Slovakia, the first battle in the long campaign that Abramovich's fledgling army waged to conquer Europe. The gulf between the sides was enormous, both in terms of class and pay packets – Veron earned more in a day than any of the Slovakians did in a year.

Ranieri had given débuts to six of the summer signings, and the match turned out to be merely a stroll for Chelsea. Joe started the game on the bench. A first-half strike from six yards by Eidur Gudjohnsen after Duff had set up the chance put them in command. Veron started on the right, which surprised those who thought he would be the central fulcrum of the side and, as predicted, Chelsea's new midfielder looked more assured when he drifted inside.

Joe became the magnificent seventh when he replaced Duff after 70 minutes. Duff had shone but a sparkling cameo from Joe brightened the match. Within five minutes of his arrival, he helped Chelsea double their lead with a strong run into the penalty area. His neat pass found Gudjohnsen who was about to shoot when the Zilina defender Michal Drahno took the ball off his toes and elegantly curled it past his own keeper and into the top corner.

In his post-match press conference, Ranieri singled out Joe for praise. Abramovich missed the match, watching it instead from his yacht.

The Chelsea bandwagon rolled into Liverpool for the first Premiership match of the Abramovich era, with the Russian and his extensive entourage there in force. The Premiership held its collective breath – at last, everyone would get a chance to see what this new team of superstar individuals could conjure together. And it was not forgotten that they had been assembled in a spree that saw spending over the summer soar to more than the rest of the league put together.

This match was the first of a series of epic encounters with the Merseysiders. Joe did not start the game, as his abilities to change a game would be exploited to their maximum effect when introduced in the latter stages; Ranieri believed that his silky skills would be best employed as a dynamic, dazzling substitute. The eleven who started that match were: Cudicini, Johnson, Terry, Desailly, Bridge, Lampard, Geremi, Duff, Veron, Gronkjaer and Gudjohnsen, with Hasselbaink, Gallas, Cole, Forsell and Ambrosio on the bench. In less than two years, nine of the squad would no longer be at Stamford Bridge.

Joe made his first Premiership appearance for Chelsea after 74 minutes when he replaced Duff, by which time, Chelsea were leading by a solitary Veron goal. It was his first and last Premiership goal for Chelsea.

Liverpool equalised a few moments after Joe was introduced. Bridge rashly brought down El-Hadji Diouf for an obvious penalty. Cole's England buddy Michael Owen missed at the first attempt, tamely slotting the ball past Cudicini's post. Rather surprisingly, he was ordered to retake it and he scored at the second attempt. The old warrior Hasselbaink, a second-half substitute for Gudjohnsen, eventually won the game for Chelsea in the dying seconds, firing home Lampard's through ball, giving Jerzy Dudek in the Liverpool goal no chance of saving it.

Abramovich was delighted with the win and, if results continued in this vein, Ranieri would seem to have secured himself quite a future with the new-look Blues. The future was not quite so rosy for Liverpool manager Gérard Houllier, who would leave the club at the end of the season.

Chelsea's spending continued unabated as Adrian Mutu and Hernan Crespo joined Chelsea to send the spending spree above the £200 million mark. Mutu made his début the following week against Leicester after signing from Parma for £15.8 million. The 24-year-old Romanian had scored 17 goals in Serie A the previous season and was bought to add superstar firepower, which he did with a tremendous goal. Mutu's right-footed drive rebounded off the defensive wall and, without breaking stride, he drove in the rebound with his left foot. On this sort of form, it seemed at first glance that the money had been well spent.

Once again, Joe made a cameo appearance, coming on for Duff ten minutes from time and quickly setting up a chance. This would prove to be the pattern favoured by Ranieri at the time – keeping Joe on the bench until he was unleashed late in the game to make his mark. Joe did start the game in the Champions League second leg against Zilina, though, and Chelsea comfortably won the match 3-0.

It was a time of great uncertainty at Chelsea; the club was in a state of flux following the massive changes in personnel, and Chelsea was no different from any other club full of cliques, hierarchies and power struggles. The players who had been there the longest would ordinarily hold the most sway over the dressing room, although they might not actually be the sharpest tools in the box. Even in the early days of the Russian revolution, it was obvious that the players who wielded the most influence were Terry and Lampard, whose authority and reputations grew as Chelsea became more successful and more respected. Lampard had recovered his form after an uncertain start and slowly blossomed into one of the finest midfielders in the world. By the same token, Terry, the only player to break through from the youth side, continued to grow as a defender and a leader, being made captain of Chelsea and earning a place in the England squad. In the Ranieri regime, both players developed to become the consistent spine of the team, while others came and went around them.

One of the unwritten laws of the game is that a new player cannot ask for the ball, become an instant star or drive the team. With such an influx of new talent, though, the old codes were being rewritten as player after player jumped at the chance of staking his claim in the new hierarchy. Huge egos and personalities were the order of the day as individual players vied to exert their importance and status. Already, Veron and Makelele were trying to establish some sort of foothold in the dressing room which would enable them to have complete control of the team, but it was the Terry/Lampard combination that would eventually dominate. Huge emphasis was placed on the importance of the English factor, with the core of the team being made up of English players. Terry and Lampard were at the heart of things, and Bridge, a close friend of Terry's, was given the role of left-back to make his own.

Joe's progress was drastically curtailed at the start of his Chelsea career for a number of reasons. He was still a youngster, with little to show for his career so far, so he could not compete in terms of status with such world-class players as Desailly. Another was that Ranieri's time at the helm was coming to an end. Abramovich seemed to doubt Ranieri's ability to fulfil the master plan of achieving massive success – titles and trophies – immediately.

Joe was also unsettled by having to move into a West End Hotel. He had always lived in Essex with his family and at first badly missed their security and support. Also he was finding it hard to work with Ranieri. He told *Esquire* magazine: 'The first 6 months were difficult under Claudio. I separate what I think of Claudio as a person and as a coach. As a person I liked him; I thought he was a nice guy. But obviously as a coach he wasn't right for me. It was frustrating. I was always fit and training hard and I'm not one to go complaining to the press. People probably assumed "Joe is unhappy" and I was, but I never came out and said it. I don't want to rock the boat because I'm a professional and you just want to keep your head down and train hard.'

Blackburn forced a 2-2 draw at the Bridge in a run of three successive Premiership home games. Mutu scored again and Joe came on seven minutes from time. While displaying an undeniable brilliance on the ball, Mutu also had an unfortunate knack of blaming everyone else but himself for his own errors. One ploy that he seemed to use frequently was to complain that others could not keep pace with his speed of thought. The unfortunate Wayne Bridge found himself on the receiving end of some scornful stares and it was no surprise when he was replaced by Joe.

The other Cole – Andy – was the match star for Blackburn, scoring both their goals. This was partly due to the fact that Raineri was finding it particularly hard to find the right combination and formation for his midfield to operate successfully. Veron was largely ineffective, showing some great touches and control but being unable to come up with any particularly dominant play.

The next home match was against Tottenham, for whom there was not a great deal of love lost, and who had not enjoyed much recent success at Stamford Bridge. The last time they had won at Chelsea was when Gary Lineker had netted the winner.

Joe came on for the last 17 minutes but set up two goals in his best performance so far in a blue shirt. Mutu scored twice in that match to take his tally to four goals in three games. There was no doubt, the player who was emerging with the greatest distinction during this initial period was Mutu and, out of all the megastar recruits, he still looked the best value.

Spurs took an early lead through another of Joe's ex-West Ham team-mates Freddie Kanoute. It was a fine effort that shook Chelsea out of their lethargy and, after 34 minutes, Frank Lampard headed Chelsea level. Two minutes later, Duff set up the tricky Mutu to put Chelsea ahead. It was Duff's only telling contribution to the match and it came as no surprise when, after 73 minutes, Joe replaced him.

With his first touch, he put Mutu in for the third Chelsea goal. It looked all over but Spurs hit back to try and make a game of it. Kanoute scored again after a mix-up in the Chelsea defence. Joe moved centre stage, though, and helped to wrest control back for Chelsea before any more damage was done. His sublime forward pass was sufficient for Celestine Babayaro to control and cross for Hasselbaink to score from close range.

Joe admitted that he had not had the best of preparations for the match. He had opted to stay in the Chelsea hotel overnight but, at 5.30 am, the fire alarm went off. Joe did not vacate his room, though, steadfastly refusing to leave his bed. The England star was claiming that he needed the rest with the Spurs game looming in a few hours.

After the game, Joe was quick to praise his team-mate Mutu. 'Adrian is so sharp, he reminds me of Michael Owen. From what I've seen, he is already a great player who is going to get better and score lots of goals for Chelsea.'

A few days later, Joe flew out to the Czech Republic to play against Sparta Prague in the Group G Champions League match. His cameo against Spurs was not enough to earn him a spot in the opening line-up as Ranieri – or the 'Tinkerman' as he had become known, because of his penchant for rotating the squad, and making sweeping substitutions during games – made seven changes from the team that had thumped Spurs. Sparta's only plan was clearly designed to frustrate Chelsea at every turn, by denying them any space or time, and while Joe sat out a wretched game on the bench, a scrambled goal from the Chelsea defender Willie Gallas five minutes from time was the only bright spot.

Joe did not feature in any reserve games for Chelsea. The superstars did not turn out in those type of games as the reserves side was full of young wannabes. Consequently, Joe had a lot of time to fill and turned to his love of music. The Chelsea hero loves guitar music – his current faves are the Arctic Monkeys, Kaiser Chiefs (great Leeds fans) and Hard-fi. But his all time favourites are Oasis, the Manchester lads who, in the 90s, were the biggest band in the world. As *NME* once said, if Oasis didn't exist, it's hard to believe anyone would have had the gall to invent them. The focal point of the band, the Gallagher brothers, were rabid Man City fans. Colin Bell, City's most iconic player, featured on the cover of their first album. The first CD Joe ever bought was *Morning Glory* – it contained his favourite song 'Wonderwall'. At 13 he went to see his idols at Knebworth Park. His mother Susan was worried because little Joe was stuck on the station at four in the morning unable to get home due to the massive crowd. A quarter of a millon people (or six sold-out Chelsea home games) flocked to see the Gallagher brothers, at Knebworth.

Joe did get off the bench after almost an hour at Molineux, in the subsequent Premiership clash against Wolves. Crespo joined him on the field and chipped in two goals in the 5-0 romp. Wolves were looking down and out in the Premiership.

Another home Champions League fixture loomed against the Turkish champions Besiktas. It looked a formality against a side that had lost all of their six previous Champions League away games, but it turned out to be a disastrous night for the Blues as the Tinkerman made five changes from the previous match. They went down 0-2 as his gamble of playing three at the back misfired horribly. Serious questions were now being raised about Ranieri's judgement as Chelsea lost for only the second time at home in 42 European games. Worryingly, too, for the club executives and owner, 11,000 seats were unsold for the fixture.

Joe did not feature at all in the match. The problem for Ranieri was that his squad read like a *Who's Who* of the best players in Europe. Now he had even more options – with a full-strength squad available, he had 32 names at his disposal. In 5 Premiership matches, he had used 23 players, and a staggering 25 in the 3 Champions League matches. Nobody was clear as to what his best eleven was, least of all him; the talent was just too abundant, and too high-profile to be content warming the bench.

Against Besiktas, Ranieri employed three centre-backs plus wing-backs; the structure of a back four was discarded. The trusted 4-2-4 formation which had earned Chelsea a Champions League spot the previous season was ditched. Gallas struggled on the left, and Terry was always exposed for pace when dragged out wide. Geremi was no right-back and his failure to spot the overlap led to the first Turkish goal. A defensive error between Desailly and goalkeeper Cudicini gifted the striker Sergen his second goal.

The three at the back allowed Veron to play in his favoured role of central midfield but, again, the Argentinian, despite his many feints and flicks, found it hard to adjust.

Joe had replaced Veron 12 minutes from the end of a turgid 1-0 home win against Villa a few days earlier. One of the few cheers of the afternoon was when the substitution took place. The *Sun* was already announcing that it had all gone 'Pete Tong for Veron'. Emmanuel Petit, the unsung World Cup winner, was the pick of the midfield, while Jimmy Floyd Hasselbaink scored the winner after Sorensen had blocked a piledriver from Lampard.

Three away games followed in quick succession. In the first, Chelsea won 2-1 at Middlesbrough, but it was a terminally drab contest. Crespo headed the late winner from a perfect Duff cross, with Joe replacing Gronkjaer 12 minutes from the end.

It was becoming clear that the Chelsea players and the fans were anxious for some consistency in terms of the line-up and the formation. The press was also pointing out that Ranieri was more than capable of being over-elaborate in his constant changes, and that this was having an adverse effect on morale, the quality of play, and would start to affect results directly. His formation at the Riverside appeared to be 4-1-1-2-2, with Makelele playing as a sweeper and Gronkjaer and Duff as the wide men. Lampard therefore found himself isolated in the central midfield spot, often being outnumbered 3:1. For all his stamina and ability, Lampard clearly needed more support and a more effective formation within which to operate.

A goalless draw with Birmingham followed, with Joe making his full Chelsea début. He played 66 minutes before going off with cramp. Joe was pleased with his performance and, despite the lack of a goal, the fact that the result took Raineri's side to the top of the Premiership. Joe hoped that it would kick-start his season and said that he was desperate to keep his place for the forthcoming fixture at Highbury. 'I'm desperate to play against Arsenal and, if I get the nod, I'll be right up for it. I had to come off with cramp and it was difficult finding space, but I thought I did a good job. It meant a lot for me to start. I thought I've done well coming off the bench and, after my first start, will get fitter and stronger the more games I play.'

Joe was at the front of a midfield diamond against Birmingham and believed that he was playing in his best position, as opposed to the wide left berth he mainly occupied at Upton Park. 'I'd love to play in the middle. That's my natural position and, hopefully, I'll get the chance to play there again soon. It's where I want to play, but I've not played there for three years.'

Ranieri replaced Joe with Duff, who was ordered to take over Joe's role in central midfield but, towards the end of the match, he started drifting out to his preferred left wing. Lampard was not the dominant force he usually was, and had a poor match. The Italian coach praised Joe by saying, 'Joe played well behind the two strikers [Hasselbaink and Crespo]. Of course, we are not used to playing with one midfielder behind the strikers and it will take time to adjust. I will try him there again but maybe not next match. Joe knows I like him and he can be the key to open the door.'

As the Arsenal game approached, Ranieri's golden team now had the opportunity to test itself against the very best. But despite the revolution that had taken place at Stamford Bridge, and the sheer depth of quality that the team undoubtedly had, Chelsea were still not yet ready to overthrow an Arsenal team that had displayed an unrivalled level of skill and consistency over several seasons. The full impact of Abramovich's vast wealth upon the English game was yet to be felt, although it was starting to dawn on many in the game what the implications would be.

Ranieri did not play Joe in his starting line up at Highbury, and a disappointing day for the young star was made worse by an Arsenal win. The Gunners' great run of form in battles with their London neighbours continued with the 2-1 win, Edu giving them an early lead with a deflected free kick. Within three minutes, Crespo levelled the score with a fabulous strike. It was Ranieri's fifty-second birthday, and the goal – a cute side-step and a blistering drive from 25 yards – must have seemed like the most perfect present.

A rare error by Chelsea keeper Cudicini presented Arsenal with all three points. Robert Pires's cross was horribly fumbled by the Italian international and the ball rolled loose for Henry to score a tap-in.

Lazio visited the Bridge four nights later. It was a vital match for Chelsea following the shattering loss to Besiktas; they simply had to win. Joe was on the bench, and Chelsea started brightly. Things looked bleak for them when Simone Inzaghi squeezed between Terry and Gallas to head home after 39 minutes, the Chelsea defence having lost concentration after clearing a corner. The Lazio striker appeared to have sent Chelsea's hopes crashing, but Chelsea's pedigree and commitment were tested fully that night, and the team proved that they were there for the long haul.

The English backbone of Lampard and Terry established themselves as the core of the side, with Veron, back in the side after a three-match absence, again flattering to deceive. Swaggering around in the first half, his influence dwindled in the latter stages of the match. Lampard was taking the game to the Italians, though, and 12 minutes into the second half he levelled the game with a goal that has since become his trademark. The impressive Duff found Gudjohnsen, who controlled the ball perfectly and crossed low to the edge of the area. Lampard, drove on from midfield, and in one fluid movement crashed a marvellous, swerving shot into the top right-hand corner.

Veron then went off to be replaced by Gronkjaer. With his first touch, he crossed to the near post where the predatory Mutu slammed a right-footed shot against Jaap Stam; he scored from the rebound with his stronger left foot. Joe replaced the exhausted Mutu three minutes from time, and had little chance to make any impact. His team had done their job, though, with Chelsea winning the game and topping their group.

Joe started his first home game of the season when Kevin Keegan's Manchester City were the visitors the following Saturday. Lazio had carved out some chances at the end of the game and, with a hard game to come in Rome, Ranieri was taking no chances. Joe linked up well with Mutu, who was the Man of the Match, setting up Hasselbaink for the only goal of the game after 33 minutes.

Of the vast array of talent on display, Mutu had become a huge favourite with the Chelsea fans, but Veron had yet to win them over. Joe was regarded as a work in progress, a player of fantastic potential, but one who had yet to deliver consistently at the highest level. He would have to be given a consistent chance to shine, and then deliver on a regular basis, for the fans to take him to their hearts.

Robbie Fowler was playing for City that afternoon, another maverick, but one who was now at the opposite end of his career. Unlike Joe, Fowler had proved his worth and quality on the field – he'd got the medals and international caps to prove it – but he was now struggling with form and fitness, and had shown only glimpses of the player he once was. When he first burst on to the scene, with six goals in his first four games for Liverpool, the boy from Toxteth was compared to the greatest goal scorer of all time –Jimmy Greaves. Bad luck and controversy meant that he never really achieved the world-class status that seemed rightfully his, although a bullet header in the first half brought a wonder, point-blank save from Cudicini, and served as a brief reminder of what might have been.

After the glamour of the European games, Chelsea's next opponents were Notts County in the Carling Cup. The Midlands club had a grand pedigree, having been one of the founding clubs to have formed the original football league, but they were now in serious debt and struggling near the foot of Division Two. Around the time Joe was born, Notts County had won at Stamford Bridge on their way to promotion. Those were the dying days of the Mears family dynasty, and Chelsea were drifting aimlessly, seemingly heading for obscurity. How times had changed.

That game against Notts County was a landmark moment for Joe, who scored his first senior goal for Chelsea. Hasselbaink was in fine form, and had put Chelsea in front early on. Notts County showed tremendous spirit, equalising on 27 minutes with Barras heading home a corner. The lanky striker gave the home defence a hard time all evening.

Gudjohnsen equalised before half-time, and scored again on the hour from the penalty spot, after Gronkjaer had been fouled by the County keeper, Mildenhall. Joe replaced the Danish winger soon after and, despite appearing on paper to offer little in the way of a real contest, the game continued to deliver some really exciting action. Notts County refused to lay down and, in front of an excited 35,000-strong crowd, threw everything into attack. Bob Dylan once said, 'When you got nothing, you got nothing to lose... ' and playing with a complete lack of restraint, Stellard impertinently scored for Notts County with five minutes to go, raising their hopes of a massive upset. Marco Ambrosio was making his Chelsea début in goal, and gifted him the chance after a mix-up.

Chelsea's strength and resilience were again tested, and the Premiership side eventually gained the upper hand, as Joe won the tie with Chelsea's fourth goal of the night.

Joe had had a terrific match and was Chelsea's outstanding player, earning praise from his manager. 'This was his best performance of the season,' Ranieri said, and he was prompted to include Joe in the starting line-up for the next match at Everton.

Merseyside had seldom been a happy hunting ground for the Blues, and the match looked finely poised with Everton missing some good chances, and Terry enduring an uncharacteristically shaky defensive display. The Londoners found themselves under sustained pressure, but still managed to go ahead through Adrian Mutu, who scored the only goal of the game with a flying header from Geremi's low cross early in the second half.

After the match, Ranieri was full of praise for Joe's skills, and seemed to hint that Joe would figure more extensively in his plans as the season unfolded. 'Everything he did was the right thing. I have a lot of confidence in him... he is quick when he needs to be, then slow. Every time he received the ball, he made things happen.'

Joe was clearly relishing his time on the pitch, and was keen to make the most of every opportunity Ranieri gave him. 'I am loving it,' he said after the match. 'To play at such a high level at a demanding place like Everton is very pleasing. I am still learning and I feel I am getting better with every game now. I am happy with the way I played and the way I am progressing... I aim to keep playing the best I can and stick to my game, then it is down to the manager. But the main thing is that Chelsea win, whoever plays... '

Wayne Rooney, on the other hand, had a quiet match, while speculation over his future continued to rage. Like Joe, prior to his departure from West Ham, Rooney was now carrying that great weight of expectation; he was the new kid on the block – and a remarkably gifted one at that – who promised so much, but was unlikely to achieve greatness while remaining at the club that had nurtured and supported him. The press had been full of stories about Abramovich being about to table a bid in the region of £35 million for Rooney, a price that looks a bargain now given his consistent brilliance for club and country. The Toffees at the time were fighting a trading loss of £13 million and had debts in excess of £30 million, so Rooney's departure was no longer a matter of 'if', but 'when'.

Chelsea's next Champions League fixture was away in Italy to play the return match against Lazio. After the nail-biter at the Bridge, Chelsea anticipated another tense affair in the white-hot cauldron of Lazio's home ground, the 82,000-capacity Olympic Stadium, which they share with Roma.

Joe was on the bench as Ranieri returned to his birthplace, where, as a boy, he had supported and played for Lazio's bitter rivals Roma. Veron seemed happy to be back facing his old club as well. 'I will have extra stimulus,' he said. 'It will be a special match. Once I get on the pitch, though, I'll be concentrating on the game and I will forget about those feelings.' Twenty minutes before kick-off, he indulged in a lap of honour of his own, walking the perimeter track with a Lazio scarf draped around his neck.

The coach opted for a four-man midfield of Lampard, Veron, Makelele and Duff. Veron set up the first goal when his brilliant free kick was spilled by the former Ipswich goalkeeper Matteo Sereni. The ball rebounded off Crespo, another ex-Lazio star, who scored off his chest against his old club.

The match hinged on the Lazio defender Mihajlovic being sent off at the start of the second half. Mihajlovic, a hard-man defender, was dismissed for two bookable offences on Duff. Throughout the game, he had been involved in a running feud with Mutu, whom he allegedly subjected to constant racist abuse.

Sereni was at fault again after 70 minutes when he failed to hold Lampard's stinging shot and Gudjohnsen made it 2-0. Duff, whose skill and pace had terrorised the lumbering Lazio defence all night, scored a brilliant solo goal to put Chelsea 3-0 up five minutes later. Joe came on for Veron immediately afterwards, and Lampard wrapped up the win by clipping home the rebound after Sereni had blocked Gudjohnsen's goal-bound effort.

The only blight on an otherwise superlative performance

was the dismissal in the last minute of Glen Johnson, Joe's former West Ham team-mate, for stupidly kicking the ball away. It was his second offence after earlier being penalised for fouling Muzzi.

Overall, this was perhaps the best performance in Ranieri's reign so far. Even Zola turned up on the night to see his old team-mates and took the time to praise Joe for his contribution.

Another after-effect of that win in Rome was the strengthening of Chelsea's credibility as a bona fide side, and not just a hastily assembled group of self-serving, superstar showboaters. There was now no denying the quality and sense of purpose in the side and the rest of Europe had to sit up and take notice of the team's steady progress. But not everyone in Chelsea colours had managed to silence the critics, and the jury was still out on some of Ranieri's more unorthodox tactics. As for Joe, he'd done enough to earn some respect from his fellow professionals and the fans – but as a peripheral member of the squad, he still had a great deal to prove.

3

In the Wings

'I aim to keep playing the best I can and stick to my game,
then it is down to the manager. But the main thing is that Chelsea
win, whoever plays, as long as we keep on winning.'
Joe Cole, November 2003

AFTER THE BLUES' glorious triumph in Rome, the T-shirt
sellers on the Fulham Road on match days were quick
to jump on to the bandwagon. Most of them had a *Gladiator*
theme, after the smash-hit film starring the pugnacious Russell
Crowe. The kings of the Colosseum – Lampard, Duff and
Crespo – featured on most of the clothing, brandishing swords
and shields as their great victory was commemorated. The
DVD of the the Ridley Scott film is one of Joe's all time
favourites. The mantra of 'strength and honour', Crowe's
battle cry to his troops, was frequently heard in the Chelsea
dressing room at the time.

A fragile Newcastle, then managed by Bobby Robson, were
next up to test themselves against the new Roman army.
Ranieri picked an unchanged side for the first time since
March and, in front of Bernie Ecclestone, Abramovich's guest

for the afternoon, Chelsea raced into a 3-0 lead by half-time with goals from Johnson, Crespo and a Lampard penalty, awarded when Newcastle's O'Brien committed a professional foul on Mutu, for which he was subsequently dismissed.

Joe came on for the exhausted Mutu after 64 minutes; this was now the ninth occasion this had happened in twelve Premiership appearances. Duff and Gudjohnsen added further goals to dispel any doubts that the new Blues were not deadly serious contenders for major honours. Joe was being dubbed 'Joe 90' in the tabloids after the Gerry Anderson cartoon character, but he was not unhappy at the way things were going for him, or uneasy over the set-up at Chelsea, and spoke to the *Guardian* about Ranieri in glowing terms, saying, 'He's an Italian Kevin Keegan, always smiling and making jokes. He's an enigmatic character, I have a lot of faith in him and how he can improve my game. I like his honesty; he will always tell me what he thinks. He has no trouble getting his point across and he is definitely the man to lead Chelsea to a lot of success over the coming years.'

Joe started Chelsea's Premiership clash against Southampton, and played for almost an hour before giving way to Jesper Gronkjaer. Wing-back Mario Melchiot slotted home the only goal for the Blues following a clever overlap, but it was a scrappy game and few players, if any, covered themselves in glory. Chelsea were depressingly ineffectual and had not really deserved the three points. It was in this match that Joe displayed one of his most outrageous pieces of skill. This party piece involved him standing on his left leg and swivelling to kick the ball with his right foot. He had first tried this out in the Youth Cup final against Coventry.

The next match was against Sparta Prague in the Champions League. Joe, in the side for the injured Veron, was the best player on the field in a 0-0 draw. Tord Grip, Eriksson's assistant, was impressed by his tight ball control and accurate passing. Joe provided pace, penetration and width on the left flank as Chelsea tried to break down a stubborn Czech side. Apart from an elaborate back-heel that gifted possession to Prague, Joe had an immaculate game. Geremi replaced him towards the end as Chelsea squandered chance after chance. They had qualified, though, and, once again, Cole was singled out for praise by the Italian coach.

On the following Sunday, Premiership Champions Manchester United visited the Bridge in another test for Ranieri's side. Joe was in the starting line-up and won the penalty from which Lampard was again successful. Lampard's growth as a footballer and influence on the pitch that season was very public and unstoppable; Joe's was far less obvious, but he was subtly contributing an enormous amount to the team's overall quality and results.

The arrival of French international Makelele for £16.6 million from Real Madrid enabled Lampard to push forward; it was no secret that the Congo-born player was one of the best defensive midfielders and playmakers in the world, whom Ranieri described as the 'battery for his fantastic watch'.

Duff looked likely to start the match but Ranieri opted to start with Joe at the tip of his diamond formation, with Lampard and Geremi the wide players in midfield. During the first half-hour, Joe worked hard in and around the United box to lose his marker, Silvestre, create openings for his team-mates or latch on to any loose balls that came his way. In the 27th minute, he darted into the penalty area to pick up Crespo's neat, flicked pass. Roy Keane immediately challenged him, and referee Alan Wiley pointed to the spot. It was a nailed-on penalty.

When the protests from Keane, Giggs and others had finally subsided, up stepped Lampard to send keeper Tim Howard the wrong way.

Joe could have clinched it on the stroke of half-time. The ball rebounded to him off Ferdinand but he blasted inches over the bar with the goal at his mercy. Joe was the replaced 15 minutes later by Duff.

Now that Joe had departed, Keane was able to drive United forward, and they pushed up for the last quarter of the game. Cristiano Ronaldo, Manchester United's young and brilliant Portuguese winger, came on for the last 20 minutes, and he proceeded to terrorise Chelsea down the right wing, as Giggs marauded down the left. The thin blue line stood firm, though, to record their sixth consecutive clean sheet.

Already, the seeds of the title-winning side were being planted. A rock-solid defence and industrious midfield are essential requirements of a successful, modern-day side, although more work still needed to be done in the areas of attacking play and capitalising on striking opportunities.

The victory put Chelsea on top of the table and they were made 5-4 favourites to win the title; Arsenal were a point behind, and were still unbeaten.

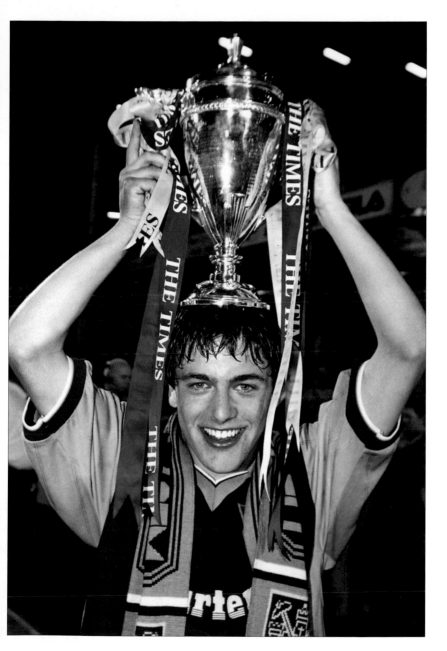

Joe started his professional career at West Ham United FC. An
obvious talent from early on, here he holds aloft the FA Youth Cup
after the victory over Coventry in the 1999 final. *© Cleva Media*

Above: West Ham United Youth Players celebrate their victory in the FA Youth Cup Final. Joe can be seen in the middle, centre right, caught up in the jubilation after they thrashed their opponents 6-0. © *Cleva Media*

Below: Joe cuts a fine, composed dash as he takes a leading role in the 1999 Inter Toto Cup v Finnish side FC Jokerit. © *Cleva Media*

Chelsea v West Ham, November 1999, and Joe Cole runs past Chelsea legend Gianfranco Zola, who was to leave Stamford Bridge a month before Joe's arrival for £6 million in August 2003.

© Cleva Media

Above: A 16-year-old Joe launches the Adidas Grassroots Partnership with future England boss Kevin Keegan.   © *Rex Features*

Below: Three years later and Keegan presents Joe at a press conference before the England World Cup qualifier against Germany in October 2000.   © *PA Photos*

Above: Joe heads the ball during training at La Manga prior to the vital qualifying game against Greece, June 2001. © *PA Photos*

Below: Joe meets Prince Philip at Upton Park while the Queen looks on. Her Majesty was quick to congratulate Joe on his selection as the youngest member of the England squad for the 2002 World Cup.

© *PA Photos*

Joe took time to feature in Sven-Goran Eriksson's England set-up.
Here they are seen together in March 2002, a matter of weeks before
the start of the World Cup. In the event, he appeared only once as a
substitute against Eriksson's home nation, Sweden. *© PA Photos*

Above: Cole sports another new haircut during a pre-season training session in late summer 2002.
© *Getty Images*

Below: Not only deadly in open play, Joe scored a belter of a free kick against Serbia-Montenegro in June 2003.
© *PA Photos*

Above: Joe signs for Premiership giants Chelsea alongside Juan Veron, as they display their new shirt numbers with manager Claudio Ranieri.

© *Rex Features*

Below: Later in 2004, a cool Joe Cole arrived in Portugal for the Euro 2004 competition.

© *PA Photos*

Paul Smith, Chelsea's interim executive, said at the time that the club would not baulk 'at spending £50 million' on a player. Who exactly the player was he did not say.

After the Lord Mayor's show against the champions, Chelsea had a more mundane fixture against Reading in the Carling Cup at the splendid Madejski Stadium. The ground was named after their owner, a scaled-down Abramovich, who had made his money in the motor trade. The Blues scrambled home with a 1-0 win, the eleventh time so far that season they had prevailed by the slenderest of margins. Jimmy Floyd Hasselbaink scored the match-winning goal, and Joe played the first half before Makelele came on to replace him. American goalkeeper Marcus Hahnemann pulled off an astonishing save to deprive Joe of a goal early on.

The same thing happened at Leeds the following Saturday. Joe was about to pull the trigger when defender McPhail slid in from nowhere to dispossess him, averting an almost certain goal. Leeds were rock bottom of the Premiership at the time and were teetering on the edge of freefall into financial oblivion. There was little love lost between Chelsea and Leeds – it was a bruising, fiercely contested match, with both Alan Smith and Paul Robinson in the Elland Road line-up. Leeds were managed by Eddie Gray, who had been a central figure in the 1970 Cup Final, that eventually went to a replay at Old Trafford, which Chelsea won in extra time. Former Chelsea chief executive Trevor Birch, who had been unceremoniously replaced by Peter Kenyon, was now at Leeds, and had managed temporarily to stave off the financial meltdown.

Back on the pitch, Jermaine Pennant, on loan from Arsenal,

put Leeds ahead after 18 minutes with a brilliant solo effort. Pennant, like Mutu, was an explosive but unpredictable talent; once the most expensive teenager in football, his career had all but stalled at Highbury. His personal life had been perpetually linked with ill-discipline and drink problems and would eventually be sacked from Arsenal. On his day, though, he was a formidable player with a great deal of skill. Now at Birmingham, Pennant has been making a real effort to rebuild his career.

Joe was replaced by Crespo at half-time. He was very closely marked and could find no space to work his magic. Lampard was dead-legged and limping, but Duff equalised near the end to salvage a point.

Joe was finding things at Chelsea very different from his time at Upton Park, as he explained to Tim Lovejoy in the *Esquire* interview: 'When I was playing for West Ham it was like a completely different sport. You go out there for Chelsea and you know you've got to take the game to teams, so for me that's perfect. Some games at West Ham, I didn't see the ball for half an hour, 40 minutes and the player I am, I want to help out and get my foot in. Sometimes I was doing too much, defending too much, tracking back. It took me six months to adjust to Chelsea.'

Joe sat out Chelsea's next European trip. This time, they travelled to north-west Germany to play Beskitas in their final Group G match, which was played in the grand AufSchalke Arena in Gelsenkirchen. UEFA had ruled it should be switched from Istanbul following a spate of suicide bombings in the Turkish city, but Besiktas felt aggrieved and accused Chelsea of 'running from terrorism'.

There was, though, a massive ex-patriate Turkish population in that region of Germany, so there remained every chance of a deeply intimidating atmosphere for the English players to contend with, as well as verbal abuse and missiles thrown from the stands. Sure enough, despite a decent number of English fans, Chelsea faced an uphill struggle. Again, Ranieri gambled by only playing three at the back, but it paid off with late goals from Hasselbaink and Wayne Bridge.

It was Bridge's first goal for Chelsea and, in a few months, he was to score one that would prove to be even more significant. The final was to be played in that stadium and Chelsea were very keen to return in the Spring.

From the lofty heights of the Champions League, Chelsea were brought down to earth rather quickly with their next Premiership match against Bolton at Stamford Bridge. John Terry commented after the match that Ranieri had been quick to focus on the next task in hand. 'Straight after the game, the lads were all happy but the boss came in and told us to forget about Besiktas. He said that Bolton were a good side and told us to start thinking about them. He said there's no point in going back to the Bridge after winning 2-0 and throwing it all away by not beating Bolton. That sums him up.'

Now was the time for Chelsea to push on and consolidate their position at the top of the league but, as so often proved to be the case that season, when the going got tough, the big guns ended up firing blanks.

Joe was on the bench again and watched as Crespo headed the home side into the lead on 21 minutes. The lead was wiped out, though, when Bolton deservedly equalised through Bruno

N'Gotty, and the visitors went on to dominate the second half. Chelsea looked tired and, at times, were almost overrun in midfield, badly missing the strength and relative experience of Veron and Petit. Veron had a back injury which had troubled him for months, and World Cup-winner Petit was slowly recovering from knee surgery.

Frank Lampard was Chelsea's busiest player but, 13 minutes from time, he was replaced by Joe. John Terry, who had a poor match, made his most telling contribution by gifting Bolton three points in the dying moments, when he deflected a cross from substitute Henry Pedersen into his own net.

After the match, Ranieri stated that his players were trying too hard to make an impression, and he was not above some succinct – albeit ungrammatical – comments about his team's efforts when he said later, 'We play very crap. We forget everything. Bolton play very well, we only watch them.'

Chelsea next travelled to Villa Park in the Carling Cup, where they had crashed out previously in successive FA Cup semi-finals in the 1960s. History was to repeat itself.

Joe started on the wing with Lampard rested for once, although his record-breaking Premiership run was still unaffected. Jimmy Floyd Hasselbaink played up front as the lone striker. Neil Sullivan, the ex-Tottenham keeper, came into the side to replace Cudicini and, as the match unfolded, Joe shone again as the most influential player, while an unbalanced Chelsea side struggled to make any impression.

Terry was given a torrid time by the Villa star Juan Pablo Angel, who beat him for pace to score the first goal. Chelsea's only reply was a couple of long-range efforts by Joe that tested the Villa goalie Thomas Sorensen. Ranieri brought on Lampard at half-time for Makelele, who was not playing well in a side that was struggling to find inspiration. The Blues improved with Lampard's introduction, and Crespo (on for Duff) added strength to the attack. The Argentinian set up Joe for a deserved equaliser, but they were unable to capitalise on it. Villa scored the winner 12 minutes from time when Sullivan failed to hold another stinging drive from Angel, and Gavin McCann smashed in the winner from point-blank range.

Chelsea seemed to be struggling up front, having scored only eight goals in the equivalent number of games. Mutu, after a sensational start, was struggling to maintain his form and his lethal strikes in front of goal deserted him. Crespo was finding it hard to adjust to the tempo of the English game, although he was on target in the next match away to Fulham. Joe came on after seven minutes when Duff dislocated his shoulder. Crespo's goal, six minutes from time, brought a great deal of relief to the away supporters and the manager, who must have been wondering how the assembled talent on display could find scoring so difficult.

Chelsea lost their chance of the championship on Boxing Day when they were savagely mauled by Charlton and ended up losing 2-4. It was their heaviest defeat of the season and the one that did most to undermine their confidence and show the rest of the Premiership that Abramovich's new, gleaming outfit was far from the finished article. The defence that had proved to be so solid was exposed time after time. Johnson looked particularly vulnerable and, once again, Terry's lack of pace was ruthlessly exposed. Speculation was also rife in the press that Ranieri's reign would soon be over. With a series of indifferent performances, and the Tinkerman unable to juggle the outstanding array of talent effectively, the storm clouds were gathering, and it would take a mighty effort, or a miracle, for Ranieri to convince his employers that he was still be the best man for the job at the end of the season.

Marcel Desailly's glittering career was also coming to an end. At 35, he could not be expected to compete at such a consistently high level. Joe started the match in Duff's role but found it hard physically to make any impression.

Two days after their defeat at The Valley, a shell-shocked Chelsea entertained Portsmouth, who had had little joy in recent encounters with the Blues. Ranieri's men regained some of their dignity – and a little self-respect – when they ran out comfortable 3-0 winners, in which the high spot was a blistering drive from Lampard for the second goal. Joe was rested after the Charlton debacle and played no part in the game.

Joe was on the bench for the 2-2 Cup draw at Watford, which turned out to be a strange match played out on a dreadful pitch, that also served as the home ground for Saracens rugby club. Chelsea trailed twice, but a rare penalty from Gudjohnsen and another Lampard goal earned them a draw.

Liverpool earned their first Premiership win over Chelsea when they managed a 0-1 victory at the Bridge on a freezing cold January night. Joe started the match, but was unable to make any real impact on the game, Ranieri pushing him wide to try and to prise open the Liverpool defence. After a slow start, he found the rhythm of the game and, after 30 minutes, he took a pass from Makelele on the edge of the box and his sublime flick put Gudjohnsen in to smash a shot just over the bar.

Three minutes later, Bruno Cheyrou exchanged passes with Emile Heskey before thundering a shot past Cudicini. It was about the only significant goal that Cheyrou was to score in his brief career at Liverpool, but it was a beauty.

Joe was inexplicably substituted by Ranieri on the hour, and any chance Chelsea had of rescuing the game went with him. Liverpool were without their megastars Owen and Gerrard, but they were still capable of containing Chelsea easily. According to the Liverpool manager, Gérard Houllier, Chelsea were made to look 'ordinary'.

The difficulties in front of goal continued for Chelsea, and Mutu particularly was picked out for criticism. The Romanian was a shadow of the player that had exploded on the scene just a few short months back. Already, rumours were circulating about his lifestyle choices, and about his attitude to the game, and in his book, *Proud Man Walking*, Ranieri says that Mutu 'had all the skills and flair, but to win championships things have to be right between the ears'. His other strike partner, Crespo, also came in for criticism.

Chelsea had lost three of their last five games, two of them at home. After the defeat to the Reds, Abramovich had a 40-minute 'shut door' with his Italian general. Raineri emerged later bloodied but unbowed. He said that he would be continuing to manage the team, and that Abramovich was still being patient as Chelsea were being rebuilt. Most observers, though, felt that the writing wasn't just on the wall for Ranieri, but that the wall had been entirely covered in graffiti.

JOE COLE

A brace of 4-0 victories in the next two games, however, earned Ranieri some breathing space from the Soviet firing squad. Joe contributed to both victories, the first of which was away at Leicester. The Chelsea star helped his side to a decisive victory when he set up the opening goal for Hasselbaink. Melchiot threaded the ball through for Joe, whose low cross was slightly deflected by a Leicester defender. Hasselbaink reacted quickly and instinctively adjusted his balance before back-heeling it into the net. He added a second when his thundering free kick was deflected in off a defender.

In a hectic finish, Joe was replaced by Gallas and the substitute Mutu scored his first goal in 13 matches to make it 3-0, and there was still time for Babayaro to run through for the fourth, whereupon he treated the crowd to one of his trademark somersaults in celebration.

Joe lasted the whole 90 minutes against Watford in the replay at the Bridge; it was the first time he had played an entire game that season. Mutu scored two and the old firm of Hasselbaink and Gudjohnsen chipped in with a goal apiece. Joe made the third goal (Mutu's second) with a wonderful long pass that really set the crowd buzzing.

Off the field, Veron's Barnes Common mansion was burgled by a drugged-up home invader wielding a machete. The injured midfielder's children were threatened and £50,000 worth of valuables was snatched in a terrifying ordeal which unsettled the Argentinian superstar even more. Crespo's future wife was also a guest in the house, which added to the striker's problems over settling down in London.

Scott Parker joined Chelsea from Charlton for £10 million

in January 2004 to stiffen the midfield even further. Joe and he were both graduates from the Lileshall academy and were good pals. The tough-tackling, crisp-passing Parker had dominated in the 4-2 thrashing of Chelsea a few weeks before. It was generally considered that he was one of the quickest players with the ball at his feet in the country and, naturally, Charlton were bitterly disappointed to lose their brightest star to Abramovich's empire. Their chairman, Martin Simons, had originally told Abramovich to 'get lost'. The press were quick to draw a comparison with Joe, and pointed out that he was yet to play a full 90 minutes in the Premiership. The fact was not lost on Parker himself, who made it quite clear that he understood that his days of being a first-choice team player for Charlton were long gone. He said that his move was inevitable, given the financial incentives, and the lure of top-flight domestic and European football, but he was realistic about his chances of actually playing regularly in the first team. 'It's a squad game, and that's what I'm willing to do… It can only make me a better player going to Chelsea.' The fact that he had to wait until October to make his first Premiership start is an indication of just how much competition there was in the squad at the time, and how much patience Parker would need to see out his four-and-a-half-year contract.

Reports were also circulating that Chelsea were looking at a Dutch winger called Robben and that a deal had already been set up to purchase a new goalkeeper in the summer called Cech from Rennes for £9 million.

A Sunday afternoon fixture against Birmingham was next on the agenda. It finished goalless and two precious points were lost. Chelsea still remained third, six points adrift of Arsenal. Joe hit the post in the first half, but it was a frustrating game and he again gave way to Mutu on the hour.

Joe then went to Scarborough for the Fourth Round FA Cup tie. In the 1980s, Chelsea had suffered an embarrassing defeat there, but now the clubs were a world apart. Scarborough had now fallen into the Conference and Chelsea were on their way to becoming one of the most powerful clubs in the world. When the draw was made it was reported that Joe did not even know where Scarborough was.

Terry scored the only goal of the game early on. Melchiot nodded on after Chelsea had worked a short corner and Terry scored from a yard out. Joe played all 90 minutes, but failed to shine. It was not only his geography that had let him down. Nine minutes from time, Gallas clearly handled in the box but no penalty was given, to the disgust of the home fans. Scarborough made £500,000 out of the day, which secured their future for the next two years.

Joe was suspended for the 3-2 win at Blackburn, having been punished for an incident that had occurred while he was still a West Ham player. In April 2003, there had been a fracas on the pitch between Bolton and West Ham players at the Reebok Stadium, during which Joe allegedly used 'abusive or insulting language' towards the fourth official. He was fined a total of £15,000, and received a two-match ban.

When Joe was not in the side he would spend time with his mates and try to watch as many games as he could. One of his pals from his school days he kept in touch with was Jay Bothroyd – another gifted prodigy. At one time he was in

Arsenal's star-studded youth-team, but was shown the door for not quite making it. He drifted down to Coventry and whenever Chelsea were in town Joe would go and watch his pal. He later plied his trade at Perugia. Gaddafi's son was on the books at the same time and the President had a plan to play a girl in Serie A. Joe must have had some interesting chats with him.

Meanwhile, Scott Parker made his Chelsea debut and was quietly impressive. Ranieri again shook up his midfield, polishing the diamond that was the central framework of his side. Against Blackburn, he employed both Makelele and Petit at the back of the diamond. The ex-Arsenal and Barcelona star did a fine job of shielding the back four. Lampard was at the tip of the diamond. And while Ranieri tinkered, neither Joe or Gronkjaer were able to establish themselves in the side on a regular basis.

The astute insight of Di Canio, explained in his auto-biography, rang very true at that time; when he said, 'Cole needs to be challenged, he needs to be stimulated. Coaching somebody like him is difficult, but you cannot apply the same standards to everybody. You need to make him feel hungry, you need to make him feel like he still has a long way to go – which he does.'

The noose was tightening around Ranieri's neck, and the man applying the pressure was Peter Kenyon. The tough chief executive had been headhunted by Abramovich, having quit Manchester United to join Chelsea in September 2003. On 'gardening leave' for five months, he hit the ground running once he was free to commence his duties formally at the Bridge. Within weeks, former chairman Ken Bates had quit the club and had been replaced by the urbane, Ivy League lawyer Bruce Buck. Bates said he was resigning from Chelsea 'due to a clash of Eastern and Western culture'.

It became an open secret that Ranieri would not be in charge after the season was over. It was noticeable now that the Stamford Bridge hierarchy were mumbling that anything less than winning a trophy would mean that the season had been a 'failure'. The normal excuses – the gradual rebuilding process taking time, or allowing a period of grace for the team to gel – all now apparently counted for nothing. Silverware was now no longer a bonus – it was a necessity.

The second match of Joe's suspension saw him sit out the home game against Charlton. The midfield was severely depleted – Duff, Makelele, Petit and Geremi were all ruled out, and Scott Parker was precluded from playing under the terms of his transfer. Chelsea scrambled home 1-0 courtesy of a Jimmy Floyd Hasselbaink penalty. A rather indifferent match was perhaps best summed up when Eidur Gudjohnsen replaced Hasselbaink for the last 16 minutes, and he did enough to be voted the Sky TV Man of the Match. Chelsea were still six points behind Arsenal, who they were to meet in the Cup and league in the coming weeks.

First, though, there was a trip to Portsmouth in mid-week, for which Joe was named as a sub. Parker looked like he had a decent Chelsea future ahead of him when he struck in the 18th minute to score his first Chelsea goal. In doing so, he became the 17th different player that season to score for the club and it was only February. Parker revelled in his midfield tackling role as Portsmouth battled hard to save the game.

Crespo came on for Mutu, whose form now was increasingly erratic. The Chelsea striker chested in the second goal when Hasselbaink's drive rebounded off the bar and fell directly into the path of the Argentinian. Joe was on for Parker by this time, and was able to impress quietly on left flank.

Chelsea had not beaten Arsenal in a major match at Highbury since Easter 1990. There had also been a League Cup victory in 1998, but both teams had fielded weakened sides. Ranieri had high hopes that Chelsea might break their 15-match losing streak when they trooped off at half-time a goal up. In that half, they had played their best football of the season and were clearly the better side. Arsenal were without the fabulous Thierry Henry, who was nursing a foot injury.

Mutu had given Chelsea the lead on 41 minutes when he left defender Kolo Toure for dead before smacking home a splendid left-footed shot into the bottom corner of Lehmann's goal. It was probably the best goal he ever scored for Chelsea. Sadly, though no one could have possibly guessed at the time, it was the last one he would ever score for the Blues. Gronkjaer had been unlucky earlier on when his header was ruled out for what later turned out to be an incorrect offside decision. Parker had a fine first half, competing very effectively in a personal duel with the Arsenal captain Patrick Vieira.

After the restart, Ranieri moved him to the left flank, which gave Vieira the freedom denied earlier. The Frenchman was fired up for the game and drove the Gunners forward time after time and, eventually, Chelsea collapsed under the almost ceaseless pressure, with the young Spanish winger Jose Antonio Reyes turning the game on its head. Up until then, he had been largely anonymous, like Gronkjaer, both spending the game hugging the touchline. Then the Chelsea defence allowed Reyes too much room when they failed to press the ball after it was cleared from a corner. Edu rolled it to the ex-Seville winger, who carried the ball forward before unleashing a tremendous rising shot that flew past Cudicini. In trying to reach the shot, the Italian keeper suffered a recurrence of a groin strain and had to be substituted. Neil Sullivan replaced him and, within minutes, Arsenal had scored the winner.

Vieira, now dominating the game, brushed aside Parker's challenge and tucked a sublime pass inside Melchiot and the heavy-footed Terry. Reyes burst on to it and beat Sullivan with a crisp finish. Chelsea's belief had drained away. The travelling Blues fans, who had spent most of the game abusing the watching Sven-Goran Eriksson, sat silently in the Clock End. Ranieri tried to save the game by replacing Mutu and Gronkjaer with Gudjohnsen and Joe, although this seemed a rash decision as Mutu had been the only Chelsea player causing them problems.

Joe struggled to find the pace of the game, and to link up effectively with Hasselbaink. The game slipped away and Chelsea crashed out of the FA Cup. Ranieri said that Chelsea had lost the plot in the second half. Abramovich turned to give him a curious smile at the final whistle.

That game proved that, above all, Arsenal were a team that worked for each other, and that Chelsea were merely a collection of individuals. They lacked a surprise element, and their strike force seemed to lack the class to turn the game around when it was slipping away from them.

IN THE WINGS

Joe had studied Reyes throughout the game. Both had started their new careers with the biggest clubs in the capital tentatively, and both had seemed sometimes disorientated by the speed of events and their newly acquired fame. It was clear now, though, that even when he was struggling, Reyes had an admirable willingness to chase back and try to win tackles.

The following Saturday lunchtime, Arsenal visited Chelsea in the Premiership. This game was set up wonderfully as an opportunity for Chelsea to avenge the recent defeat to their London neighbours, and Eidur Gudjohnsen gave Chelsea a dream start, firing home after just 27 seconds.

Arsenal hit back, and Dennis Bergkamp began running the game. Now 34, his legs had gone but he was still capable of some sublime football. On the quarter-of-an-hour, Vieira robbed the insipid Makelele and found Bergkamp in space. He completed the one-two with an exquisite return back to Vieira, who galloped into the box to shoot easily pass Cudicini. Edu sealed victory six minutes later when he seized on a loose clearance to fire Arsenal in front.

Joe came on for the ineffective Geremi, but was unable to break down the Arsenal defence. The gulf between the two sides still looked as vast as ever. Joe's work in the penalty box still lacked ruthlessness and precison. He was working very hard in training and still had fire in his stomach, but had little direction.

After the Arsenal double over Chelsea, the Blues had a Champions League fixture against VFB Stuttgart. They maintained their 100 per cent away record in the competition with a efficient display in the Gottieb-Daimler Stadion in which they beat VFB by a solitary own-goal, and in which Joe was only able to contribute for the last minute of the match.

Chelsea lacked style but the foundations for the iron-clad spine of the team were being laid with the Gallas/Terry/Lampard/Makelele combination that was starting to emerge.

Sandwiched between the Stuttgart ties was a Premiership visit to Manchester City, which Chelsea won 1-0, when Gudjohnsen, who came on for Joe after 64 minutes, grabbed the only goal.

Stuttgart played well at the Bridge in the return match. No goals were scored, although Chelsea went through by virtue of the own goal scored in Germany. Ranieri's team had scored only twice in four Champions League home games. Once again, there had been no place for Joe in the opening line-up. Joe tried to console himself by buying a new car. He was a self-confessed petrolhead and enjoyed driving. His first ever car at West Ham had been a Golf, and at one time he had owned a Hummer, the armoured car that looks more at home in Iraq than leafy Essex.

The pressure on Ranieri was now immense, with his only salvation being to win either the Premiership or the Champions League, and the rumour mill was working overtime with speculation over Sven-Goran Eriksson as a possible successor.

Ranieri's strategy seemed designed to avoid losing at all costs, so he opted for a bizarre 4-5-1 formation, particularly as they were leading in a second-leg home match against a competent, but not outstanding, side. Ranieri tried to convince the press that he had started with a 4-3-3 line-up, saying, 'I wanted to keep possession of the ball and put them under pressure with three strikers – Damien Duff, Jesper Gronkjaer and Crespo.

The idea was to play 4-3-3 and close down their flanks, Gronkjaer on the right and Duff on the left, but they had too much space to play through and we closed down space on the edge of the box.'

Scott Parker made his Champions League debut for Chelsea but made little impression and was eventually replaced by Geremi. He had made his name with Charlton playing in the centre, but Ranieri was playing him out of position on the left. Mutu came into the fray for Duff with less than ten minutes left. In that time, he contrived to miss two chances that he would probably have converted easily given the form he showed when he started his Chelsea career. Duff was playing in his first match since the Fulham game in December when he injured his shoulder. The Irish superstar was at his most effective when he was given a free role to play his orthodox winger's game – his forte was beating defenders on the outside with his penetrating runs and firing over accurate crosses. Ranieri had switched him inside, though, to support the beleaguered Crespo.

Duff was left wondering about his future at Chelsea when he heard that they had cut a deal to buy Arjen Robben for £12 million from PSV Eindhoven. Peter Kenyon had masterminded the purchase of Holland's hottest property with Frank Arnesen, who was also destined to join Chelsea. Robben had signed a pre-contract and eventually joined Chelsea at the end of June. The acquisition of Robben was a massive blow to Manchester United who had been trailing him for months, and they simply could not compete with Abramovich's buying power. Given the influx of even more raw talent, Joe Cole appeared to be pushed down the pecking order even further.

4

Heroes and Villains

'When I signed, Claudio Ranieri had also signed Veron, Geremi, Duff and we already had Frank. I probably had the smallest reputation, and sometimes reputations go before performances in football. I didn't have the right opportunities.'

Joe Cole, December 2005

AFTER DISPOSING OF Stuttgart, the draw for the Champions League quarter-final threw up a mouth-watering opponent for Chelsea – Arsenal. The first leg would be at the Bridge. Just over eight miles separated the clubs geographically, but at that point in the season, the gap between them was massive.

Before that game, there were a couple of Premiership matches to negotiate. The first was against Bolton and, once again, Joe started on the bench but came on for Crespo after 65 minutes. Two late goals from Terry and Duff won the points for the Blues, with Joe setting up Duff's goal. He made a strong run and supplied a neat pass to Jimmy Floyd Hasselbaink, who then crossed low to Duff, who scored easily.

Joe nearly rounded it off with what would have been the

goal of the season; he rounded N'Gotty and stepped inside Emerson Thome, and fired past the Bolton keeper Jaaskelainen. The Bolton defender Charlton cleared off the line, though, to deny Joe his wonder goal.

In the next fixture at home to Fulham, Joe replaced Damien Duff with 20 minutes to go. The withdrawal of the Irishman brought jeers from the Matthew Harding Stand. Duff had already scored what proved to be the match-winner in the 30th minute and had terrorised the Fulham defence all afternoon. The introduction of Joe was seemingly another baffling decision by the 'Tinkerman' as it diminished Chelsea's attacking options, although Joe did help to suppress Fulham's growing midfield superiority. Ranieri was apparently saving Duff for the Arsenal game and it would seem that Joe was regarded solely as a midfield makeweight, and not considered sufficiently influential to warrant a regular place in the side. Unfortunately for Joe, it was accepted that he would only get to participate fully in the big matches if other higher-profile players had sudden dips in form, or if there were injuries. As a fellow professional, Joe would not have wished either on his team-mates... but part of him must have wondered what on earth he had to do to get on the team sheet, and get a decent run in the side.

The build up to the 157th meeting between the two London sides was unique, even though it was the fourth time the teams had met that season. There was talk of a pair of tickets for the game, with the face value of £42 each, exchanging hands for a street value of £1,000. Ranieri joked in the pre-match press conference that he should be referred to as the 'dead man walking', but added, 'I am still moving. It is difficult to kill me.' He was offered support by Arsène Wenger, who said, 'I find it strange that he is under pressure… I have sympathy for him.'

Despite this, the Arsenal coach still insisted that his team would go for the jugular to pile more pressure on his stressed opposite number, and go for it they did, with a breathtaking first-half performance against an under-performing Chelsea team. They gave the home side a lesson in flowing football that was some of the best they had played throughout their record-breaking run. From that display, Arsenal looked firm favourites to become the first London side to reach a European Cup semi-final. Ranieri may have found some solace in the reaction of the crowd, who chanted 'There's only one Ranieri…' throughout the match.

Once more, Joe was consigned to the bench with Duff, reckoned by many to be the match-winner, returning to the side. Ambrosio continued in goal in the absence of Cudicini, and Marcel Desailly and Scott Parker were included to add steel to the team. Lampard clashed with Vieira early on.

After 53 minutes, Chelsea took the lead when Gudjohnsen charged down Lehmann's clearance to slide home. Chelsea were in front for six minutes but a bad error by Terry let Robert Pires steal in front of him to head Ashley Cole's cross home. It was the first goal against the Blues in Europe in 560 minutes of football.

Joe came on for Parker and Desailly was sent off after receiving a second yellow card. The second was for a foul on Man of the Match, Vieira. Edu had a brilliant match, but Joe could make little impact in the remaining minutes as Arsenal ran down the clock. The mountain ahead was of Everest proportions; Chelsea had to score at Highbury in the return to have any chance at all of progressing to the semi-final stage.

All the while, the pressure was intensifying on Ranieri, with pictures appearing in the tabloids of Kenyon and Eriksson in discussion. The only hope he had of avoiding the sack was to win the Champions League and, even then, it was doubtful if he had any long-term future with the club.

Joe started the match against a Wolves side already on their way down. The Chelsea crowd were fully behind Ranieri still and spent most of the game denouncing Sven-Goran Eriksson. In a bizarre match, late substitute Jimmy Floyd Hasselbaink scored a hat-trick in the last 12 minutes to win the game for the Blues. Melchiot gave Chelsea an early lead but two errors by Terry led to goals by Camara and Craddock.

Joe's performance came in for widespread criticism after the game. A comparison was made with Chris Waddle, the ex-Tottenham and Newcastle forward, who was as famous for his clichéd 1970s mullet haircut as for his dribbling and ball skills. The end product was often lacking, and Waddle's tendency to dribble with his head down infuriated coaches. Joe's display that afternoon was similarly dogged with tactical naivety and over-elaboration. Only intermittently did he produce any real class.

Some of this loss of form must have been due to Ranieri constantly tinkering with his line-up and formation, which prevented several of his stars from settling into any sort of consistent form. For a while, Joe was switched to a central striking position. With his back to goal, Joe found it very hard to make any impact. His game was simply not suited to the strength and tactical nous required to hold up the ball, turn and muscle past experienced defenders. Eventually, Ranieri brought Hasselbaink on and replaced Joe with Parker. It was a roller coaster performance, with Chelsea managing to score five times, but seemingly unable to keep things organised in midfield or defence.

For the Champions League semi-final, Joe was on the bench at the start of the game with Duff picked ahead of him. Arsenal went in front just before the break, after a breathtaking half of tight, tense football. Henry's downward header rebounded off the heel of Freddie Ljungberg straight into the path of the Spanish star Jose Antonio Reyes. The man who had dashed Chelsea's FA Cup hopes scored instantly, firing the ball past Terry and the brave Ambrosio. Arsenal could have capitalised on their lead and asserted their superiority early in the second half, but Chelsea re-grouped at half-time and came out fighting.

Within six minutes of the restart, Chelsea were level. Makelele's long-range shot bounced off the chest of Lehmann to Lampard, who drove home the equaliser. As the game wore on, Ranieri gambled by going for broke and, with seven minutes of normal time still remaining on the clock, he put Joe on for Duff. Crespo, his other big-match player, came on for Hasselbaink.

Immediately, Joe nearly set up the winner with a swerving run and clever flick to Eidur Gudjohnsen. The bigger the game, the better Gudjohnsen seemed to play, with the Icelandic forward blasting in a drive at the Arsenal goal, but Ashley Cole, who was to figure in the Chelsea headlines in the coming season, cleared it off the line.

The chance to win the game seemed to have gone, and both sides seemed to have settled for extra time when up popped Gudjohnsen again to put in Wayne Bridge for a simple goal. On the final whistle, the Chelsea players couldn't contain their joy and relief, and Joe was as ecstatic as anyone in celebrating the victory. It was a famous win for the Blues, and now that so many big names had crashed out of the Champions League, the trophy was there for the taking.

Chelsea confounded everybody with their wonderful victory at Highbury to reach the semi-finals for the first time in their long history. Ranieri was vindicated for his team selections and the effort he had put in to build a great team spirit at the club. It was Arsenal's first defeat at the hands of Chelsea in 18 games.

Now Chelsea were in the semis and, if the press was to be believed, they already had one foot in the final. Their opponents were Monaco, who had surprisingly beaten Real Madrid. The whole of Europe had been anticipating a really mouthwatering clash, with Abramovich's new-look All-Stars against the tried and tested Galacticos and their array of world-class talent – Beckham, Zidane, Ronaldo et al. Monaco, though, had put paid to that, and now feared no one.

In the other semi-final, Porto – coached by the rising star Jose Mourinho – were drawn against Deportivo. In the previous round, they had knocked Manchester United out, 3- 2 on aggregate. A bizarre offside decision given against Paul

Scholes, which disallowed a legitimate goal, had helped them through. The subsequent events at Chelsea – its management team and results on the pitch – might all have been so different had that goal been given. Porto might not have gone on to win, and Mourinho would most definitely not have garnered the attention and acclaim that brought him to the forefront of European football. How often in football do we see the success or failure of a particular team or individual rest on a single crucial decision, a dazzling piece of individual skill, or a heartbreaking error? Mourinho's march towards European glory was certainly a special one, and it was charmed, as well.

Joe would have loved to have crossed swords with the Spanish giants. He was learning Spanish, and he loved the climate and the relaxed lifestyle. In his spare time he travelled to Valencia to watch a Spanish League game. Above all, he was a huge fan of the football. Perhaps one day he would play out there but for now, everything was focused on establishing himself at the club he had loved since he was a lad. So few people realized he was a dyed-in-the-wool Chelsea fan. It was always assumed that because he had made his name at West Ham and chosen them to start his carrer with that they were his first love. This was despite the fact he hailed from North London. Joe kept his allegiance to the blue flag a secret when he was at Upton Park, correctly judging that it would hinder his progress.

Before Chelsea could enjoy their biggest challenge on the European stage for years, they had a trio of Premiership matches to focus on, and it was crucial to their title ambitions that they put the defeat of Arsenal to the back of their minds.

JOE COLE

On Easter Saturday, Middlesbrough came to the Bridge. Duff was rested and Joe Cole started the game. It was a landmark game for him, as he actually completed the full 90 minutes for the first time in Chelsea colours.

Joe was Chelsea's most threatening forward, and looked the best player on the pitch. Veron came on for the injured Makelele after 57 minutes, his first appearance in five months and, like Joe, he performed very well.

The real test for the team on this occasion, though, was how well they would deal with the post-match euphoria after the events at Highbury. Despite playing positively, the team failed to capitalise on opportunities, and Lampard, of all people, spurned two easy chances to win the three vital points. They still had a mathematical chance of the title but, when the game petered out to a 0-0 draw, Ranieri conceded that Arsenal were champions.

On Easter Monday, Chelsea travelled to Villa Park for a tough match against Aston Villa, and Ranieri decided to rotate the squad again, with Joe spending all but the last 20 minutes on the bench. In all, there were eight changes from the Boro game. Mutu made a rare appearance but, by then, his extravagantly decadent lifestyle was taking its toll. Crespo scored two tidy goals but the problem for Chelsea was that Villa scored three. Peter Crouch, the 6ft 7in striker, was playing up front for Villa and set up two of their goals. Like Joe, he had been a keen Chelsea fan as a youngster. The defeat obviously piled even more pressure on Ranieri. Abramovich watched the match stony-faced as Villa rampaged through Chelsea's defence and, as they did, all mathematical chance of overhauling Arsenal disappeared.

BLOWING BUBBLES... BUT NOT FOR EVER

Everton forced a scoreless draw at the Bridge in the last game before the trip to Monaco, and the England manager was in the 41,169 crowd to assess the contributions of some of his key players, and to look out for potential recruits to the national squad. Joe, Terry and Lampard were of particular interest at the time, with the latter already being hailed as the most improved player of the season, and becoming one of the most influential midfielders in Europe.

Joe, on the other hand, had not had nearly as much opportunity to shine in a Chelsea shirt that season, and had not really progressed in the way he would have liked. In the Everton game, he only produced flashes of the verve and confidence he had produced on a regular basis for West Ham.

Another young player of immense potential at both club and national level, Wayne Rooney, was playing one of his last games for Everton and the pressure seemed to be taking its toll. He was capable of blinding brilliance on the pitch, but also had an immature edge to his game which often led him to commit howling errors of judgement through his aggressive, physical approach. At one stage, he kicked out in frustration at Joe and, fortunately for the pair of them, he missed.

Joe's most commendable contribution to the match was a beautifully controlled run with the ball at his feet into opposition territory in the second half that brought an ovation from the crowd. Only a foul by Gary Naysmith halted his progress just outside the box, and German centre-back Huth's powerful free kick was easily cleared by the Everton defensive wall. Gronkjaer replaced Joe ten minutes from time as the game fizzled out into stalemate.

A few days before the Champions League semi-final against Monaco, Ranieri was allegedly quoted by a Spanish newspaper as saying, 'I already have the Abramovich sword embedded in me. I'm convinced that even if I win the Champions League, I will be sacked.'

Subsequently, these comments were denied by Ranieri, but it was clear that whatever the main protagonists had said or thought or done, most observers of the game believed that Abramovich's sword had been embedded for a while, and had probably been pulled out already to allow him to bleed to death. He did have the opportunity, though, to make his departure that much more difficult for the Chelsea board to orchestrate, if he brought home the most prized trophy in Europe.

The Stade Louis II is a shabby, functional ground built above a car park. Chelsea took 1,500 fans with them, desperate to see their club make the final. They had become favourites to win the Champions League in front of Monaco, Deportivo and Porto. The omens were not good – history dictated that Chelsea Football Club had one consistent factor in almost a century of unpredictably – they won games they were expected to lose (Arsenal being the latest example), and lost games they were expected to win.

Didier Deschamps was the young, much lauded Monaco coach, who had spent a year at Chelsea as his long and glittering career came to an end. Deschamps was one of the three French World Cup Winners who had spells at Chelsea, Marcel Desailly and Emmanuel Petit being the other two.

Petit spent 12 years at Monaco and was full of misgivings about Chelsea's chances there. He reasoned that Chelsea would find it very difficult to get anything out of the game in the compact stadium, which holds 15,000 fanatical supporters. Deschamps was an attack-minded coach, and Petit was particularly concerned about the pace Monaco were able to deploy up front.

This proved to be chillingly accurate, because the home side, although reduced to ten men, ran out 3-1 winners on the night. Joe Cole was named as a substitute but never figured in the match. Ranieri gambled, but failed with his team selection and substitutions, although it is debatable whether the Joe Cole of April 2004 would have had the confidence and ability to change the game sufficiently to alter the outcome.

Ranieri was slaughtered in the press for his team selection and changing strategy throughout the game, but it was also true that he was let down badly by his normally impregnable, Serie A-type defence. Melchiot conceded a free kick after 15 minutes that Prso headed home, and it became only the second goal Chelsea had conceded away from home in the competition. Crespo equalised soon afterwards from Gudjohnsen's scrambled pass. One of the most iconic images of that time was Crespo celebrating on the track after he had scored. In the foreground is the famous Mears family lion crest, banished by the Bates regime, but a symbol of the old Chelsea – the Chelsea that Joe Cole had fallen in love with when he was a ball boy. That night Joe was just another Chelsea fan watching the death throes of the Ranieri era.

At the break, Ranieri made the decision that probably sealed his fate, replacing Gronkjaer with Veron. Things might have turned out differently had Joe had a full half to work his magic, but Ranieri was determined to stick with players who were not performing well on the night, and who were not capable of breaking down a stubborn Monaco defence. Gronkjaer was having a poor match, but Veron was only half-fit, and there was some speculation over the reasons why Ranieri would have risked the Argentinian. Some believed that Veron represented Ranieri's greatest dilemma, in that he felt he had to say to Abramovich, 'You bought him, so I will play him.'

Things started to go wrong for the Blues when volatile defender Desailly clashed with Fernando Morientes, the Monaco striker, in an ugly brawl. Then Makelele clashed with Zikos, and the Chelsea midfielder collapsed as though he'd been shot. The Monaco player was unlucky to be sent off.

Now that Monaco were down to ten men, Ranieri gambled by bringing on Hasselbaink in place of Melchiot and switching Crespo out to the right midfield. Parker went to right-back to cover for Melchiot but, within six minutes, he was replaced by the lumbering Huth. All the subs had been used, and Joe was unable to join the fray. What was needed at that stage was more width to stretch the ten men of Monaco, but Chelsea played all night with a very restricted pattern, which allowed them painfully little scope. The player that Joe has now become would have had a field day on the flanks.

Chelsea were unsettled by the changes; Monaco replaced their goal-scorer Prso with the defensive midfielder Edouard Cisse, who had played with Joe at West Ham the previous season. He was a player in the Essien mould, and was thought by many West Ham fans to be very underrated. In fact, his inclusion was inspired, as Cisse nullified the Lampard threat and, in the last 15 minutes, Chelsea fell to pieces.

Ranieri commented later to the *Daily Telegraph*, 'We lost the plot, everyone wanted to do something more, run with the ball and not pass it to the strikers. It was the worst 15 minutes I've seen from my team this season.'

Morientes destroyed Chelsea's dream with a superb second goal. Fernando Morientes was on loan to Monaco from Real Madrid and, having just turned 28, he had already won the European Cup three times and was Spain's durable main striker with an impressive record of a goal a game. He was a class act.

20 minutes from time, Giuly took a short pass from Cisse and put through Morientes, who left Terry standing, and lashed the ball into the Chelsea net. As the final whistle approached, with the Chelsea defence overrun, Nonda nipped in front of Terry to make it 3-1.

Abramovich left the ground in tears, and asked the Italian coach to join him on his luxury yacht *Le Grand Bleu*, but Ranieri politely declined the invitation, stating that he wished to stay with his team in an attempt to lift their flagging spirits. They were to have a post-match meal together, and Ranieri wanted to hold a post mortem. In effect, this could easily be described as a last supper.

As Joe left the ground to board the bus to the hotel, the Monaco fans taunted the Chelsea team. Abramovich returned to his yacht for a muted get-together with his nearest and dearest, but the evening finished early, leaving the billionaire to retire to bed. He could not sleep, though, so he returned at about 2.00 am to the team hotel and convened a meeting with his chiefs-of-staff – Peter Kenyon, the head of his investment company Eugene Shivdler, and the American chairman of Chelsea, Bruce Buck.

Perhaps Ranieri's biggest error was his constant use of the diamond formation. With players like Veron, Lampard and Joe at his disposal, he felt committed to using it. The successful sides in England had generally played 4-4-2, and when Ranieri deviated from this tried and tested formation, problems arose.

Around that time, the name of Jose Mourinho was being mentioned as a possible replacement for Ranieri. He had apparently come from nowhere to establish his credentials as the top coach in Europe; he had yet to prove himself among the European greats, although his ambition and self-marketing skills were undeniable. Some commentators voiced doubts, though, over his preference for the long-ball game, a ruthless midfield and a Scrooge-like defence.

On the Saturday following the Monaco defeat, Ranieri took his exhausted troops to Newcastle, never an easy trip at the best of times. Joe was included in the team and scored his first Premiership goal for Chelsea after just five minutes. Frank Lampard set the chance up for him by winning the ball in midfield and finding Joe just inside the Newcastle half. Joe raced through the Newcastle defence after a high-speed exchange of passes with Lampard and, unchallenged, Joe squeezed between Woodgate and O'Brien before slipping the ball through the legs of the Newcastle keeper, Shay Given. Joe told the *Telegraph* that the feeling of putting one in the net was, 'Like going to heaven for a few seconds'.

Sir Bobby Robson, then managing the Magpies, sat shaking his head in disbelief, as the consistent weakness of his team in defence – a problem that was to plague his successor, Graham Souness, as well – continued to undermine Newcastle's challenge for league honours.

Joe, very productive that day, nearly scored a second goal when he darted into the box yet again with a brilliant piece of skill that set him up for a shot. As he steadied to fire home, O'Brien, chasing back hard, did just enough to force Joe to slide his shot just wide. In moments like that, games are won and lost.

Ameobi equalised for Newcastle two minutes before the break, which undermined the good work Chelsea had achieved in the first 40 minutes. Early in the second half, the prolific Shearer, in the left-hand channel, swivelled past Desailly to thunder in Newcastle's second. It was his 22nd Premiership goal of the season and as good a goal as he had ever scored in his illustrious career.

Back came Chelsea, driven on by Joe in his most committed performance of the season, to try and salvage the game. Full of feints and flicks, including a sensational back-heel, Joe was a constant threat. The Blues bombarded Newcastle in the closing stages with virtually every player having a strike on goal. In the 94th minute, Terry hit the post from point-blank range. It was a woeful miss and confirmed the slight loss of sharpness in his play over the preceding weeks. The broadsheets, though, and the *Telegraph* in particular, were strongly of the opinion that Terry was the man to supersede Beckham as England captain – sooner rather than later.

And the man to supersede Ranieri? All talk was now of Robson's former interpreter, Mourinho, who had worked with the grand old man of the English game at Porto, Sporting Lisbon and then at Barcelona for a total of eight years. Robson was on record as rating him very highly, having experienced Mourinho's hunger for success, his intelligence and deep understanding of the demands of the game. Pictures also appeared in the press at the time of a covert meeting between Abramovich and Mourinho's agent.

There was one more Premiership game to play before the return leg against Monaco – Southampton at the Bridge. Chelsea scored 4 times in the last 30 minutes in what was little more than a stroll for them. Joe played for 80 minutes before being replaced by Veron, who still looked unfit. When he was substituted, Joe received a great ovation from the crowd who were warming to his skill and application. Once again, Joe was the pick of the Chelsea side.

Looking forward to the Monaco clash, Joe and his team-mates were well aware that they had a mammoth task to overturn the 3-1 deficit, although scoring twice, and keeping a clean sheet, would be sufficient to see them through. Monaco would not be easy to break down, though, and they had already shown the threat they posed up front.

Ranieri welcomed the media to the press conference before the game by saying 'Hello, my sharks... welcome to the funeral,' and admitted that he was definitely going to be leaving Chelsea, and that he even knew the name of his replacement. He also announced that Joe Cole would start in what was arguably Chelsea's most important game in the club's history. He confirmed the confidence he had in his young English star by saying, 'I believe in Cole... he has a brilliant future. It's important that he tries to do everything very, very calmly.'

It was two goals they needed, and Chelsea did not disappoint. Joe helped Chelsea race to a 2-0 lead, and the prospect of a glorious end to the season, with Chelsea contesting the Champions League final against Mourinho's Porto, who had won their semi the previous night, seemed a distinct possibility.

Joe was only one of three of Abramovich's signings who started the game. Gronkjaer put the English team ahead after 22 minutes when his speculative cross ended up in the net. It was a piece of luck out of the blue that sent the crowd wild and contributed to the sort of atmosphere not heard at the Bridge since the heyday of Osgood and Co. Gronkjaer admitted after the match that it had been a fluke shot.

Joe had a chance to score again when the Monaco keeper Roma failed to hold a shot from Geremi. The ball squirted out towards Joe, who had the time to control it but rushed his attempt and sliced horribly wide. How different might things have been, had Joe managed to retain slightly more composure at that moment? The desperate swipe he took at the blocked shot was emblematic of the main flaw in his game at that time. Ranieri, with a great deal of foresight, had identified the need for calm, and it was this that might have provided the entire Chelsea team, and Joe in particular, with the dominance that they so desperately needed that night.

Gudjohnsen hit the bar and Hasselbaink missed a sitter in

the high-octane battle that followed, as Chelsea pushed forward with ever increasing urgency. One of Monaco's strengths was the counter-attack, so they were never more dangerous than when they were under pressure. Morientes had a goal-bound effort deflected by Terry, ending up thumping into the post. It was a portent of things to come.

Lampard scored Chelsea's second a minute before the break, unleashing a pile-driver that nearly burst the net. At this stage, Chelsea were in the ascendancy, and looked odds-on favourites to go through to the final. Ranieri's more cautious approach, to stifle the Monaco midfield and front line, seemed to be paying off.

Chelsea's euphoria was short-lived, however, as Monaco immediately equalised straight from the re-start. Danger man Rothen crossed from the right, Morientes rose majestically to power a beautifully directed header against the bar, and the ball rebounded back on to the Argentinian Ibarra's arm, and back into the goal. Cudicini and Joe led the Chelsea protests, but Anders Frisk let the goal stand.

The game was all but over then, although there were still 45 minutes left to play. Chelsea seemed to lose their stomach for the fight; Terry was run all over the pitch by his nemesis Morientes, and could not inspire his team. Lampard, after his first-half exertions, faded badly as his influence waned.

Morientes destroyed Chelsea on the hour, just as he had done in Monte Carlo. Rothen put him through after a clever build-up, and he brushed Terry's challenge aside before slotting the ball home past Cudicini. Joe tried to rouse Chelsea, but with an aggregate score of 3-5 to overcome, realistically it was game over. Ranieri brought on Johnson to try to curb the threat of Rothen, but it was too little, too late. Most of the team left the field in tears; the feeling that night was that they would never have a better chance of lifting the Champions League trophy.

Who knows how things might have turned out, had Chelsea come through against Monaco, and then faced Mourinho's team in the final. Mourinho himself watched the match from the West Stand at Stamford Bridge, a guest of Abramovich's 'hospitality', and said that he was on a prolonged spying mission of his opponents in the final.

After the bitter disappointment of the defeat to Monaco, Chelsea played out the season with a 1-1 draw at Old Trafford and a 1-0 victory over Leeds. The Danish winger Gronkjaer scored in both games. He was another player in the Chelsea squad who had occasionally given truly world-class performances, but who had never really had the chance to establish a first-team place.

Joe set up his goal at Old Trafford when he played Gronkjaer in from Geremi's corner. Chelsea really should have won the match; Parker came on for Joe 13 minutes from time, was shortly after Huth had been sent off for a hideous tackle on van Nistelrooy. Ranieri then changed things again by sending Johnson on for Melchiot, with Johnson moving to the centre of the defence to plug the gap left by Huth's departure. Gronkjaer was slotted into Melchiot's position, but then Ranieri inexplicably brought Babayaro on to replace the goal scorer. A careless error by Cudicini, when he spilled a cross from Silvestre, gifted van Nistelrooy a late equaliser. The draw clinched second spot for Chelsea for the first time in their history.

Joe was named as Man of the Match in Chelsea's last game of the season against relegated Leeds. Without Abramovich, Chelsea would probably have been making the same journey as Leeds, down and out of the Premiership, with star players being sold off and huge debts threatening to bankrupt the club. It was ironic that Ken Bates was eventually to take over as chairman of the Yorkshire side.

Joe Cole played all 90 minutes of that last match of the season, and finished on a high, making 58 accurate passes out of a total of 74. It was predominantly the Joe Cole show, with the overall team performance improving a little in the second half.

That match against Leeds was Ranieri's last game at Chelsea, although even in his last few weeks at Stamford Bridge, he left a tremendous legacy, in orchestrating the transfers of goalkeeper Petr Cech and the Dutch winger Arjen Robben. They have gone on to become two of the most consistent and high-performing players in the Premiership.

Porto eventually won the European Cup, easily beating Monaco 3-0 in Gelsenkirchen. Within minutes of receiving the trophy, Mourinho removed his winner's medal from around his neck and left the rostrum. It was a gesture that suggested to the world that he was disassociating himself from Porto. Later that evening, he announced that he was joining Chelsea in a four-year deal worth £5 million per annum.

Jose Mário dos Santos Mourinho Félix was nicknamed 'the gunfighter' in Portugal because of his extraordinary ability to keep his cool under pressure. Today, the man from Setúbal has become the most talked about and publicised figure in the European game. The story of Joe Cole is, in many ways, also the story of Jose Mourinho; the rise of Joe Cole is linked directly with the arrival of the Portuguese manager at Chelsea, and their relationship has been pivotal to the success that Joe has enjoyed since Ranieri's departure.

Mourinho's father was a footballer who kept goal for Vitóra de Setúbal and Portugal. Jose, educated in élite schools, was a quiet lad, always well groomed but, rather like the teams he coached, he was also austere and highly disciplined.

He shared a very close relationship with his older sister Teresa, with whom he grew up. Unlike his father, he was never a good footballer and Bobby Robson was surprised to hear that he had never played football at a professional level. Despite his self-importance, and his willingness to pontificate on every aspect of the players and officials, Jose's career never progressed beyond Rio Ave, an amateur team coached by his father, but he never made the first team.

Instead, he took a degree in PE, but his talents as a coach only came to light when he took a coaching course run by former Scotland manager Andy Roxburgh, who had been a huge influence on the career of Pat Nevin - a 1980s Chelsea legend and another favourite player of Joe Cole.

In 1992, Sporting Lisbon needed an interpreter for Bobby Robson and Jose landed the job. Once again, it was a case of not what you know, but who you know; Manuel Fernandes was a friend of Mourinho's, and was Robson's assistant at Sporting. Jose's job was to pass on Robson's instructions to the team, and also to relay the feedback and any comments back to the former England coach. Jose thrived on the responsibility and was soon coaching, scouting, writing match reports and generally getting involved in every aspect of team management.

Poor results for Sporting Lisbon meant that the duo was fired, whereupon an opportunity arose at FC Porto. Their fortunes improved and, in three years, they won two championships and two super cups. Another four years were spent at Barcelona, Robson and Mourinho taking over from the great Johann Cruyff, where they changed the strategy of the team and tactics.

When Bobby departed the Nou Camp to join PSV Eindhoven, Mourinho wanted to go with him but Robson urged him to stay in Spain because he felt that he could learn more from working with players like Kluivert, Figo and Rivaldo. The Portuguese coach found it difficult building a relationship with Robson's successor, the demanding Louis Van Gaal at first. Jose stayed, though, to help him win the championship and Spanish Cup. His main duties were giving reports on the opposition and scouting for new talent in the lower leagues.

Mourinho returned to Portugal when van Gaal went to Holland as technical director for Ajax. Serra Ferrer was the Dutchman's replacement, having climbed the coaching ladder at Barcelona. Many fans thought that Jose should have been given the job as coach, but he was expected to continue as assistant to Ferrer. Jose, however, had had enough of being regarded as the support act, and felt that the time was right for him to step out of the shadows and take on the leading role.

For this reason, he turned down the chance of working with Robson again, this time at Newcastle.

Around that time, Mourinho's sister, Teresa, died from septicaemia, a complication of diabetes. This had left her practically blind after a period of substance abuse. It was a difficult time for Mourinho as he adjusted to the tragedy, and waited for the right career opening to come along.

Mourinho used the time to compile what he called his 'bible'. This was a dossier on everything he knew about coaching – all aspects of the technical, physical and, perhaps, the most important of all, psychological elements of the game were logged and analysed. Mourinho was a man with a plan, and that plan covered even the smallest of details. This has been the secret of his success – his preparation, his focus, and the fact that he has always known what he wanted to achieve, and the means to deliver. Basically, his approach on the pitch was very straightforward refinement of the high-tempo pressing game favoured by Ranieri.

Mourinho had a short and, ultimately disappointing, spell at Benfica, lasting only three months. He would claim later that 'they' were against him from the start, but he never specified who 'they' were. Having only just arrived at the club, he dropped some of the popular players and antagonised some of the younger squad members by decreeing that they had no future in the game. Then he criticised the entire structure of the club.

While Mourinho had clearly worked his way up into full-scale management through hard work, dedication and technical brilliance, it would appear that he struggled with the demands of some very complex working relationships, a requirement of anyone in the high-profile, high-pressure role of club management.

After a further period of unemployment, Jose took a modest job with the mid-ranking Portuguese club União de Leiria. Eventually, he took up the top job at Porto, where, in his second season, he won the Portuguese League and Cup double, and the UEFA Cup, which was won in extra time in the Olympic Stadium in Seville with a 3-2 win over Celtic. Henrik Larsson equalised twice for the Glasgow side, but a late winner clinched the treble for Mourinho.

The next season saw him win the title again and scoop 'the big one' – the Champions League. His relationship with the club deteriorated, though, especially with the chairman Pinto da Costa, and that is probably the key to his personality. Mourinho controlled his image as tightly as he did his midfield. The coach had an almost pathological shyness, which he masked with his apparent arrogance and combativeness. For example, all childhood pictures of Jose were banned from being shown in the press. All interviews, press conferences and statements were carefully scripted before released for public consumption. The look he cultivated was carefully styled and contrived. Sometimes, he would appear unshaven in front of the cameras, but it was always carefully engineered designer stubble. Jose was by far the smartest dressed of all his contemporaries. Abramovich, by contrast, appeared completely unconcerned about his own media image, choosing to dress in informal, almost sloppy, casual clothing.

Mourinho almost waged psychological warfare on his

opponents. Perhaps that is what appealed to Abramovich; not only did he want to win every game, but he also wanted to destroy the opposition. The game plan was to build a dynasty that would relentlessly win everything year after year after year while crushing any rivals. Soon, his players would start to reflect this passion to dominate as never before, and the language they used was highly revealing. Robben spoke of the psychological damage a win at Highbury would do to Arsenal's title ambitions; Terry spoke of demoralising the opposition by constantly winning games. Mourinho's original strategy, that of combining the experience and technical skill of the coach with a form of psychological warfare, was one that he would continue to refine as he took the reins at Chelsea.

When Mourinho arrived at Stamford Bridge, nothing would ever be the same again.

5

Football Special

'He's a great fella and he does his job fantastic. He can have
banter with the lads as well, and there aren't many in the game
who can do that and command as much respect as he does.'
Joe Cole on Jose Mourinho

MOURINHO'S FIRST PREMIERSHIP game was a
microcosm of what was to come – a 1-0 home win
over Manchester United. It was a dismal affair, with the only
highlight being Gudjohnsen's close-range goal at 15 minutes.
Chelsea had six new faces in the first game, who made their
debuts at various stages throughout the match – Cech, Ferreira,
Carvalho (both signed from Porto), Kezman, Smertin and
Drogba. Didier Drogba was signed from Marseille for the
princely sum of £22 million, a mere drop in the ocean of Roman
Abramovich's vast wealth. Wenger commented at the time that
Chelsea had destroyed the transfer market. As for those who
were not in favour with the new manager, both Veron and
Crespo were loaned out to Inter and AC Milan respectively.

The pattern of Chelsea's play was pure Mourinho from the
start – from the moment they scored, Chelsea were only

interested in preserving their lead. United, without van Nistelrooy and Ronaldo, had 60 per cent of the match, but were unable to break down the Blues. The Chelsea midfield sat deep with their back four almost on the 18-yard line. There was no space behind them for United to exploit. Not one Chelsea midfield player broke forward after that first goal.

Joe Cole wasn't even on the bench for the United game. Mourinho had had doubts about his fitness following a foot injury he'd picked up during a pre-season tour to America, during which Chelsea were keen to build their profile in the minds of the US public. Joe had featured briefly on the tour and had scored against Roma in the first half of a match played in Pittsburgh.

Mourinho suffered some barracking from the United fans situated behind his dug-out and, by the following season, the away fans were moved to a corner of the Shed End. Football fans have long memories, and it had not been forgotten that Jose had made a 50-yard victory dash down the touchline when Porto had knocked the Reds out of Europe.

Joe told *Esquire* that Mourinho had been like a breath of fresh air to Chelsea: 'He'll definitely tell you when you are doing well, he'll tell you when you're not doing well. Jose's more than a manager, he's a psychologist as well, and he does things to get the best out of players. Personally I think he's got a crystal ball in his office.'

Joe grabbed his chance in the next game, though, when he came on as a substitute at Birmingham and scored the only goal of the game. Joe replaced Geremi after 63 minutes and, five minutes later, he scored with a low, firmly struck 20-yard drive, deflecting in off the Birmingham defender Martin Taylor. Chelsea held out for their first away points of the season, despite the fact that Cech had a nervous game flapping at crosses.

After the match, Joe said to the press, 'We haven't produced the football we want to play, but we will, don't worry about that. The most important thing at this early stage of the season is getting results… And I'll say to people who criticise the way we're playing at the moment – judge us on the football we will reproduce next May when it really matters. Other teams have questioned our spirit and they're wrong to do that. We know we can play better and that's a nice, comfortable feeling for us.

'It'd be a bit worrying if we were playing at the top of our game and only winning 1-0. We know there's a lot more to come and we think it's going to be good for us this year. What we need to do – which we didn't do here or last season – is get the second goal to kill games off. We'd like to get two or three up so we can take our foot off the pedal and rest a bit – although the manager wouldn't want to hear us talking like that.

He said a few things at half-time, but they were positive. He told us to get out there and get a result, and that's what we did.

'The difference now is that, when I look in the manager's eyes, I can tell he believes in me. I've not felt that before. Now I really feel the trust of the manager and that helps. I just want to run games and win medals for this club.'

It was highly significant that, just a few games into the season, Joe was talking about trust and belief. Already, Mourinho had instilled belief in his players, despite his apparent indifference to most things around him.

Joe was in the side that travelled a few miles across the river to south London to play Crystal Palace a few nights later. Joe was the only exponent of any panache or style in another functional display as Chelsea ran out comfortable 2-0 winners. The joy among the Chelsea fans as they made it three straight wins was unalloyed.

Wingers Robben and Duff were both missing through injury, with Robben having been ruled out indefinitely following a crunching tackle from Dacourt in the Roma game on the American tour. Zenden, Stanic, Hasselbaink and Desailly were also out, but for them, it would be permanent – they had departed the club in a flurry of pay-offs.

Lampard, Makelele and Tiago formed the three-man unit in midfield, with Joe out on the left flank. Mourinho had given him the task of being the creative spark in the side. Joe fulfilled his brief expertly, and supplied a steady supply of decent balls for Drogba, who put Chelsea ahead after 28 minutes from Babayaro's cross.

Joe almost scored with a fierce drive that forced the Palace keeper Speroni to make a fine save and then, on 73 minutes, Chelsea scored their second through Tiago. He had followed Jose to Porto from União de Leira, as had Paulo Ferreira and, when Tiago rejoined his mentor at Chelsea, Jose said that he would make him 'a great player'. The following summer, Tiago joined Lyon. He had been a great presence in the dressing room, and Mourinho was said to have regretted his departure hugely.

Immediately after Tiago's goal, Joe was replaced by Geremi as Mourinho sealed the midfield even tighter, and he deployed his 'resting' trick, encouraging his team to keep possession of the ball by constantly interchanging passes while they recharged their batteries.

Joe was subsequently tasked with the left-wing role for the next three matches. The first of these was at home to Southampton, with James Beattie becoming the first player to score against Chelsea that season when he volleyed past Cech after just 13 seconds. The Saints striker then, bizarrely, equalised for Chelsea with an own goal, and Lampard scored the winner from the spot.

Villa became the first side to take a point from Chelsea when they held them to a 0-0 draw at Villa Park. Drogba hit the post from a move started by Joe, and Mourinho openly displayed his customary contempt for borderline decisions going against his team when the referee failed to award a penalty for a trip on Drogba later in the game.

At this early stage in the season, it was beginning to look as though Chelsea had only an outside chance of the Premiership title. Arsenal had rattled in 16 goals in their first 4 matches and set up a record of 43 unbeaten games. Chelsea, though, were just two points behind them. Mourinho had settled on his first-choice strikers and back four – they were virtually picking themselves – but the fiercest competition for places was in midfield. Lampard and Makelele were automatic choices, with Joe, Duff, Tiago and Smertin competing for the remaining two places. Robben, when he was fit, would also make a very persuasive claim for an automatic place.

Spurs took a point from Chelsea as they drew 0-0 for the second successive week. Mourinho, openly and energetically contemptuous of Spurs' defensive approach, accused their London rivals of 'parking a bus' in front of the goal. The truth was that Chelsea found it impossible to break down the resilient Spurs defence.

Duff replaced Joe the following week at Middlesbrough, with Drogba grabbing a late winner to take the points.

The first of Chelsea's Champions League matches pitched them against Mourinho's old side Porto. Shorn of their guiding light and asset-stripped of several of their best players, they were a pale imitation of the side that had lifted the European Cup just a few months previously. Mourinho showed no compassion whatsoever as Chelsea strolled to a 3-1 victory.

Joe was a substitute, but did not get on the pitch. Smertin gave Chelsea an early lead, and second-half headers from Terry and Drogba settled it. After the match, a disgusted Porto fan spat at their former coach as he walked down the tunnel; the fan was Helder Mota, who had earlier made a death threat to Mourinho. Mota was a lieutenant in the Super Dragons, a more political and militant Portuguese equivalent of the Chelsea Headhunters, a hardcore group of fans who organised violent street battles against rival fans. When Mourinho arrived at Porto in January 2002, he had insisted that the team learnt the chants of the Dragons to motivate them, and he also knew that the hardcore fans had a powerful influence over the running of any club. It was a power that even Abramovich could not buy.

Rumours circulated that Mourinho had fallen out with the Dragons, although the exact reasons were never clear. Mourinho then made a fatal error of judgement in comparing

Porto to the mafia-ridden town of Palermo in Sicily. This made him subject to even more anger and abuse from the fans than for leaving Porto with two years left on his contract.

Joe only played for 52 minutes against Liverpool in the first of the club's five clashes with the Reds that season. He scored the winner, earned himself an England call-up with his performance and received a stinging rebuke from Mourinho. It was perhaps his most important match up to that point in his career, as it turned his life around completely.

Liverpool were without their best player, Steven Gerrard, who had turned down a lucrative move to Chelsea in the summer. The travelling Liverpool fans had brought with them a banner in honour of their hero, depicting a set of scales. On one side was Gerrard's heart and, on the other, Abramovich's money. As The Beatles sang in the 1960s, 'Money can't buy you love… ', it appeared that it couldn't buy Gerrard's switch of allegiance either. Managed by Liverpool's new boss, Rafael Benítez – like Mourinho, a highly regarded coach, but in a more modest, self-effacing mould – Liverpool were struggling to adjust to the changes in their fortunes. 'Rafa' had won the Spanish title and the UEFA Cup with Valencia the previous season. It was Ranieri who inherited Benitez's legacy at Valencia, having departed Chelsea with a handsome pay-off, but things did not go well for him in Spain and he was soon on his way again after a string of bad results and an early exit from the Champions League.

A few nights before the Chelsea–Liverpool game, the Reds had been soundly beaten in Greece by Olympiakos and looked to be heading out of Europe. Not even seasoned gamblers, even with Abramovich's wealth, would have been willing to wager a few pounds on the Merseysiders winning a major honour that season.

Joe came on when Drogba went off with a muscular injury, which kept him out for several weeks. Joe made an immediate impact, setting Paulo Ferreira away down the flank to cross for Lampard to send his diving header wide.

Joe continued to make his presence felt and early in the second half he smashed a shot into the side netting after another exchange of passes with Ferreira. Then he let fly with a half-volley that the Liverpool keeper, Kirkland, managed to block, with Harry Kewell heading the clearance away. This was not the first time Joe had tested Kirkland's resilience – the first time Joe had lined up against Kirkland was when Chris was at Coventry and West Ham put nine goals past him in the FA Youth Cup Final.

Joe finally beat him after 64 minutes with a well worked free-kick. Joe was also behind the move which led to the free kick; a clever back-heel from him found Smertin, who was chopped down by the classy midfielder Xabi Alonso. Lampard made as if to shoot for goal with one of his trademark piledrivers, but he subtly clipped the ball instead for Joe, who had cleverly lost his marker, and swivelled to send the ball into the net with a right-footed shot. It was the eighth goal out of the last ten that had come from a set piece, and Lampard had been involved in six of them.

Liverpool were unable to lift their game to salvage anything, despite pushing up in numbers, and Chelsea had to consolidate to hold on to their meagre lead. Alonso, normally so imperious in midfield, had a woeful game and wasted a number of free kicks.

Mourinho, meanwhile, was visibly infuriated at Joe's failure to track back in the closing minutes. Joe was endlessly positive, though, always looking for a way to open up the game and attack. He was recognised by the pundits as Man of the Match, an award that seemed in some dispute as soon as the Special One had an opportunity to offer his thoughts. Mourinho, in his inimitably sullen style, remarked, 'Joe Cole gave us some dynamism and scored a goal. But after that I needed 11 players defending, but I only had 10. Joe Cole still has a lot to learn. He has to improve if he is going to do it for club and country. He didn't do enough after the goal. I can make him better. He wants to become better. He has two faces – one is beautiful when he attacks with the ball. I want to keep that face. The other face is not so good defensively, and I don't like it so much. Players must not just try to please the crowd. It's me who picks the squad.'

In Porto, Mourinho had been tough on anybody he felt was not contributing to the cause. Star striker Benni McCarthy was dropped after a night out in Vigo two days before a crucial clash with arch rivals Benfica.

Mourinho was clearly not averse to heaping public indignity on anyone who incurred his displeasure, and who he believed was not in tune with his game plan and strategy. The warning for Joe was clear – do your job the way I want it to be done, or you won't play. Fortunately, Mourinho was also so confident in his managerial skills that he publicly declared that he could take a great player and make him a world-beater –

ego or not, at least Joe would benefit from the boss's attention, and his desire to develop his young stars to help them achieve their potential.

Mourinho's leadership style had come under scrutiny over this period, and some criticised him for his arrogance, and public denouncement of one of his players. It was becoming clear as the season rolled on that Mourinho would do things his way, and behave however he wished, rather than pander to a critical press, or try to be popular for the sake of it. Mourinho is narcissistic and, unlike other leaders who might employ compassion and collaboration, he is wholly convinced of his god-given talent, and will impose his will, come what may. And if that involves criticism of his players immediately after a match, then so be it.

Of course, the risk he runs is that of potentially alienating his squad, the board and the fans. In 1973, the great Chelsea Cup-winning side was destroyed because of the personality clash between its manager and its star players, Peter Osgood and Alan Hudson. The players' dissatisfaction lay in their unhappiness with the standard of management and coaching they were receiving. The manager, Dave Sexton, was an average player whose career was cut short by a knee injury; he had been a better player than Mourinho, but he was no Hudson or Cole.

The row that sparked Osgood and Hudson's departure was with the then-coach, Dario Gradi, about the correct technique to head a ball. Gradi had one of the longest careers in the game, but incurred the duo's wrath because they had no respect for his methods. This was based simply on the fact that they were top-class players and he was not.

The Osgood–Hudson affair ended badly. Both players chucked their careers away with mediocre sides. Dave Sexton was sacked, Chelsea were relegated and almost bankrupted in a downward spiral. It is safe to say that Chelsea never fully recovered from the fallout of the fiasco until Abramovich appeared on the horizon three decades later.

Brian Mears was chairman of Chelsea from 1969–81 and was at the helm during its rollercoaster ride from riches to rags. He has said:

'In those days, the club always sided with the manager. Peter and Alan were grand lads and marvellous players but they overstepped the line and had to go. It cost us everything, ultimately, but it was a point of principle.

'Today, it is all different – the players have the power by virtue of their tremendous wealth. They are better advised with their own managers, agents and advisers... Mourinho's criticism of Joe Cole would have sparked no end of trouble in the '70s. Joe Cole is probably the nearest thing we have to Alan Hudson in the modern game – tremendous natural ability, plus the element of the unexpected, which is sadly missing from so much of the modern game. I can imagine what Alan would have said to Mourinho if he trooped off the field after a match-winning performance to be criticised in such a manner.

'Mourinho's side brought the glory back to Chelsea, thanks to Abramovich funding it, but, to me, they are the Leeds of 1970... the work ethic above everything.'

To his credit, Joe took his punishment on the chin and showed no sign of being aggrieved by Jose's rebuke.

Subsequent reports in the press seemed to suggest that few believed Joe would learn from the experience.

If Mourinho was disappointed with the work ethic of his team after a game that they'd won, one can only assume that he was absolutely livid when they lost their only Premiership game of the season away to Manchester City in October 2005.

Kevin Keegan was manager of City at the time and, on the morning of the match, he was asked if he liked Mourinho as much as Ranieri. The ex-Liverpool superstar shook his head and smiled. Keegan had tracked Joe Cole when he had managed Newcastle and was known to be an admirer of the England international. Keegan would be the first to admit he was a self-made player, and he had a great deal of respect for the truly gifted. When Alan Hudson was seriously injured in a road accident, Keegan had been one of the first to offer his assistance, such was his regard for the ex-Chelsea man as a player.

Prior to the City match, Joe had been on England duty in Azerbaijan, and Abramovich had arranged for his private jet to fly him, Lampard and Terry home. Their team-mates had not been so lucky, having to take the red-eye FA charter flight, dropping off the Northern players at Manchester first, then landing at Heathrow. London lads like Joe's pal Defoe stepped off the plane at 5.00 am.

Even though Joe arrived back at the Bridge in double-quick time, Mourinho kept him on the bench until he replaced Tiago with just over 23 minutes to go. The match against Manchester City had been scheduled for a tea-time kick-off, and Chelsea never really got going. Despite having over 60 per cent of the possession, Chelsea could find no way through the stubborn City defence.

The only goal of the game came after 11 minutes when Ferreira collided with Nicolas Anelka in the box, and the troubled Frenchman scored from the subsequent penalty. Keegan thought that Ferreira should have got more than a yellow card, but Mourinho was convinced that Anelka had been fouled outside the box. The Frenchman had long been a thorn in Chelsea's side, with his sheer pace being too much for Terry to deal with. Known as 'Nico' by Robbie Fowler, he was a diffident, self-centred character, whose bankrolling transfer from Arsenal to Real Madrid had given him 'mega-star' attitude. He had found it hard to settle at City, and only sporadically showed the form that had earned him vast sums at two of the biggest clubs in the world, but against Chelsea, he delivered.

For the first time since his arrival in England, Mourinho looked flustered and seemed unable to come up with any decisive tactic to ease his side back into the game. The confident, opinionated, tactical genius of the previous week's press conference suddenly looked vulnerable, and he wasn't helped by the Chelsea attack performing woefully. Mateja Kezman had signed during the summer for £5 million from Robben's club PSV, but was looking anything but a Premiership striker. It was a pretty safe bet that Chelsea replica shirts with 'Kezman' emblazoned across the back had been bought before the start of the season. Gudjohnsen and Duff also struggled to make any impact. When Joe came on, he similarly seemed a little out of sorts, and failed to make any positive impact.

Chelsea now trailed Arsenal, who were still unbeaten, by five points. For the only time that season, grave doubts were expressed about Chelsea's ability to win the Premiership, and there were particularly huge question marks over their potency as an attacking force. Mourinho, though, had been making the point all season that Chelsea should not be judged until his full squad became available for selection. That meant the inclusion of Robben, who was approaching full fitness at last after his ankle injury.

Next, there was the matter of the Group H home fixture against CSKA Moscow in the Champions League. The Russian press were dubbing it 'Abramovich v Abramovich', with the oligarch having personal and business links with CSKA. Sibneft, the oil company that he had a majority shareholding in, had paid CSKA £10 million a season to have the company name on their shirts. UEFA seemed unconcerned by the Russian's links to both clubs, with far more fuss at this stage being made over Mutu, who had tested positive in a drugs test. Mourinho refused to comment on the situation.

On Chelsea TV, Joe was jokingly asked if he would contemplate a loan move to CSKA. Joe said that he would find the winters too cold and the food not to his liking.

Chelsea started well, with Terry scoring in his third successive Champions League match when Gudjohnsen headed on Lampard's corner. The strategy of exploiting Terry's size and aerial ability against foreign opposition was nothing new – Chelsea had been using that approach for decades, since Tommy Lawton had wreaked havoc among the Moscow Dynamos a few months after the end of World War II.

Likewise, David Webb, a tough-tackling, aggressive centre-back, had plundered vital goals on the way to Chelsea, winning the European Cup Winners' Cup for the first time in 1971. Defender John Dempsey had even blasted the winner against Real Madrid in the replayed final.

The tactic of throwing Terry forward was certainly not original, but it was highly effective, and had been reaping dividends in the Premiership as well.

The feeble CSKA defence caved in again when Eidur Gudjohnsen hit the second. The 2-0 win was a welcome return to form, but Joe was not called on to play that evening. He froze on the bench all night as the temperature plummeted.

Joe started the game against Blackburn in the Premiership, but was subbed by Robben after just over an hour. Gudjohnsen had already scored his first hat-trick for the Blues, the first having been set up by Joe with an exquisite through-ball that the front man threaded past the onrushing Brad Friedel.

That afternoon was the start of the Arjen Robben 'roadshow', in which he gave fans a taste of the dazzling footwork and sheer audacity that would characterise many subsequent performances for his club. For the last half-hour, he ran Blackburn ragged and set up Duff for the fourth.

Their win meant that Chelsea cut the deficit behind Arsenal to just two points as the Gunners lost their amazing unbeaten record in a 0-2 defeat at Old Trafford.

Joe retained his starting place in the side for the visit of his old team West Ham in the third round of the Carling Cup. He was good-naturedly booed by the 6,000 travelling Hammers fans every time he was on the ball. The more serious abuse was reserved for Frank Lampard, who was cruelly jeered when he came off the bench.

Joe was the outstanding player on the pitch and ran the game against his former club. Early in the match, Joe found Robben, who had switched to the right. His shot was deflected into the path of Kezman, whose instant volley was tipped away by Hammers reserve keeper Jimmy Walker. That was the story of the evening, as Walker stopped almost everything Chelsea threw at him. Twelve minutes into the second half, though, a splendid through-ball from Joe put in Kezman to score from 18 yards with a low shot into the corner of the net. It was his first goal in 557 minutes of playing for Chelsea. That was an extraordinary statistic, as this was a player who had scored 105 goals in 112 games for PSV.

Joe was denied again later in the match by a fine save from Walker. Lampard came on 20 minutes from time and, within ten minutes, his penalty, given for a foul on Robben, was brilliantly saved by Walker. Lampard had done everything right, smashing the ball low towards goal, but Walker somehow kept it out. The West Ham fans were delighted, and made sure that Lampard was in do doubt about what they thought of him.

Minutes later, he had a chance to make amends, but his rising shot hit the bar. Frank desperately wanted to score against his old club to put an end to the torrent of abuse aimed at him.

Kezman was hit by a missile thrown from the stands, as tensions threatened to boil over. After the match, some of the

West Ham travelling support clashed with the police, in scenes that were reminiscent of the crowd troubles of the 1980s.

Anton Ferdinand, brother of Rio, and another of West Ham's potential stars, nearly saved it for Hammers when he headed against the bar with Cudicini flat-footed.

Joe said after the game to the *Sun*, 'Frankie gets more stick from the West Ham fans than us. We left the club under different circumstances. But the stick he gets drives Frankie on. He is desperate to get his first goal against West Ham.

'Their keeper did so well against us. Whatever we threw at him, he kept us out. I thought I had scored two goals.'

The MP for Newham at the time was Tony Banks, a die-hard Chelsea fan, who watched the game from the West Stand. It was to be the last time he watched the two London sides fighting it out, as he died of a stroke in January 2006. It had been Banks, a former Minister of Sport, who, at the time of the acquisition, had ordered an investigation into Abramovich's dealings, and the management of the Blues' affairs.

The events that happened over the next few months were the most important in Joe's career, and they helped to shape his future. The emergence of Arjen Robben, thanks to an astonishing burst of form, changed the whole team pattern and raised Chelsea to a different dimension.

Joe started another Premiership game against West Bromwich Albion on 30 October 2004, but was replaced by Robben at half-time. The Dutchman proceeded to tear West Brom apart with a marvellous display of wing play, with the Blues winning 4-1.

In midweek, Chelsea travelled to Russia for the return with

CSKA, and Joe was dropped to the bench. Robben scored on his European debut and the splendidly-named Vagner Love missed a penalty for the Russians, blazing it high into the stand behind the Chelsea goal.

Robben scored again the following Saturday when he grabbed the winner against Everton, then flying high in third spot. Joe remained on the bench as he saw Chelsea claim top spot in the Premiership for the first time that season. Observers now wondered whether Mourinho's all-stars had the consistency and determination required to maintain their supremacy, or would they fold under the increasing pressure to deliver a much needed return on Abramovich's massive investment?

Joe was back in the side for the Carling Cup game at Newcastle, in which Mourinho made seven changes from the team that had started against Everton. Joe played for 70 minutes in temperatures not much warmer than those in Moscow; he was then substituted by Lampard, although the score remained goalless after 90 minutes. Then Mourinho sent on Gudjohnsen and Robben in extra time, and they both scored. Gudjohnsen netted his sixth goal in six games, and Robben neatly tucked his away after a sublime run.

Joe is a great one for superstitions. Like most footballers he believes luck plays a great deal in continued success, and he performs a series of pre-match rituals. He always tries to duplicate the same pattern of behaviour from the last time he won. For example, he never touches the ball in the dressing room and makes sure his right foot goes on to the pitch first. Only then is he in the mood to play.

Perhaps these rituals paid off, as Fulham were next to be

obliterated in front of their own supporters with Chelsea rattling in another four, a common outcome in that wonderful spell of form in late autumn and early winter. Robben went into overdrive, dribbling, making goals, scoring and demoralising the opposition with his searing pace. His talent was undeniable, and defenders found him simply unplayable at times.

The Fulham manager, Chris Coleman, said that Chelsea had played them off the park and tipped them for the title. Given the wealth of talent in the squad, Mourinho currently had plenty of options in all positions – unfortunately for Joe, this meant that the opportunities for him to play himself into the starting eleven were few and far between. He only watched the Fulham match from the sidelines, and would have been further frustrated at Mourinho's comment around this time, when he stated that, 'It is impossible for him [Joe] to play in my team as a midfielder.'

The Portuguese coach had Tiago, Smertin and Parker as his water carriers, with Lampard and Makelele as the engine room of the side. Robben was universally acknowledged at that time as the best winger in Europe, with Martin Jol, the Spurs manager, already comparing him to Johan Cruyff. Duff, who had flattered to deceive since his arrival from Blackburn, had now proved that he could play with Robben. The way ahead for Joe seemed blocked at every turn. It appeared that he would have to make do with infrequent appearances in the lesser competitions, or cameo roles as a sub, if his career under Mourinho was to continue to develop. Only injuries to others, or a significant contribution in a significant match, might start to cause the manager to rethink Joe's status within the squad.

Bolton unexpectedly grabbed a point at the Bridge in a 2-2 draw and became the first Premiership side to score twice against the Blues. At one stage, Chelsea were two goals up, but allowed the battling Northerners to come back into the match. Again, Joe did not manage an appearance.

Joe was selected in midfield, though, for the home Champions League tie against Paris St Germain. Chelsea, with a 100 per cent record in the competition, were eight points ahead in their group and the match was a bit of a non-event. After missing an early chance to put the Blues ahead, Joe dug in and played efficiently. He lasted the full 90 minutes as the game petered out to an uninspiring 0-0 draw.

Chelsea returned to Charlton, but without Joe. Duff opened the scoring and Chelsea steamrollered the Addicks 4-0.

Chelsea seemed to have struck a rich vein of form as they prepared to cross Bishop's Park to play Fulham in the quarter-final of the Carling Cup. Fulham, that night, were a different proposition to the side that had crumbled a few weeks earlier. Duff opened the scoring yet again, and Lampard hit a late winner after Fulham had equalised. Joe came on as sub for Robben, but the game was all but over by then.

Lampard dedicated his winning goal to his grandfather Bill Harris, who had died the day after the Charlton game. Lampard comes from an incredibly supportive family, with his father, Frank Sr, making a point of seeing all of his son's matches. Harry Redknapp, the former West Ham manager and mentor to the young Lampard and Joe, was often to be heard singing the praises of his young protégés, particularly as Lampard had started as a much-pilloried struggler at West

Ham, but had now become one of the best midfielders in the world. Joe had yet to match his colleague's status within the game, and within the hearts of the fans.

It is interesting to note that Joe comes from a council estate whilst Lampard grew up in the privileged world of a footballer's family. Frank grew up in a mansion in Romford near where Joe was to move to when he eventually hit the big time. Frank went to an expensive private school in Brentwood and came away with 9 CSE'S at grade 'A'. Joe's qualifications were the stacks of honours he won in junior football. Frank was linked with a string of female celebs. His former girlfriends are rumoured to include pop goddesses Liz McClarnon of Atomic Kitten and Suzanne Shaw of Hear'Say, and ex-Eastender Martine McCutcheon. He was also allegedly linked with Jordan before her marriage, whilst Joe has lived his private life out of the spotlight. His girlfriend, Carly, is a normal girl who coped admirably in an abnormal world.

Newcastle were back at the Bridge for a Saturday lunchtime game. Joe wasn't even on the bench, as the gritty Magpies controlled the game for an hour. Then Lampard scored and the roof fell in. Three more goals followed through Drogba, the mercurial Robben and Kezman from the spot. It was Kezman's first goal in the Premiership and was greeted with a strange display of congratulations from the team. Despite Mourinho's desire to outflank his critics, and to endorse the Serbian striker's credentials, the truth was that Kezman never made any real impact. It was significant that he never scored in the Champions League for any of his teams.

Drogba, too, was enigmatic as a first-choice striker, having given some blistering performances for his national team, the Ivory Coast, but never quite delivering on a consistent basis for Chelsea. At times, he could be mesmerising, using his strength and skill to destroy even the best defences. But the jury was still out over his commitment to the team, and his apparent willingness to crumble theatrically under soft challenges rather too easily, when staying on his feet and taking his chances might have won the team better opportunities to score. At this point in the season, it seemed extraordinary that Chelsea achieved such success with those two strikers who cost nearly £30m.

Constant rumours were circulating around this time that Jermaine Defoe was to join Chelsea as Kezman's replacement in the January window from Tottenham; it was also rumoured that Joe Cole was going to make the reverse trip to Tottenham as part of the deal. Spurs would have loved to have obtained Joe Cole even if on loan. Once dubbed 'The Bank of England' side of football, they have lived in the shadow of Arsenal for decades and now their bitter enemies Chelsea towered above them. Cole was the type of player that they had employed in their salad days of the early 60s. Joe, however, was determined to fight for his place at Chelsea. He told the *Sun*: 'When you're at Chelsea, every day training is an opportunity to impress, an opportunity to fight and make an impression on the manager.'

Defoe also played down the move to Chelsea, but urged the director of football at Tottenham, Frank Arnesen, to sign his former West Ham team-mate. In the event, the only person to move was Arnesen, who was recruited to help build up the youth development system, being appointed Head of Development and Scouting.

The situation over Adrian Mutu's future at Chelsea was coming to a head at this time, with his alleged drug-taking and speculation over his extravagant lifestyle being constantly debated in the press. Chelsea had signed the Romanian from Parma for £15.8 million, as he had scored 18 goals in 31 appearances in what is universally regarded as the toughest defensive league in the world. He was also captain of his national team, and had just been appointed club captain. So Mutu had the class, the skill and the experience to deliver for Chelsea, given the right psychological conditions to enable him to achieve his potential. Those conditions never materialised. Things started to go wrong when his marriage crumbled, whereupon the tabloids exposed the cracks in his personal life to every reader in Europe.

Chelsea eventually took the decision to sack him; some believed at the time that what he really needed was a guiding hand, and that anyone who had seen his early games for Chelsea would have known that he was worth saving, because players that good do not come on the market that often. Mourinho, though, either decided not to intervene and fight for the player, or he believed, like the Chelsea board, that Mutu was past redemption.

Juventus rescued him. Fabio Capello told him it was his last chance because they paid nothing for him and could sack him without any loss. In 2006, Mutu's rehabilitated career made him Juventus's second-highest scorer. Unfortunately for Chelsea, the latent class that they paid £15.8 million for is now being employed for Florentina's benefit after leaving Juventus.

Of course, Chelsea had the resources, personnel and manager to avoid having to suffer any long-term damage from the affair, and were able to continue on a fantastic run despite the sacking of one of their prized assets. Such an outcome would have had a disastrous effect on other club in the Premiership.

The case of Mark Bosnich (sacked by Chelsea in 2002) was very similar. Bosnich strove to rebuild his life after being the first high-profile player to fail a drugs test. Mark always claimed that he unknowingly took the Class A drug after a drink had been tampered with. The ex-Manchester United keeper was a great Chelsea fan and maintained that the 11 games he played for them were the finest in his career.

Next, Mourinho took Chelsea back to the Estádio do Dragão in Porto for the Champions League return fixture. It was a non-event, really, but the fans were very hostile, and the situation was inflamed by the Porto president Jorge Nuno Pinto Da Costa calling Chelsea 'a small, nothing club'.

Joe didn't even make the bench for the game. Wayne Bridge was given a rare chance playing on the left of the midfield diamond. He ran hard, but his distribution was poor. Duff, again Chelsea's best player, gave them the lead, but Porto equalised on the hour. The most competitive duel of the evening was between Porto's Maniche and his ex-team-mate, Ferreira. Maniche later moved to CSKA Moscow before ending up at the Bridge for a spell.

Porto were the better side on the night, and it was the South African striker Benni McCarthy, causing Terry all sorts of problems, who grabbed the winner. That win meant that Porto qualified for the next stage of the competition.

Next on the agenda was a trip across London to Arsenal for the game that would truly test their title aspirations. Following the Champions League victory in March, however, Highbury did not seem quite so daunting. Joe, though, again was not part of the squad.

A global audience of 600 million watched Henry fire Arsenal ahead within two minutes but Terry equalised after some slack defending. Then Henry, alive to the possibilities of taking a quick free kick on the edge of the box, cunningly steered the second Arsenal goal into an empty net while Cech was still lining up his wall.

Mourinho was incensed that the goal had been allowed by Graham Poll, the referee, who had apparently asked Henry if he wanted to play the ball early. The truth was that the Chelsea defence were not alert to the danger, and had been caught napping.

Gudjohnsen equalised for Chelsea early in the second half with a simple header, making the most of Arsenal's potential weakness at the back.

On the Saturday before Christmas, Norwich came to the Bridge. Championship talk was rife and another 4-0 victory put Chelsea five points clear. The usual suspects scored – Duff, Lampard, Robben and Drogba.

Villa came to the Bridge on Boxing Day. In the past, the Christmas fixtures had sometimes thrown up unusual results or bizarre events, such as the 5-5 draw between Chelsea and West Ham in 1965, or even a 7-4 victory over Portsmouth in 1957.

At Christmas 2004, the atmosphere for the game against Villa was muted. Duff had struggled to justify his £17 million price tag, but since the emergence of Robben, the boy from the Ballyboden housing estate had been showing his true potential. Once again, he ended up being the match winner for Chelsea, scoring the only goal in a poor match.

Joe must have had a miserable Christmas; from a professional viewpoint, his decision to join Chelsea had been sound, as the Blues looked to be on the threshold of greatness. Personally, though, he must have wondered if he was ever to get a chance to show what he could do. The question of a move from his beloved Chelsea was still in the air. Joe loved playing football more than anything. With the 2006 World Cup campaign looming he knew he had to be playing regularly to have a chance of making the squad. Cole's strength was getting the ball down and running at players. In the trench warfare of the Premier League midfield it was becoming increasingly difficult to find any space to make those runs. The dilemma was causing his glittering career to stagnate, but shortly a solution was to be found and the whole situation would turn around.

6

Silver Lining

'The best feeling in the world is when you come away
with three points away from home.'
Joe Cole

GEOFF HURST ONCE said that, in football, 'the good times do not last for long, but the bad times don't last too long either.' The West Ham legend could have been talking about another West Ham hero because things were going to improve for Joe Cole. Despite the problems, he had kept a positive attitude and told the press he was still happy at the Bridge.

Chelsea travelled to Portsmouth for what was considered to be the first of two tough away games in four days; the second was a trip to Liverpool. Chelsea were starting to look invincible but, no matter how many points they had accumulated and how few goals they had conceded, there was still speculation about a bad patch, a 'blip'. If it was ever going to happen, then it would be at places like Fratton Park and Anfield.

Portsmouth was a tough game – the fans had history. The

hooligan crews had clashed frequently in the 1980s and it was always an uncomfortable place for a Chelsea fan. The fact that the Londoners were now the richest club in the world had intensified the animosity towards even the ordinary fans. Anyone supporting Chelsea was now considered a band-wagon jumper and a glory seeker. Chelsea, though, had always had a huge away following. Even in impoverished times, they would have a hardcore support of about 4,000. To those fans, used to mediocre strikers and suspect defences, the massive leap from middle-table grafters to mega-star world-beaters took some getting used to, but they accepted Mourinho's brand of football more readily than some fans might. The satisfaction for the moment came from beating teams who used to lord it over them. Style and good football could come later.

Portsmouth went hard at Chelsea in the first half. The midfield in particular struggled to close things down when they lost possession, and Lampard was being man-marked out of the game by Faye. An animated Mourinho reminded them at half-time exactly what was at stake, and he sent on Gudjohnsen and Joe.

When Joe entered the fray, he started to find extra space and Faye could not concentrate on keeping Lampard pinned down. Towards the end of the match, Joe set up the first goal. He moved the ball forward and gave Lampard the chance of his first strike at goal. Robben then took matters into his own hands when Lampard appeared to have lost the opportunity, scoring with a low drive.

Portsmouth, stung by Chelsea's goal, threw everything forward in desperation to salvage something. In injury time,

Joe received the ball at his feet, controlled it and scored from about 20 yards out with a marvellous curling drive. A brilliant solo goal, conjured out of nothing. It was absolutely vital, as Portsmouth were threatening and Chelsea were under severe pressure.

The significance of that goal was not lost on the fans or the Chelsea manager. Some of the hardened Chelsea fans rushed to the front of the stand to greet Joe as he ran towards the away supporters in celebration, and Mourinho catapulted himself out of his seat to display uncharacteristic emotion. He often remained seated, disconcertingly impassive when the rest of the Chelsea bench were dancing with joy. Against Portsmouth though, the relief that their lead was unassailable, and that the league title – the first for 50 years – was virtually theirs, was too much to contain.

Joe started the New Year as he had finished it, scoring the only goal at Liverpool on New Year's Day 2005. Duff had been taken off to allow Joe into the game. After 76 minutes, his low drive went in off Jamie Carragher. It was a tight match, and Chelsea were fortunate to have survived what appeared to be a certain penalty when Tiago blatantly handled in the box.

But it was results that counted and, at the end of the holiday period, Chelsea had amassed maximum points and had a five-point lead over Arsenal. Barring a horrendous dip in form, the Championship trophy was almost on its way to Stamford Bridge. The two games Joe had played such a vital role in winning had destroyed any lingering doubts over Chelsea's durability, and with Joe forcing his way back into the reckoning with those performances, Chelsea now had another potent weapon to deploy on a more regular basis.

Joe played for an hour against Middlesbrough in a Premiership game the following Tuesday evening. Drogba killed the game in the first 15 minutes with two simple goals, with Joe being involved in the second. Having been hacked down on the left wing, Joe won a free kick, which Lampard delivered to the penalty spot where Drogba headed powerfully home. Sickness and injuries forced Mourinho to use Joe in a more restrained midfield role, in which he had to curb his natural inclination to push forward. Clearly, Mourinho was still trying to find Joe's best position. By virtue of the fact that he was such a talented player, he could adapt to virtually everything he was asked to do. Tiago replaced him during that game and Joe was keen to make clear it was tactical. He explained to the *Daily Telegraph*, 'The boss explained why I was taken off. I don't want to reveal the details but it was a positive reason. I want to nail down a regular place in the team. I've played central midfield in a 4-4-2 before with some of the best players in the world.'

The truth was that Joe had been replaced because Mourinho was fearful of losing another 2-0 lead, as had been the case at the Bolton home game. Across town, Shaun Wright-Phillips, another young star who was rapidly becoming an attractive proposition for many of the top clubs, scored at Highbury to earn Manchester City a point and increase Chelsea's lead still further.

Lowly Scunthorpe came to the Bridge the following Saturday for an FA Cup match. Mourinho seemed a little ambivalent about the competition, but went through the motions. Scunthorpe played better than many of the Premiership sides who had appeared at Chelsea that season, and at least were prepared to carry the game to the champions-elect, which was certainly more than Middlesbrough had been prepared to do earlier in the week. Most Premiership sides were set up to deliver a damage limitation exercise, which was one reason why there had been so many low-scoring, unexciting matches at the Bridge.

In the past, there was always the possibility that a good side could come away with something from Chelsea. Similarly, even mediocre Chelsea sides had always been able to beat superior opposition, with the 1978 side being a prime example. Chelsea were newly promoted to the big time, and twice in one season handed out beatings in the Cup and the League to the great Liverpool side that won the European Cup that year, and who fielded such greats as Alan Hansen, Kenny Dalglish and Graham Souness. Times had changed, and with Chelsea now being the team to beat, everyone they played made sure that things were kept tight, and often uninspiring.

Joe made the first 11 for that FA Cup game, and was voted Man of the Match. Scunthorpe did their best to steal the headlines by scoring first, and the League Two side led for a glorious 18 minutes while the world waited for the biggest upset in the history of the FA Cup. Much of this early disarray was due to Mourinho's eccentric choice of back four – Johnson, Watt (who moved to Swansea), Smertin (in Terry's place) and Morais (a right-footed midfield player at left-back).

Kezman scored the only decent goal in his brief Chelsea

career to level. Ironically, it was against a team that probably least deserved it. Chelsea's second came when Drogba's cross was turned into his own goal by the Scunthorpe skipper Crosby. The minnows continued to make and squander chances before Gudjohnsen lashed in a third.

After the match, Mourinho offered an interesting perspective to the *Daily Telegraph* on Joe's contribution. 'He was fantastic. Now he thinks the game, not as an individual but as one of 11 players. He understands what the team needs and what he has to do when we don't have the ball.

'He is improving a lot, a completely different player. He can play on the left, right or as a pure midfield player. He's a good boy. Instead of being sad and crying or speaking to you, he wants to improve. He wants to ask why and where is the mistake.

'I keep saying to him he doesn't need to show his talent because I think everybody knows he has that. I told him he needed to show me he could play in a tactical way and, at this moment, his evolution is big in that sense.'

Mourinho also had an interesting theory about the FA Cup, in that Premiership sides should always play against smaller teams away from home. Jose was the perfect host, personally conducting the Scunthorpe team around the Bridge for a tour and, afterwards, laying on sandwiches, autographs and shirts.

From League Two strugglers to one of the most successful clubs in the history of the game – Manchester United. The next round of the Carling Cup saw the Red Devils come down to the Bridge on a grim winter's evening. Joe was again in the starting line-up, standing in for the suspended Robben.

Slotting back into his role on the wing, Joe had a great first half, displaying some classy touches on the wet surface. At one stage, his pass was perfectly delivered to Duff, who should have done better than scuff the shot.

In the second half, Joe, visibly tired was replaced by Jiri Jarosik, who had joined from CSKA Moscow. The lanky Czech international had impressed Mourinho in the Champions League clashes. He was the latest in a long line of midfield players whom Mourinho had employed to combine great skill and toughness with versatility, as the manager attempted to find the most balanced but flexible solution to the demands of the various competitions. Joe, though, was the only Chelsea player capable of matching the flicks and tricks of United's Ronaldo, and the much lauded Rooney struggled to make any impact as the Shed taunted him.

Joe had a chance of breaking the deadlock when Tim Howard, United's keeper, hit a weak clearance to him. Joe instantly lobbed it back, but it went just wide as Howard vainly tried to scramble back into position. The game then petered out to a 0-0 draw, which would have satisfied United, but frustrated Chelsea.

After the match, Mourinho's dissatisfaction with the result was plain to see, as he claimed that Ferguson's personality had overawed the referee. 'It was a question of a big personality influencing another person without so much prestige in the world of football... a bit of pressure and a few clever words can change a little the way you think.

The second half was fault after fault, diving after diving. Dive and fault and fault and dive.'

Joe came on for Duff in the next match at White Hart Lane with 11 minutes left on the clock. Chelsea were leading by a first-half Lampard penalty, and he scored again in the last minute to clinch a 2-0 win. It was their sixth straight Premiership win without a solitary goal conceded. For Spurs fans, it was particularly depressing as it was now 30 League matches since Spurs had beaten Chelsea, stretching back over the previous 15 years.

Joe was again in the starting line-up for the Premiership clash against Portsmouth, and played the full match. It wasn't Joe who stole the limelight that day, though. It became another Arjen Robben showpiece as he almost single-handedly destroyed Pompey. The Dutch winger scored one and set up Drogba for two others. Chelsea dominated from start to finish and enjoyed 70 per cent of the possession.

Next up, the Blues travelled to Old Trafford for the second leg of the Carling Cup semi-final. Wenger had recently damned the Premiership leaders by comparing them to a matador waiting for the bull to tire, and it turned out to be prophetic, as the killer blow was delivered five minutes from time.

Joe was on the bench and only came on from Robben in the dying seconds. Lampard, after losing the close attentions of Roy Keane, gave Chelsea a first-half lead with a typical finish from Drogba's pass, which was cancelled out by Giggs's sublime lob over Cech.

With Rooney on as a sub, United looked the more likely winners. The grace and guile of Giggs was a constant threat to the Chelsea defence. Then the matador struck, as Duff arced over an in-swinger of a free-kick from the left, from well over

40 yards out. It bounced and flew into the net past Howard.

It was enough to put Chelsea into the final at Cardiff against their old adversaries Liverpool. It was Mourinho's 42nd birthday, and to celebrate, he had brought with him a £240 bottle of 1964 Barça Velha from Portugal. However palatable the vintage, though, it probably left a sour taste in Alex Ferguson's mouth that evening. It was Ferguson's first defeat in 19 domestic semi-finals and another indication that blue was the new red.

In recent years, the Carling Cup had been seen as being the lesser of the domestic tournaments, the one in which the big clubs tended to blood their youth players and second-string journeymen. Mourinho and Ferguson, though, had been forced to use it as another theatre of war in their battle for global supremacy.

Chelsea had another cup on their agenda in their next match against Birmingham at the Bridge. Joe was in a re-shuffled side as Mourinho rested some key players. Joe had another excellent game and particularly linked up well with Jiri Jarosik, who also showed some neat touches. Joe received applause from his own bench for some of his neat footwork, something that had not happened too often before.

Robert Huth, the giant Chelsea defender, scored the first, and Terry scored a late second. Chelsea were still fighting on four fronts, with the Premiership, the crowning glory for any top club, being the most secure accolade at this stage in the season. If Chelsea's win at Portsmouth had set the foundations for the title win, perhaps the game that they won at Blackburn was the one that convinced everyone. In his post-match press conference after the Birmingham game, Mourinho was as critical of Robben – whom many regarded as the shining star of this newly formed Chelsea team – as he sometimes had been of young Joe.

He said 'I was not pleased with Robben. Damien played better. Robben told me he was keeping energy to play better against Blackburn Rovers on Wednesday.' Mourinho never seemed satisfied, even with his match-winners, yet in that period following his return to fitness, no player had conducted himself better or contributed more to Chelsea's dominance in all competitions than Robben. Mourinho had a deep distrust of skilful players. It was as if he refused to place control of his destiny in anyone else's hands (or feet) but his own. In an interview with *Jornal de Noticias* in January 2004, he said: 'I wanted players with titles, zero; money, little.'

Mourinho is a highly complex character. He finds it easier to mould players with no ego or self-confidence and so it was no surprise that the two players he criticised the most were the most skilful.

Robben carried on in the same vein at Blackburn, and showed how astute he had been in conserving his energy. Within five minutes, he scored an absolute gem of a goal. Gudjohnsen put Robben through and he simply tore down the left wing, eventually turning defender Lucas Neill inside-out before scoring with a hard, left-footed drive past Brad Friedel. Seconds after scoring that wonder goal, though, the Blackburn defender Aaron Mokoena's crunching tackle caught Robben's foot with enough force to break some bones. It ruled him out for some time and compromised Mourinho's attacking options. Sadly, that was the last goal he scored in the 2004/05 season and, despite sporadic periods of brilliance since, he has yet to recapture the full majesty of that spell.

Joe came on after Robben's injury, but was under strict instructions to play deep all evening. Joe had become one of Mourinho's utility players, a flexible stop-gap who could be trusted with various roles, but his strength was to dazzle and run at defences in the attacking third of the pitch. His defensive duties went against Joe's instincts, as he was itching to press forward and make the game safe.

Blackburn pushed up on Chelsea, with Robbie Savage and Paul Dickov sparing no blushes as they tore into the Blues' midfield and defence. Chelsea hung on, regrouped, and hung on again. Cech then brilliantly saved a penalty from Dickov, and proved that night that he had become the pre-eminent goalkeeper in the Premiership, having beaten Peter Schmeichel's record for the longest unbeaten run in the top flight.

Mourinho's side had never been put under such intense pressure in a Premiership game, but they held firm. Joe was everywhere, helping in front of the defence, tackling back but still trying to set something up. Whenever he got the ball, the Chelsea fans' spirits lifted as he tried to set up counter-attacks, and he was sufficiently confident to perform an exquisite step-over late in the game, that had the crowd roaring their approval.

When the final whistle blew, Mourinho was first on to the pitch to congratulate his players, but refused to shake hands with Hughes, displaying the same contemptuous behaviour that he would repeat at Highbury later in the year. What was undeniable about Mourinho's strategy that night, though, was that the team had played for each other, in the face of some thoroughly unpleasant challenges. They had won because they had played as a unit, and were more than the sum of their individual parts.

Manchester City were next to visit the Bridge and left with a point after forcing a 0-0 draw. In doing so, they became one of only two sides Chelsea failed to beat in that record-breaking season. As had been the case in Manchester, Chelsea were unable to find a way through their defence, and again they found an opposition keeper, David James on this occasion, in majestic form. After 62 minutes, Mourinho sent Joe on for the disappointing Kezman. City held on, though – and could have won the game through a Robbie Fowler late header – and Mourinho played them a rare compliment, saying, 'they defended like us.' He also made a point of saying that he did not see the City star winger Shaun Wright-Phillips in the game.

Chelsea travelled back up to Merseyside to play at Goodison. In the war of words that had raged since Mourinho's arrival, Sir Alex Ferguson had hinted that 'Chelsea will find it difficult when they come north'.

The display of solidarity at Blackburn, though, undermined that theory completely. There now seemed to be no obstacle that this all-conquering Chelsea team could not overcome. The Everton game hinged on Beattie's early dismissal for a foolish challenge on William Gallas. Beattie had not had a great season against Chelsea, having scored at both ends for his former club, Southampton, at the Bridge. It was a bitterly cold day on Merseyside.

Joe had another solid game, diligently defending as well as

attacking. He had become another of Mourinho's grafters, a player with enormous quality, but who was just as important in a spoiling role, tracking back for the team, making crucial tackles, flinging himself in front of dangerous balls and generally harrying the opposition into mistakes.

Chelsea used to have a player called John Boyle on their books in the 1960s and early 1970s. He was a tough young Scot with massive potential that was never really unleashed. Like Joe, his best position had never been found, and he was used, particularly in away games, by Tommy Docherty to disrupt and generally break up opposition play. In some away games towards the end of this season, Joe had become a latter-day John Boyle. By this time, Joe had beefed up, and as well as being fitter, he was now stronger. This was a direct result of the special fitness methods and training introduced by Mourinho. A dietician was advising him about what he should be eating. Mourinho had also brought two assistants with him, to help him develop new techniques. Steve Clarke had made over 300 apearances for Chelsea and was very calm and composed while Brazilian, Baltemar Brito, was a passionate and fiery character. One of the most valuable techniques they taught Joe was the 'resting'trick, the ability to get the ball and 'rest'with it at his feet. This enabled Chelsea to keep possession by passing it between themselves whilst they recharged their batteries

These new techniques showed themselves in matches. Twenty minutes from the end of the Everton match, Joe fed Paulo Ferreira, who crossed to Gallas. He turned it on to the bar, and Gudjohnsen tapped home the rebound. Skill and simplicity combined in perfect harmony.

Chelsea had dominated this game, having enjoyed 67 per cent of the possession. Mourinho then battened down the hatches as he sent Jarosik on for Joe.

The statistics bore out Mourinho's faith in Joe – 27 accurate passes out of 36, and 3 tackles, on a difficult surface, out of the 25 Chelsea put in.

The next competition in which Chelsea interests were still very much alive was the FA Cup and another trip north for a difficult fifth-round tie against Newcastle. Mourinho had high hopes for this match – and for that seemingly impossible quadruple-winning season – but had to pick the squad with two vital fixtures following in quick succession – a visit to the Nou Camp in the Champions League, and the Carling Cup Final in Cardiff. So Mourinho rested six players, with Joe again starting in Robben's slot.

Three minutes into the game, Bramble dispossessed Joe out on the left, with Carr, Dyer and Butt linking to supply Laurent Robert. A perfect cross on the run found Kluivert, who out-jumped Gallas to smash home. It was a superb goal, of the highest quality, which belied the disappointment that Robert and Kluivert had been throughout their spells at St James's Park.

The Chelsea cause wasn't helped by a blizzard rolling around the stadium throughout the first half, and the Blues struggled to get back into the game. At half-time, Mourinho took his biggest gamble of the season and lost. It was the first in a series of unusual decisions and calculated risk-taking that he was to take at crucial points over the following week. They were all to become part of the Mourinho legend, and would propel him to become one of the biggest names in the European game.

Sensing that the game was slipping away, Mourinho threw on Lampard, Duff and Gudjohnsen, three of his strongest players replacing the midfield trio of Geremi, Tiago and Joe. He may well have been afraid of losing, but considering the deteriorating weather conditions and the massive games on the horizon, it seemed a reckless gesture bordering on the downright foolhardy.

Two minutes into the second half, following a challenge by Shearer, Wayne Bridge went off with a broken ankle. It was a terrible blow for Chelsea, and Shearer was cleared of any blame. Bridge's injury was serious and he was never really able to establish himself as first-choice left back again. In January 2006, he went out on loan to Fulham in a bid to re-establish his career and was rewarded with a place in the World Cup squad.

Chelsea briefly revived, thanks mainly to Duff's contribution, but then he got a knock, as did Gallas. Then Chelsea's ten men went down to nine as Cudicini was sent off for cutting down Ameobi. The game ended in total disarray for the wealthiest club in the world, with Johnson in goal and only six fit players in the outfield.

Mourinho's folly cost the club a place in the FA Cup. Jose escaped any real criticism because the next two games generated sufficient talking points to keep everyone talking for months.

The fall-out from the match against Barcelona caused no end of problems for Chelsea, and the repercussions are still being felt today. Joe started in the Nou Camp and played for 70 minutes. It was probably the biggest club match he had ever played in, with a crowd approaching 90,000. He was there on merit; the combination of great technique and a willingness to adapt his game had clinched his place.

Before the game, Mourinho continued to play with the media, refusing to name his line-up, but offering to predict Barcelona's. He had done this previously in the build-up to a Porto-Sporting Lisbon match, delighting the press with a 100 per cent accurate prediction. He pulled the same stunt on this occasion and, again, he managed to name all 11 of the Barça line-up.

Duff, who seemed to be in real pain when he went off at Newcastle, was included in the starting 11. Barcelona had clearly not been as prescient as Mourinho, and had not banked on Duff's ability to supply the front men. After 33 minutes, Duff, apparently having made a full recovery, eluded van Bronckhorst and delivered into the box. Joe raced in to meet Duff's cross, but the defender Belletti beat him to it and slammed the ball past keeper Valdes and into his own net. Belletti, it is worth noting, later joined Chelsea and won their 2007/8 goal of the season award. It was just the start Chelsea had wanted and the away goal was vital to their chances of going through. Chelsea should have clinched another within a minute when Makelele put Drogba through on goal, but he squandered the chance.

At half-time, Mourinho claimed that the referee Anders Fisk spoke with the Barça coach Frank Rijkaard. From that, a row erupted that became the talk of Europe, and resulted eventually in the resignation of Anders Frisk from refereeing. Among all the claims and counter-claims surrounding the referee's actions and subsequent press attention, he felt that he could not continue in the game. One allegation that may have had some bearing on his decision was that it had been reported that Frisk's children had been threatened by 'Chelsea' fans.

Early in the second half, having been booked for persistent fouling, Fisk had no hesitation in dismissing Drogba for a foul on the Barcelona goalkeeper. Chelsea now had a massive task to hold on to their slender lead.

The axis of the game shifted and Barça dominated, moving the ball around with an accuracy and ease that embarrassed the visitors. Lopez came on as a substitute and equalised on 66 minutes following brilliant work by Ronaldhino. Then Eto'o put the Spanish giants ahead after Lopez had deceived Carvalho. Only a stream of excellent saves from Cech in the closing stages kept Chelsea's hopes alive.

For the first time under Mourinho, Chelsea had lost two games in a row. The Newcastle game had been a freak match, and they were unlucky to have suffered such appalling weather and a run of injuries, but the defeat at the Nou Camp was different. Barcelona had given their visitors from London a lesson in free-flowing football, with Ronaldhino easily the best player on the pitch. Despite the millions Abramovich had poured into the club, no one in blue could hold a candle to him that night. Lampard had had a poor match; arguably Chelsea's most consistent player that season, he looked lethargic and struggled to find any rhythm. Terry's lack of pace was again exposed by the lightning Eto'o, and what was particularly worrying for club and ultimately country was that both players looked out of their depth at that level. The rest of the defence were overrun at times. Mourinho's credibility was now hanging by a thread. Only Joe and Cech had emerged from the game with any credit.

Mourinho then resorted to diverting attention from the result, or the performance of his team, and opted instead to attack Barcelona and the referee. Mourinho refused to speak after the match but Simon Greenberg, the Chelsea director of communications, said, 'We will be making an official report to UEFA about an incident that occurred at half time.'

With the defeat at the Nou Camp behind them, Chelsea moved on to the Millennium Stadium in Cardiff for the clash with Liverpool. Could Abramovich finally see some return on his massive investment?

Chelsea got the worse possible start, falling behind after just 45 seconds to a John Arne Riise goal. It was the fastest-recorded goal in the history of the final. Morientes – Terry's *bête noire* in Europe – was now playing for the Reds in the seventeenth final of his career. He collected the ball on the left, turned inside Terry and clipped over a perfect cross that Riise volleyed brilliantly home.

Joe had started the game and was Chelsea's most incisive player in the opening stages. Over the season, his performances may have been a little erratic, but there was no doubting his work rate, and he had found a place in the hearts of the Chelsea faithful with his willingness to work for the team. He could always trade on his affable nature and limitless skill, but now he was seen as a valuable team player. Jamie

Carragher blocked a drive by Joe as Chelsea laid siege to the Liverpool goal. The game became extremely tense for both teams, and mistakes were being made all over the pitch, with a couple of crosses from Joe going wildly astray.

There seemed to be a great deal of animosity between supporters, management and players that day. Abramovich looked uneasy and tense, and spent long periods of the game with his head in his hands. Liverpool had managed to get under Chelsea's skin in a way neither Arsenal or Manchester United ever could. The fans may dislike other clubs more, but there seemed to be real needle developing between the players and management. How much of that was down to the comments and behaviour of Mourinho himself is open to conjecture.

For a long time, it looked as though Liverpool would hang on to their lead. Jerzy Dudek, the Liverpool keeper, only had one real save to make in the first half from Drogba, a low shot after Joe had set up the chance.

At the interval, Gudjohnsen was introduced for Jarosik, and his downward header brought a snap save from Dudek, who then blocked Gallas's follow-up. Mourinho gambled again, taking off Gallas and bringing on Kezman as Chelsea went into a 3-1-2-4 formation. Gerrard should have put the game beyond Chelsea's reach but he wasted a good chance.

There were only 11 minutes left on the clock when Hamann body-checked Lampard, although Cole was openly contemptuous of the ref's decision to award a free kick rather than play the advantage. Ferreira's workmanlike set-piece skimmed a couple of defenders and Gerrard, of all people, rose to nod it past it Dudek.

Mourinho was on the touchline at the time, surrounded by Liverpool fans, having taken merciless stick from them all afternoon. As he done in Barcelona a few nights before, he chose to incite an already inflammatory situation. Mourinho celebrated by pressing a finger to his lips, apparently taunting them that they had little to shout about now. He stated that it was a gesture not intended for the Merseysiders, but to tell the English press to 'put their pens in their pocket'. This was obviously because he resented the poor reviews Chelsea had received over their recent cup defeats. On police advice, Mourinho was sent back down the tunnel and watched the rest of the match in the Sky interview room.

Joe was replaced by Glen Johnson two minutes later, with Mourinho still sending out messages through the communications director. Chelsea reverted to their traditional back four as the game went to extra time. There could only be one winner now, though as Liverpool's spark seemed to have deserted them the moment Gerrard's header flew past his own keeper. It was a crucial time of the game, with everything to play for, but they seemed incapable of bringing the game to Chelsea.

In the 17th minute of extra time, Johnston's choreographed long throw skidded off Sami Hyypia's head and Drogba tucked away the loose ball from point-blank range. Five minutes later, Dudek saved Gudjohnsen's snap shot, but the ball rolled to Kezman who scored while virtually on the goal line. Liverpool were down and out.

Mourinho's behaviour became even more unusual. At the end of the game, he insisted on shaking Gerrard's hand, as if to rub in the misery of having handed the cup to Chelsea. Of the policeman who had banished him from the pitch, Mourinho said, 'The policeman is not a football man. They are there to control the crowd. If I made a mistake, then I apologise. I am happy that I am not going to jail.'

With the Liverpool fans incensed at Mourinho's gesture, and whipped up to a fury, the manager's actions and subsequent comments seemed very naïve. In the not so distant past, the football fan base around the country comprised a hard core of vicious thugs who needed little encouragement to display their violent tendencies, or take out their frustrations on opposing supporters. Liverpool, along with every other club, had its hooligan element, and there is still an undercurrent from those times. To do anything to incite a crowd, or to ignore or even make light of the potential for violence just beneath the surface, could lead to serious consequences.

At the end of the game, Mourinho had mocked the Liverpool fans a second time by waving to the same section of the crowd to whom he'd gestured earlier. In the press conference after the game, a reporter tackled him on the waving gesture, which Mourinho dismissed by saying that he had been waving to his wife. He then warned the reporter, 'Be careful what you say... I think you can be a bad boy. I have to adapt to English football and you have to adapt to me. If not, we will have a fight.'

Once again, Mourinho's showmanship and desire to do whatever he wanted with little thought for the consequences left a nasty taste in the mouth. What was disappointing was that Chelsea had just won its first honour in the new Abramovich era, but it was Mourinho's behaviour, and apparent insecurity, that attracted much of the press coverage. Frank Rijkaard, the Barcelona boss, described to the *Sun* Mourinho's swaggering behaviour before the tie, saying, 'Someone who talks that much cannot be calm inside.'

On the plus side, Chelsea had started to deliver silverware, and they now had to be taken seriously. It may only have been a win in a lesser competition, but a victory over Liverpool, a domestic trophy and a triumphant day out for the fans at the Millennium Stadium were not to be dismissed lightly.

With the win, Joe Cole had secured the first of his professional honours. That first trophy would always mean so much to the youngster who, as a schoolboy, when he was just starting to display the first vestiges of his awesome skill, must have dreamed of days like these, and the adulation that went with them. Now, after the years of frustration and setbacks, Joe was starting to enjoy the fruits of his labour and was on the verge of winning another even more prestigious accolade.

7

We Are the Champions

'Hopefully this is the start of a very successful reign.
You can't argue with Jose Mourinho's record. He has already
put silverware on the table.'
Joe Cole, February 2005

JOE FINALLY HAD his first medal, and now he was keen to win another, more prestigious one – the Premiership. Chelsea took a step closer to the Championship trophy by winning 3-1 at Norwich, another side who were eventually to lose their place in the top flight, but who went down fighting. Joe put Chelsea ahead with perhaps his best goal of the season. It was a typical striker's goal – a run, a feint past defenders, and then a blistering shot into the back of the Norwich net which the keeper had no chance of saving.

It looked set up for another goal spree but Norwich, playing their best football of a difficult campaign, fought back. Leon McKenzie became the first player to score against Petr Cech in 1,025 minutes. A truly amazing statistic in the modern game, which has been modified to hamper the abilities of goalkeepers, and provide more goals, through such introductions as the lightweight balls that curl wickedly in the air, and restricting to keeper to a kicked clearance after a back pass. Cech, and the defence in front of him, could feel justifiably proud of that record.

Chelsea were momentarily rocked back on their heels, but soon they were pushing up. Kezman, temporarily rejuvenated by his Cup-winning strike in Cardiff, restored the Blues' lead with another close-range goal. When Carvalho headed the third, it was all over.

Then Barça visited the Bridge in the return leg of their epic clash. For those lucky enough to be present, it was one of the most fantastic matches ever played in Chelsea's 100-year history. Joe played a huge part in the event, having a hand in two goals and looking completely at home in a match featuring some of the greatest talent in world football. He lasted for the full 90 minutes, made 10 accurate passes and 4 tackles.

The match was refereed by Pierluigi Collina, who replaced Anders Fisk after he had quit the game in the aftermath of the fixture at the Nou Camp. Chelsea raced to a 3-0 lead in the first 20 minutes playing easily their greatest spell of free-flowing football under Mourinho's austere reign. The Blues coach gambled again by putting Kezman up front as a lone striker with Gudjohnsen breaking from deep. It worked perfectly for 20 minutes and, by that time, Chelsea had built an almost unassailable lead.

Gudjohnsen scored the first. Truly a big-match player, the Icelandic international was one of the most underrated players in the squad. Barça later signed him. Lampard started the move by dispossessing Xavi and sending Kezman away to cross to Gudjohnsen, who controlled the ball beautifully, glided around Belletti and scored with a low right-foot shot.

Then Joe tore down the right, beating van Bronckhorst before firing in a speculative shot. The ball glanced off Olelguer and Valdes made a world-class stop to keep it from spinning in. Lampard was following up, though, and slammed home Chelsea's second.

Joe was far from finished; determined to make his mark, he received the ball from Kezman in the centre circle, and produced a wonderful pass to put Duff through for the third. Everything about the goal was sheer class – Joe's sumptuous through-ball, Duff's instant control, sureness of touch and crisp and ruthless finish. Delivering a pass of that quality in a showpiece match was one of the high spots of Joe's career.

Chelsea were absolutely on fire, and it looked at this stage as if the game was well and truly over. But you dismiss Barcelona at your peril, particularly given the wealth of talent on display. World-class players can turn matches, even if the team is not playing particularly well, and this occasion offered world-beaters in abundance. Chelsea had class to spare, but Barcelona had Ronaldinho, the World Player of the Year, an accolade he had earned through dazzling skill, consistency and a fantastic understanding of the game. What the game needed now, from Barcelona's point of view, was someone to gain the upper hand in midfield and unlock the Blues defence, and there was no better player in the world than the Brazilian superstar.

The game swung towards Barça when Collina awarded the Spaniards a penalty, ruling that Ferreira had handled Belletti's cross. Cech was, at the time, the best goalkeeper in the world, but even he was made to look ordinary when Ronaldinho coolly converted the kick, seemingly unaffected by the immense pressure applied by the Blues fans at Stamford Bridge.

Then, 11 minutes later, Ronaldinho scored again. This time it was from open play with a shimmy that deceived Ferreira and a brilliant, merciless, effortless finish that totally beat Cech. The goalkeeper's reputation was restored, though, when he made a point-blank save from a snap header from Puyol later in the game.

Chelsea's best chance came when Joe hit the post just before the break, with Duff failing to convert the rebound.

Barça were back in front and dominated the rest of the game. They had almost twice the possession of Chelsea, who managed just 34 per cent. The crowd were stunned as both teams trooped off at half-time after the five-goal bonanza. It had been overwhelming and a thrilling advert for the game.

After the break, the tempo dropped, as neither team could sustain the intensity of the first 45 minutes. At this point, Barcelona looked to be comfortably easing their way to a win on the away goal. When Iniesta hit the post a quarter-of-an-hour from the end, it looked all over, and it would have sealed a deserved victory. Mourinho sat disconsolately, hands thrust deep into his pockets. His team, though, were not yet beaten, and tried to exert some meaningful pressure with the scant possession that they could muster. They looked beaten, but they were always dangerous on the attack.

When Chelsea earned themselves a corner, Duff curled over a looping ball and Terry, unchallenged, headed goalwards. It was a firm header, but Valdes would have dealt with it until Carvalho impeded him and the ball ended up in the back of the net. Amazingly, Collina let the goal stand. Acknowledged as the best ref in the world, it was inconceivable that he could make a blunder on such a scale. The question marks followed him into his retirement from the game a few months later.

That goal, more than anything, won Terry his PFA Player of the Year award; it took Chelsea through against the side that had outplayed them in both games. No matter how mesmerising your attacking options, winning the Champions League is a tall order without a cast-iron defence, and Barcelona had been undone by defensive frailties. The fragile defending of the Catalan side had let in a soft goal at the Nou Camp and had collapsed woefully in the early stages of the second leg. Joe played his part in three of the five goals they had scored in the tie, but it was Carvalho's hand on Valdes that became the deciding factor of the match.

Mourinho swiftly brought on Huth and Tiago to protect the lead, and the game ended in a near riot. When the whistle blew, Eto'o who had had a poor match, accused a Chelsea steward of calling him a 'monkey'. One of Mourinho's entourage was also accused of taunting Ronaldhino and Rijkaard. The Barcelona fans then took their anger out on Abramovich, who rather unadvisedly walked across the pitch from his eyrie in the West Stand to the dressing room. They started to pelt him with plastic bottles and coins; the billionaire was used to making money hand over fist, but having loose change thrown at him was probably a new experience for him.

It was a great night for Mourinho, and served to heighten the animosity felt by many in the game, and the Catalan club in particular, towards the Portuguese coach. When he worked with Bobby Robson at Barça, in his first year things were hard for him, and the problems with Johann Cruyff stem from that time. Cruyff had been in charge at the Nou Camp for eight years before the Robson-Mourinho era. The Dutchman had been a legend as a player and coach, and was an almost impossible act to follow.

The Spanish press were harsh on the English coach and the unknown Mourinho, who was stung by a remark from the Atlético Bilbao coach Luis Fernandez after a clash at the Nou Camp. He is reported to have said, 'But who exactly is this Mourinho nobody?'

That comment was to haunt Mourinho for years, and is one of the reasons he craves publicity and acceptance. Not only does he want to rule the world, but he needs it to love him back. Barça regretted not choosing Mourinho as a replacement for Louis van Gaal in 2001, but since then there had been a lot of water under the Stamford Bridge

Chelsea were through, and again it was a shame that Mourinho's behaviour should have detracted from a fantastic first-half display by Chelsea, and a superb, virtuoso performance from the World Player of the Year. Joe also came out of the match with a great deal of credit, having played a significant part in the victory, and proving, once and for all, that he could look right at home among the best in Europe.

Joe was delighted at his performance, revealing how impressed he had been being on the same pitch as the World Player of the Year: 'Yeah, he's impressive. He's going to be one of the best of all time, He'll be up there with Pelé, Maradona, Cruyff. Without a shadow of a doubt.'

WE ARE THE CHAMPIONS

From the elation of that roller-coaster win in the Champions League, to the demands of the Premiership, and a home match against West Brom. Drogba was back after suspension and scored the only goal of a dull match on 25 minutes. Drogba was, again, a mixture of the brilliant and the bizarre, missing a stack of chances. At times, he looked as though he could go past defenders and score at will, and on other occasions his control and vision would desert him. Joe played efficiently as Chelsea moved inexorably towards the title.

Crystal Palace came to the Bridge next and went down fighting 4-1. Joe was named Man of the Match after a great performance. Mourinho was so impressed with Joe he even sent him out in his place to talk to the media after the game. Always his own biggest critic, Joe told the *Daily Telegraph*: 'It wasn't one of our best performances and we have had a chat about how we could have done more. People have seen what I'm capable of in flashes and demand that I do it for 90 minutes. They always want more. If I have an average game, people call it a poor game. They expect so much of me.'

Lampard had put Chelsea ahead with one of his unstoppable drives, but let Palace back in the game when he miskicked a corner and Riihilahti equalised. Joe restored Chelsea's lead ten minutes into the second half, after some clever footwork by Gudjohnsen. Joe met his cross and converted the chance with unerring accuracy. Kezman then poached two goals to distort the scoreline rather cruelly in Chelsea's favour.

A 3-1 win at Southampton followed, with Joe contributing another fine performance. Lampard opened the scoring with a deflected free kick; Gudjohnsen put Chelsea two up after a strong run by Glen Johnson, and then Kevin Phillips pulled a goal back for Southampton following a short corner. Gudjohnsen then made the game safe in the last quarter. The Premiership was tantalisingly within their grasp.

But before they could focus on a historic domestic league championship, they had a Champions League quarter-final clash with Bayern Munich to contend with. Munich were four times champions of Europe and had just knocked Arsenal out in the previous round. Chelsea were further up against it when UEFA ruled that Mourinho should be banned from the touchline for the two ties, because of his comments about referee Anders Fisk after the match in the Nou Camp. Mourinho was furious, naturally, believing that Chelsea had not fought his case rigorously enough, and again it was the manager's outbursts and antics that threatened to overshadow one of the most significant games in Chelsea's history.

Joe had become a regular in the side and, within five minutes, he had scored his first goal in the Champions League to put Chelsea ahead. Duff laid the ball off and Joe's 20-yard strike hit the heel of Bayern's Brazilian centre-half Lucio, and deflected past the legendary German keeper Oliver Kahn. Some papers gave it as an own goal but Chelsea officially credited it to Joe.

Bayern were well organised, though, with a better defence than that of Barcelona. They dug in, held their back line and refused to buckle. Early in the second half, Schweinsteiger equalised after Cech had failed to hold Ze Roberto's vicious, swerving drive. Joe was doing an excellent job of containing the forward runs of the Bayern back Willy Sagnol, which was an integral part of their game plan.

Lampard then smashed in two goals to put Chelsea ahead. His second was probably the best of his career as he swivelled to chest down Makelele's cross, altered his position as the ball came down and thumped home a goal of immense power. He then set up the fourth for Drogba to score from close range ten minutes from time. It looked all over and Mourinho replaced Cole, who had plagued Bayern all night, with Tiago in the closing stages. Ballack gave the Germans some late hope, though, when he scored from a disputed penalty. It was a heart-stopping moment because it gave Bayern another precious away goal. All in all, it had been another wonderful display in Europe by Chelsea and the bookies were now making them favourites to win the competition.

Birmingham visited the Bridge a few days later. As had been the case for the West Brom game after the euphoria surrounding the Barcelona match, it was a bit of an anti-climax. Chelsea did not play particularly well and it was another disappointing occasion as the game petered out into a 1-1 draw. The strain was starting to show, as the fixtures came thick and fast, and there was also the fact that Chelsea had become the team to beat, and that some lesser sides were now playing for their lives. Many teams were now adopting a highly physical, bruising approach, and were setting about Chelsea far more than in previous encounters.

Joe's first-half effort hit the post as he fought hard to lift his side. His fitness was an important factor, because as he had not been involved in quite so many matches as other members of the squad, he was not exhausted or burnt out. Walter Pandiani put Birmingham in front after Cech had fumbled Jermaine

Pennant's free kick. Drogba was sent on for Kezman and, seven minutes from time, equalised from Lampard's pass.

Then it was back to Germany for the return match with Bayern. Joe was arguably the Man of the Match and played a significant part in both of Chelsea's goals. He played the full 90 and made 12 accurate passes out of a total of 16 and, significantly, he made 12 tackles. The press were glowing with praise, referring particularly to his tackles on Ze Roberto. The *Sun* even went as far as saying that Joe was now 'the luxury - turned essential'.

Bayern tore into Chelsea form the outset, roared on by 59,000 passionate fans. On the half-hour, though, having withstood Bayern's onslaught, Chelsea scored the goal that virtually made them safe. Gallas broke on the left and found Joe, who dribbled along the edge of the box. His quick turn on a treacherous pitch made some space for a pass and, riding a tackle, he rolled the ball to Lampard who fired in a low 20-yard shot. By a quirk of fate, the ball again hit the heel of the unfortunate Lucio. As had proved the case at the Bridge in the first leg, the deflection was enough to deceive Oliver Kahn. Chelsea's good fortune did not go unnoticed by the Munich coach Felix Magath, who likened the Blues to lottery winners.

Although they were now 3-5 down, Bayern stuck to their task. Cech, who was suffering a slight dip in form by this stage of the season, struggled to deal with a header from Ballack, and was able only to tip that ball against his post. Pizarro almost burst the net from close range as he blasted the Germans back into contention.

It was still anybody's game when, with ten minutes left,

Lampard fed Joe who broke on the right. The Chelsea fans expected him to head for the corner flag where he could try and run the clock down by winning a corner or, at worst, a throw-in.

Joe had other ideas, though, and wasting time was not one of them. Avoiding the corner, he spun and cut in towards the box. Joe stopped the ball at his feet until he picked out a figure in blue, arm upraised. He then curled over a high, right-footed cross, the ball looping and then dropping precisely for Drogba to run in and meet it. The cross was perfectly flighted, clever enough to lure Kahn from his goal line, yet with just the right amount of arc to enable it to hang in the air. When Drogba's forehead connected with it, there was little doubt where it would end up. It was a goal that had been conjured up from nowhere – Joe's brilliance had enabled the Ivory Coast striker to put the game beyond Bayern, and had vindicated his manager's decision to stick with him for the last few games. On this occasion, the eyes of Europe would also be watching, and his value would soar with every deft flick and pinpoint cross.

With the score now at 3-6, it was game over. Bayern, though, were not prepared to give up, and they still had time to score two more goals in the last few seconds to give them a win on the night. Guerro equalised in the last minute and, in the third minute of injury time, Scholl netted a third. Both goals were the result of mix-ups in the Chelsea defence, which was gradually allowing the cracks to show after months of iron discipline and strain. Bayern had had even more possession than Barcelona in the previous round, but Chelsea's amazing resilience once again had seen them home.

Ballack had played well in the ties and it was no surprise when he joined Chelsea in May 2006 on a free transfer. Joe welcomed the news, telling AOL Sport, 'The more World Class players we sign, the more games we win and the more titles we will win.'

Chelsea lost 3-2 on the night, but went through 6-5 on aggregate. It was perhaps the most tense, enthralling, thrilling match Chelsea had played in the competition that season, and it meant that the Blues would meet Liverpool in the semi-finals, after the Red's triumph over Juventus. It was the first time that two English sides were to meet at that stage in the competition.

Having given their all in Europe, and triumphing again, Chelsea had to summon up their last energy reserves to meet Arsenal in the Premiership. They were 11 points ahead of Arsenal, who had all but given up the title race... but no team of Wenger's gives up easily, particularly if there is a mathematical chance – however small – of overcoming the opposition. For long periods, Arsenal were the better side, but Pires missed an early chance, and then hit the bar when he should have scored.

The game ended goalless. The name Cole dominated the match reports, but this time Joe had to share the coverage with his namesake Ashley. Earlier in the season, the Arsenal left-back had been the subject of an alleged attempt to lure him to Chelsea. A meeting involving Mourinho, Peter Kenyon and Cole was splashed all over the press. Ashley was arguably one of the best left-backs in the world at the time and, with Wayne Bridge nursing a broken ankle, Mourinho was even more anxious to fill the position. The matter was probably the last straw in the worsening relations between the two sides.

Ashley Cole took to the pitch with even more to prove than his team-mates. Strangely, he was directly responsible for nullifying Joe's threat down the right wing, as Mourinho was still not totally convinced that he was a natural winger, but his performances for Chelsea since the injury to Robben had been exemplary. Joe could also accommodate Gudjohnsen from the right, whom Mourinho was still trying to integrate in his central midfield role. The Chelsea fans, though, still saw Gudjohnsen as a striker after his successful partnership with Hasselbaink.

Joe could get little change out of Ashley Cole that night, and it was the Arsenal man who was the outstanding player on the field. A significant moment in their personal duel came when Joe slipped past an Arsenal defender and bore down on Lehmann's goal, only to be stopped by a wonderful sliding tackle from his namesake.

Fulham were the next to face the Blues, and they might have been forgiven for thinking that this was a great time to play them – if Mourinho's claims were anything to go by, then the entire squad was exhausted after their European and league fixture pile-up.

It was just a question now of when Chelsea would actually win the title. Joe was the Man of the Match again as he helped his teams overpower Fulham 3-1. Joe desperately wanted to play his part in the final stages of the Premiership and Champions League campaigns, and was determined to start in the impending semi-final against Liverpool. He knew that the only way to achieve this was to continue to perform impeccably, and make it impossible for the manager to leave him out.

Robben was almost back to full fitness and was actually named as one of the subs for the Fulham game, and Joe knew that Robben would be waiting in the wings should he fail to deliver.

And deliver he did. Joe scored the first goal of the game after 17 minutes to put Chelsea ahead. It was Joe's 7th goal in 24 Premiership games. A fine goal it was, too; Drogba dispossessed Moritz Volz and passed to Joe, who whipped a fiercely struck volley from the edge of the D that looped up over Edwin van der Saar, who would soon be on his way to Manchester United. The Dutch national keeper had no chance.

Fulham fought back and Collins John equalised from a bouncing cross just before half-time. At this stage, Chelsea looked totally exhausted and listless; Fulham looked the fresher side, and were full of running. Once again, Mourinho gambled, replacing the exhausted Joe with the revitalised Robben; Duff then went deep to full-back in place of Huth. His ploy worked perfectly as Robben treated the fans to 45 minutes of brilliance. He absolutely caned the Fulham defence, delivering a performance as good as anything he had produced earlier in the season.

Lampard put Chelsea ahead after a delightful piece of skill by Robben. In the dying minutes, Gudjonsen made it safe for Chelsea with the third after Tiago had put him through with a diagonal pass. Of the 16 players in the squad for the Fulham game, 9 of them had been Claudio Ranieri signings. Unbeaten now in 25 Premiership games, Chelsea were on the brink of collecting their first title since 1955.

WE ARE THE CHAMPIONS

Liverpool were next on the agenda, with the first leg of the Champions League semi-final to be played at the Bridge. Mourinho admitted that he would have liked to go to Anfield first. No matter how good are side are, there are only so many times in a particular season they can beat a team of similar quality. Joe's goals had already provided Chelsea with the first league double over Liverpool since 1919.

Joe played for 77 minutes before he was substituted by Kezman. Mourinho had to do without his two orthodox wingers Duff and Robben; the latter had sustained a knock while playing for Holland, which effectively ruled him out as an attacking threat for the rest of the season. In hindsight, it seemed a gamble to have let him play for Holland after his lay-off.

Joe set up Chelsea's best chance of the match for Lampard. Gallas crossed and Joe brilliantly headed down for Lampard, who had been scoring goals for fun from similar positions all season. That night, he hit the chance way over the bar.

Cech then kept Chelsea in the match by making a fabulous save from Baros's header. It was a wonderfully agile save and Mourinho said it could prove to be a match winner. So now it was all down to Anfield for the showdown. On the balance of play, Liverpool won narrowly on points, but there was everything to play for in the second leg.

Chelsea had other matters to attend to before the return leg, though – lifting the Premiership trophy. They clinched it at Bolton thanks to Lampard scoring twice, taking his total of Premiership goals to 12.

After missing the chance created by Joe against Liverpool, he looked extra-sharp against Bolton. As is so often the case with title-clinching matches, the quality of the play left a great deal to be desired. Bolton dominated for long periods and Mourinho gave his players a tongue-lashing at half time. Joe started on the bench but made an appearance near the end, and went on to play a central role in the after-match celebrations. At one point, he clambered through the hatch on the roof of the team bus, from where he squirted water on his team-mates below.

All the way back to London, the team sang and chanted old favourites, but their manager, having delivered his second piece of silverware that season, chose not to join in the euphoric atmosphere.

The shrewd money was already being laid on Chelsea retaining the title the following season. Rather than waiting another 50 years, many believed it might happen for a second time in the modern era in about 50 matches.

There was little time to dwell on winning the Premiership as, arguably, an even more prestigious accolade beckoned - that of the European Cup, and the cauldron-like atmosphere of a European semi-final at Anfield.

Chelsea could not have had a harder game at that stage. They were not just playing a battle-hardened, brilliantly coached side, but at times it seemed they had the entire City of Liverpool on their backs. The Reds were going for their fifth European Cup and, for once, Chelsea were perceived not as underdogs, but almost as the bad guys. Liverpool had been having an indifferent season in the league, but had pulled off some remarkable wins in Europe to get to the semi-final stage, but there was another significant factor that swung most of the neutral support behind them – they had not spent in excess of £150 million to assemble their squad, and that was still gnawing away at many who doubted the long-term wisdom of allowing someone like Abramovich to wield his cheque book in such a cavalier fashion. Their criticism now, though, was of a club that had won a Carling Cup final, and the Premiership, and was in the semi-final of the Champions League, so love them or loathe them, Chelsea still deserved a great deal of respect.

The league table indicated a 33-point gap between the sides, although in this one-off match, form counted for little. Desire and passion were going to count for a lot between two sides who were so evenly matched, and it was Liverpool who initially seemed the hungrier and sharper.

In a season of controversy, Liverpool's goal was one of the most discussed events. It came early on, when Gerrard, later to be named Man of the Match, put the ball through Lampard's legs and sent Baros in on goal. The Czech striker collided with Cech and Garcia headed the loose ball back into the yawning mouth of the goal. Gallas raised his leg to hook the ball away, but the referee let the goal stand. To this day, Mourinho is adamant that the ball did not cross the line. The opposing view is that Cech should have been sent off for his challenge on Baros, and that his replacement should have faced a penalty. Mourinho insisted later that it was the linesman who had scored.

Joe was Chelsea's best hope in midfield, and with Gerrard winning his contest with Lampard, it was left to Joe to create something. In the first half, he worked frantically to try and get Chelsea back into the game, and sent a terrific pass through to Drogba. The Ivory Coast striker wasted the chance and, as the game wore on, Carragher marshalled Drogba out of contention. Joe last significant effort was to fire in a near-post shot that Hamann managed to block, and then Mourinho gambled on conjuring up a winner by replacing Joe with Robben. The young Dutchman had little to offer, though, and Chelsea struggled to create any chances at all. Terry and Lampard were both carrying long-term injuries but, for the sake of the club, they kept soldiering on.

Robben's patchy performance came in for some criticism from parts of the dressing room. Chelsea slid out of the competition, having been unable to break down the Liverpool defence, which had been wonderfully orchestrated by Jamie Carragher.

The semi-final was a major disappointment for fans and the team alike. There was so much potential now at the club, but it had yet to be fully realised at the highest level. Despite Abramovich having spent several fortunes on the team, Chelsea looked increasingly fragile. Mourinho's tactics also left a lot to be desired, and many were left wondering what might have happened had Joe been allowed to run at Carragher.

When Crystal Palace had won 2-0 away at Liverpool in the FA Cup, Julian Gray had scored a sweet goal coming in from the left. His former Arsenal teamate Thierry Henry had spoken to Gray before the game, advising him to run at Carragher.

Chelsea collected the Premiership trophy in front of their own fans on the following Saturday against Charlton. There was some controversy surrounding the game, as Makelele scored the only goal of the game. This was a surprise, given that he had yet to score for the Blues in 94 games, and he had never scored for Real Madrid.

When Lampard was tripped outside the box, Mike Riley surprisingly gave a penalty. Fans – and Mourinho, apparently – were amazed to see Makelele stride up to take his first spot kick for the club. The Charlton keeper Stephan Andersen blocked Makelele's first attempt, but he managed somehow to put the ball in the net at the second attempt. Even then it barely crept over the line as the kick was sliced horribly and only a lucky bounce got it home.

Mourinho said that the arrangement for Makelele to take a penalty was only if the Blues had a 2-0 lead going into the last minute. His rules had clearly been broken.

Joe was the most dangerous player on the field and the Charlton keeper denied him a certain hat-trick with some fine saves. A flying leap that ended up with Andersen tipping a curling drive on to the post was voted the save of the match.

Chelsea wound up their epic season with two away games, the first of which was a trip to Old Trafford. This match confirmed the widening gap between two of the Premiership's heavyweights. United were 20 points behind the new Champions, and they started aggressively with a challenge from Keane on Joe earning him a booking. Chelsea fielded a virtual 'B' team, but still took control of the game, with Joe particularly impressive, moving the ball around with confidence and looking every inch an integral part of the Championship-winning side.

United took an early lead through van Nistelrooy after Rooney had opened up the Chelsea defence. Tiago levelled things up with a terrific swerving shot from 30 yards which deceived Tim Howard. It was Tiago's last goal for Chelsea and he could not have scored a better one. For a side described as 'boring' and 'robotic' by their critics, the stats indicated that they had fired in more shots on target than any other team in the Premiership.

Tiago set up Chelsea's second when his fiercely hit through ball was beautifully controlled by Gudjohnsen before he slipped it past Howard. An hour had passed and the United fans, not used to see their team so comprehensively outplayed, started to drift off home. Their disgruntlement over the destination of the Premiership title had been compounded by the news that week of the Glazer takeover.

Joe clinched a great night for Chelsea when Lampard intercepted Wes Brown's poor clearance and rolled the ball to Joe. Looking a long way offside, Joe drove the ball home for Chelsea's third. It was a fitting end to another chapter in his roller-coaster career, his eighth goal of the season in the big league. Chelsea had not enjoyed such a successful evening in Manchester since they had won the Cup there 35 years earlier.

Ex-England coach Terry Venables, writing in the *News of the World*, was full of praise for Joe: 'I have been very impressed with the way he has taken his games to new levels and he deserves his place in the team. Like any highly-technical player, there will be days when he does not perform under pressure but they are getting fewer. He is, however, a match winner and you can never have too many of them.'

There was just one fixture to fulfil – an away trip to their Cup conquerors, Newcastle. Joe was in the side from the start, and contributed to a 1-1 draw. It turned out to be a meaningless exercise, with the only lasting memory being of Graham Souness screaming at his unreliable defence. It gave Chelsea a record total of 95 points and a 12- point lead over runners-up Arsenal. Abramovich had spent a total of £280 million on players, and another £120 million on clearing the club's debts, but winning the Premiership was priceless.

For Joe, it was another priceless moment as well. Collecting his Premiership medal was the high point of his career to date, and it could sit proudly alongside his Carling Cup medal. Not a bad return on the season's efforts.

Joe's end-of-season Premiership stats were impressive, too, and showed what a contribution he had made to the team – he finished with a pass accuracy of 82 per cent, he had 2 goal assists and notched up 8 goals. For the little guy from Camden Town who started off at West Ham with the 'this is too easy' swagger and a head full of dreams, it was a wonderful vindication of his talent. This was his heyday, as he grew into a game which demanded ever-increasing pace and the ability to create space. With the assistance of Jose Mourinho, Joe had successfully developed the technical skills and tactical awareness necessary for playing at the highest level, without ever compromising his natural talent.

8
First Choice

'When I was 18 and 20 I just went out and played my football
and I was enjoying it; but I wasn't as good a player as I am now.'
Joe Cole, February 2006

THE 2005/06 SEASON started in the aftermath of the
July 7 terrorist attacks on London; Joe Cole and John
Terry, along with some representatives from Arsenal, appeared
in the London *Evening Standard* holding a message saying
'London Stands United'. The plan was for the capital's
bitterest enemies to encourage London's communities to stand
together in the face of the terrorists. It was also the summer of
Flintoff and Pietersen, with Ashes fever taking up most of the
back pages.

Chelsea had been busy in the summer strengthening their
already massive squad. The only apparent weakness in the
team, at left-back, was plugged by the purchase of Asier del
Horno for £8 million from Athletic Bilbao. Del Horno had
attracted the attention of Mourinho when he scored the winner
for Spain against England in Madrid the previous November.

Asier left Chelsea in the Summer of 2006 joining Valencia after failing to establish himself.

The defence looked as solid as ever, but it was in the midfield area that Chelsea were to invest a sizeable chunk of Abramovich's wealth. This naturally heightened the speculation over Joe's future at the club, particularly as the Blues had flirted with Steven Gerrard for a second time, and it looked certain at one point that he would join them. Less than six weeks after lifting the European Cup in Istanbul, the Liverpool captain announced that he was quitting Anfield. A British record fee of £35 million was mentioned but, once again, the 'deal' fell through. Gerrard, in a complete turnaround at the last moment, declared that he was staying on Merseyside.

As if stung into action after this rebuff, Chelsea immediately purchased the pacy England winger Shaun Wright-Phillips for £21 million from Manchester City, which amounted to nearly 50 per cent of the five-year sponsorship deal Chelsea had secured from Samsung. Arsenal had also been keen to sign him, and Wenger rather sourly suggested that Chelsea had paid twice his real value. Shaun, of course, rejoined City in a cut-price deal in the summer of 2008. The relationship between the two clubs was strained at the best of times, but it would be placed under even greater pressure as the season unfolded.

Michael Essien, the 22-year-old French Footballer of the Year, was added to the mix for a fee of £24 million from Lyon, after a summer of haggling with the Lyon president Jean-Michel Aulas. The tough-talking Aulas demanded, at one stage, to meet Abramovich personally to thrash out the finer points of the deal. One of his memorable quotes was that he would not sell Essien cheaply as he was not 'wearing a beret and carrying a baguette'.

Essien turned out to be a wonderful buy, a phenomenon, and he soon proved to be a real powerhouse of a player. Born in Ghana's capital city, Accra, he was the youngest, and only boy, of five children. Like Joe, he had had a tough start to life when his father James left the family. He joined the Corsican club Bastia and then moved to French champions Lyon for £8 million where he quickly established himself as one of the top midfielders in Europe. His major strength was his versatility; in two seasons at Lyon, he played in defence, mainly at centre-back, right-midfield and right wing. Laid back and multilingual, Essien was Mourinho's ideal player in that his inter-changeability meant that he could slot in anywhere.

The £45 million influx of talent to bolster the midfield raised serious questions about the present squad members. Since Abramovich had landed at the Bridge, his average monthly spend had been in excess of £10 million and, naturally, with spending like that, no one could be 100 per cent guaranteed of their worth to the team. You never knew when the next superstar might suddenly become available. Joe was sitting on a beach somewhere reading the papers every day about Chelsea signing Wright-Phillips and Eissen in his position. His thoughts must have gone back to the time when he first played against Wright-Phillips on the astro-turf surfaces in Camden. Both of them had been very small and very young at the time.

Joe still had another year on his contract to run and both parties were set to hold talks about extending his contract at the end of the season. Tiago, who had played efficiently in Chelsea's Championship season, made the reverse journey to Lyon for £6.5 million and, although the ex-Porto player had failed to reach the level of acclaim of his team-mate, Joe, Mourinho gave him a glowing tribute when he left the Bridge.

Scott Parker's transfer to Newcastle did not bring any tributes from Mourinho, who never really gave him a chance during his time wearing blue. First Robben, and then Joe, had stolen his thunder.

Chelsea's first major game of the 2005/06 season was the curtain-raising Community Shield at the Millennium Stadium against Arsenal in Cardiff. Joe was on the bench as the Champions started with the wing pairing of Duff and a rejuvenated Robben, who had both been pivotal to Chelsea's fortunes the previous season. Two long ball goals from the much maligned Didier Drogba won the trophy for Chelsea. Arsenal had more possession but could not make it count. Apart from Fabregas's 65th-minute goal, cleverly set up by Freddie Ljungberg after a defensive error, Arsenal barely threatened Cech's goal. Joe came on towards the end for the lacklustre Duff and almost grabbed a third on the break.

The only slightly worrying note was the sight of 5,000 empty seats at the Chelsea end of the stadium. The road to Cardiff is not the easiest of journeys, although the Arsenal fans seemed not to have worried too much. Maybe, on a hot August afternoon, with England playing and then beating Australia in the amazing Second Test, football had come a little too early for some fans. For the Champions of England, it was a disappointing show from the fans.

Abramovich's supercharged outfit started the new term with a morale-boosting prize, though. In just 13 months, Mourinho had won all the domestic trophies bar the FA Cup. Wenger commented that he had won four Community Shields and nobody counted it as a trophy; he dismissed the match as a friendly. There was no doubt that the £13.7 million sale of superstar Patrick Vieira had left a gaping hole in the Arsenal line-up, and they badly missed his physical presence.

With the phoney war over, hostilities commenced the following week when Chelsea visited newly-promoted Wigan at the JJB Stadium. Wigan's wage bill was £3 million, compared with a staggering Chelsea figure of £143 million. On the field, though, the gap was not quite so marked.

Once again, Joe started the game on the bench with Mourinho employing the same line up as he used in Cardiff. After a gruelling first half dominated by Wigan, he replaced Robben with Wright-Phillips and Gudjohnsen was replaced by Joe, who operated in the hole behind Drogba. On the hour, Crespo came on for Duff and, in the last moments, the Argentinian thundered in a 20-yard drive to scrape a lame win.

Crespo had returned to Chelsea after spending a year in Serie A playing for AC Milan on loan. He had had a successful time there, and ended up scoring twice in the European Cup Final against Liverpool. Economics dictated that the 29-year-old should return home after Milan refused to do business for Ukrainian superstar Andriy Shevchenko. A

£60 million bid had been mooted, which would have shattered the previous world record. Andriy later joined the club for half that sum.

Mourinho, furious at his team's display, explained to the *Daily Telegraph*, 'There was no system. The left winger [Robben] was playing inside. The right winger [Duff] was playing on the left. The forward [Drogba] was not making the right line.'

Mourinho comforted the crestfallen Wigan manager Paul Jewell and told him it had been unfair. Wigan eventually proved to be the surprise package of the season, their unfancied team bristling with possibilities.

This early into the campaign, trouble was already brewing at Chelsea. Mourinho berated his player's performance at Wigan, stating that they were too slow and that some did not look motivated. Defender Ricardo Carvalho made a public outburst after being left out of the team. Carvalho had started 22 games the previous year and had cost nearly £20 million. The centre-back was one of the first of Mourinho's purchases and had previously played for him in his all-conquering Porto squad. The outburst was understandable as he was probably the most gifted central defender in Europe. At Chelsea, though, John Terry and Gallas always seemed to be the first-choice pairing. Gallas had to play to cover Terry's lack of pace, particularly on his left side. Terry was the Footballer of the Year, Chelsea captain and, along with Frank Lampard, Mourinho's most trusted lieutenant. It was a dilemma for the coach – Terry was reliable and a great leader, but Carvalho was technically a more gifted defender.

Mourinho, however admiring he might have been of his fellow countryman's prowess on the pitch, was swift in quelling outward displays of dissent. Carvalho was fined two weeks' wages – nearly £100,000. The press wondered if anyone else would follow Carvalho's example and risk incurring the wrath of the guv'nor, or jeopardising their careers in the blue shirt. Joe was favourite for the role, but John Terry was soon extolling the young star's virtues, telling the *Evening Standard* that Joe was a great example. 'Mourinho does not want players coming round knocking on his door every week but he does not want them to be happy about being left out. Once they get their chance, it is up to them not to sulk and to go out there and fight for their place. Players have got to have that drive in themselves to keep working hard. Look at Joe last year.

He didn't really get that opportunity at the start. We had a few injuries, he played four or five games on the bounce and that did him the world of good. He looked fitter, he looked sharper and he stayed in the side for the rest of the season. He was also man enough to take criticism on the chin and he listened to what the manager had to say. He has improved as a player and now he has his England place as well. He is an example to the other players.'

Against Arsenal in the following home match, Joe did not even make the bench and was seated in the stand not far from Sven-Goran Eriksson. It was a had been a bad week for both of them, following Denmark's 4-1 dismantling of England a few days earlier. They both watched another tedious match in which Arsenal had plenty of possession but failed to convert it in the final third. Drogba was once again the match-winner scoring the only goal of the match after replacing Crespo. The Ivory Coast striker raced on to Lampard's quickly taken free-kick in the 73rd minute, and tried to swivel to hook the ball past Jens Lehman. Instead, the ball hit Drogba's knee and bobbled into the net. It was an appropriately bungled goal in a thoroughly uninspiring game. Cech kept his 30th clean sheet in 51 games. The Blues finished the match with £70 million worth of substitutes on the field when recent signings Essien and Wright-Phillips came on.

Joe was back in the side a few nights later when West Brom were the visitors. Joe was back in the side at the expense of Robben who had been replaced by Wright-Phillips against Arsenal. There had been some tension between the mercurial Dutch player and Mourinho after he had come off in Cardiff and headed down the tunnel without so much as a glance at his coach. There was also still a little unease over his performance during the Champions League exit at Anfield and Robben's fitness problems. The situation was inflamed by his ankle injury and his outspoken views on the need for Mourinho to keep a settled side. Robben's high-speed trickery had been mesmerising at times, but rarely reached the brilliance of his early appearances. Grandiose pronouncements did not help his case.

Joe grabbed his chance and scored Chelsea's second goal in a 4-0 thumping of the Baggies. The England star opened his Chelsea account that season with a crisp drive after Wright-Phillips had set up the chance. Joe's other notable contribution during that game was when he allowed the Chelsea physio on to help him blow his nose. How much more pampered could these millionaire footballers become?

Bryan Robson rested some key players from the game in a strange team selection that handed the initiative to Chelsea. Joe's East End pal Lampard was the star of the night scoring twice and dedicating the goals to his newborn daughter Luna.

Tottenham were next on the agenda and Joe retained his spot in the side. Chelsea had not been beaten by Tottenham in the league for 31 games, so the fans were naturally confident. Del Horno, looking very impressive, opened the scoring with a neat header. Joe was on the field for 65 minutes and received a booking before being replaced by Shaun Wright-Phillips, who set up the second goal for Duff. It was another bizarre effort as the Irishman fell as he lined up the shot, and the ball trickled in off his shoulder.

Another 2-0 victory followed over Sunderland, who were lying at the foot of the Premiership and yet to score any points. They looked as though they would become cannon fodder for the rest of the Premiership this season but, as is so often the case, particularly when playing the Premiership Champions, they put up stubborn resistance before falling to goals from Geremi and Drogba. Joe did not feature in the game. Joe kept his spirits up in this period by spending time with his puppies and listening to his music. He had recently moved to Esher with his girlfriend Carly and bought a beautiful home. It was near the training ground at Cobham, Surrey, where Abramovich had bought a wonderful complex with stunning facilities. Esher was a long way from the council estate in North London where Joe had been brought up. Like Joe, the

Beatles had purchased homes in Esher when they had found fame and fortune.

Two days after the Sunderland game England clinched the Ashes victory, and Chelsea played Anderlecht in the first of their Championship League games. The final this season would be played at the Stade de France in Paris. Once again, Chelsea failed to sell out the match, the gate being 12,000 short of capacity. Joe featured briefly, coming on for Duff 13 minutes from time. Already, the fans were streaming to the exits.

Anderlecht were another poor side in the endless procession that seemed to appear at the Bridge. Going down to a record eighth successive Champions League defeat, they seemed content just to keep the score down. Chelsea won with a 1-0 scoreline, courtesy of Lampard's signature free kick. This made it six straight wins with no goals conceded, but the victory seemed hollow.

The press hammered Chelsea, especially over the gates; amazingly, Sheffield Wednesday had a higher average gate than the Premiership Champions. When this was put to him, Mourinho commented, 'It's hard for normal people to pay for tickets and you have to understand that.'

Joe had made a comment to the *Evening Standard* that he felt the admission prices at Stamford Bridge were too high, saying, 'The club has got to find a way of filling the ground. The normal fan cannot afford the ticket prices. I'm sure the club are trying to do that and attract a new generation of fans to come to Stamford Bridge.'

The press seized on this, claiming that the inflated wages of the modern players was the biggest factor in driving up the prices. Nobody was in a better position to comment on the situation than Joe, though, as he had been a fan himself and knew the sacrifice fans had to make to follow their team.

The late England legend Alan Ball, one of the class of '66, had spoken to the *Guardian* about the factors that had made the players at that time such such strong characters.

'We had this wonderful feeling that we were still part of the people. Every street in England had a footballer living in it. Not any more. They're behind big barbed wire fences, they've got security, they've got blacked-out windows, they hire clubs to go and have a night out. We were ordinary, approachable people. You were welcome to walk the streets, you were patted on the back, you were touchable, reachable.'

The main reason for the rise in Joe's profile and popularity over the years was that, to the fans, he was still reachable.

Charlton were next to meet the Champions; unbeaten at that stage, they were proudly lying second to the Blues. Marcus Bent, their pre-season signing from Ipswich, had fired them to the dizzy heights with some important goals. Shrewd observers were saying, though, that the true inspiration had been Alexei Smertin, on loan from Chelsea.

Sections of the press were also already complaining that the Premiership was virtually over. Before the season had started, chief executive Peter Kenyon had claimed that the Premiership winners would come from a 'bunch of one'. His boast now sounded more prophetic than arrogant, as Chelsea strolled to a 2-0 victory over Charlton. Crespo powered in the first and then Robben curled in a second with his first, and probably the best, Chelsea goal up to that point. Robben's goal was also a statement of intent from the young Dutchman and sounded an ominous warning to pretenders to Chelsea's crown – Robben, such an integral part of Chelsea's success the previous season, was now back to his best.

Joe came on for Robben after 79 minutes; he had started only two games so far that season, and uncertainty over his Chelsea career, as well as his place in the England set-up, began to surface. Over the next few days, a report appeared that Joe was the latest of the players inside the camp to be unsettled. It had allegedly arrived via a friend of Joe's, who stated that he had confided to him that he needed to quit Chelsea because his career was suffering and that it was time for a fresh start. However, Mourinho, fresh from his attack on Ricardo Carvalho for speaking out over his decision to exclude him from the side at the start of the season, saw no reason to speak to Joe about the report.

Mourinho said to the *Sun*, 'My reaction to the story is rubbish. It is an interview with nobody – I don't understand the source. Who is he? A friend… a friend of a friend? It is unbelievable. For me, it is nothing. Why should I speak to Joe? For what? Joe Cole was always very open to me. He was in my office last season half-a-dozen times knocking on my door to speak to me. He asked me why he wasn't playing and what he could do to improve. I feel this is ridiculous.'

Mourinho added that it would be odd for Cole to request a move as the transfer window wouldn't re-open for three months, and stated that, while he knew the phrase 'there's no smoke without fire', 'if there is a fire, there is a stupid fire, because it's a fire that has to burn for three months. And with the rain in England!'

Like Ranieri before him, Mourinho could not resist spicing up comments with his unique brand of humour, much of which was lost in translation, but was intended to bring a smile rather than a scowl.

Aston Villa were the next visitors to the Bridge and actually had the audacity to score a goal. The *Sun* had offered a £10,000 reward to the first team to score against the Blues, with the money going to charity. Luke Moore scooped the prize, giving David O' Leary's side the lead, but two goals from Lampard, dispatched with great aplomb, restored the status quo and made it seven straight wins. Joe did not feature in this match.

Then came two stressful trips to Anfield in the space of four days. The first was a midweek Champions League fixture. Chelsea were desperate for revenge after their exit in contentious circumstances the previous season, and Liverpool were anxious to defend their fifth European Cup. The game was a massive disappointment as both teams ground out a dull draw. Joe sat out the game on the bench.

Chelsea's ultra-conservative style stoked up the perennial controversy about 'boring' Chelsea. The Kop chanted the insult throughout the match, as the Blues frustrated the Reds. Mourinho left Merseyside refusing to comment on penalty claims made by Liverpool.

Joe started for Chelsea for the first time in weeks when the teams met up again on the warm, early autumn Sunday afternoon. The match was completely different from the dismal Champions League tie. Cardboard-and-foil models of the European Cup had been waved at Roman Abramovich on the previous Wednesday, but the joke may well have been on the fans, as the multi-billionaire augmented his riches even further after the sale that week of his Sibneft organisation. Reports indicated that he could have been as much as £7.4 billion richer, surely enough money to ensure the continuing domination of the English game by Chelsea Football Club.

That day, though, was all about the Premier League, and simple pride in your team and club. Lampard put Chelsea ahead from the spot, after Traore had hacked down Drogba. Lampard was given terrible stick by the Kop, mainly over his weight. He was appearing at the time in an ad for the *Sun*, and it was no surprise that anyone paid by Murdoch to advertise that particular tabloid would receive sustained criticism. The Liverpool fans were still incensed by the *Sun*'s reporting of the Hillsborough tragedy in 1989, after which circulation was severely affected in the Merseyside area.

Stephen Gerrard equalised for Liverpool and the Kop went nuts as the Reds briefly threatened to make a game of it. Damien Duff punctured the raucous atmosphere when he put Chelsea ahead on the break after some dazzling footwork by Drogba.

Joe then blasted Chelsea 3-1 ahead on the hour with a close-range shot. The ex-Hammer had his best game of the season so far and his match-sealing goal capped a performance of sustained effort and skill. Substitute Geremi zipped in and added a fourth in front of the now mute Kop. The Champions League defeat of the previous season was now consigned to history, and Mourinho took some comfort from demolition of one of the Blues' fiercest rivals on their home turf. The strength of the central midfield trio of Lampard, Makelele and Essien meant that Joe, formerly a central-midfield player, had been employed more on the wings. The switch to the wings was the key to the transformation in his game. Mourinho had now convinced Joe that he was a flanks player.

It was Liverpool's heaviest home defeat in 36 years, and a record win for Chelsea on a ground that had been a graveyard to so many of their dreams in earlier times. Prior to the match, Liverpool had topped the list of teams that had the best record against the Blues. They had won 57 games out of the total 123 played. Just a few seasons before, a four-goal rampage at Anfield would have seemed unthinkable.

Cole told the *Metro* that 'people have said that we are boring but we don't get enough respect for being champions. We are having to adjust to different situations every game we play. But we showed the quality we have and can make the adjustment against any opposition. It comes with the terrority of being champions. It is the British mentality that people get shot down when they are so successful. We have to guard against any complacency. He went on to say, 'It is always a tough game for us when we face Liverpool. You have to battle hard against them and win your fair share of tackles. It does seem to be something of a grudge match when we face them at the moment.'

The press were ecstatic about Chelsea's performance. Perhaps that was the day that Chelsea clinched the title. It had apparently become a one-horse race with bookmaker Paddy Power paying out already to punters who had backed them to win the League. They were nine points ahead of nearest rivals Charlton, and defender William Gallas was talking in terms of sealing the title by the New Year.

Joe ended the speculation over his discontent and possible departure by stating, 'Leaving is not something that crosses my mind. When you are at Chelsea, every day at training is an opportunity to fight and make an impression on the manager. When you get chances, they are big. I have enjoyed everything I have done at Chelsea. I have had some great moments and some frustrating moments, but I love being around the place. I am still learning and feel like I can go on another few levels as a player.'

Joe was boosted by being included in the top 55 stars shortlisted in the FIFPro World XI Player awards, ranked alongside Galacticos like Brazil's Ronaldo and Adriano, Ukraine's Andriy Shevchenko and France's Thierry Henry. England had 10 players in the world's top 55. Lampard and Terry were the other Chelsea players included in the England contingent.

Joe was now rubbing shoulders with the great and the good of world football, yet his place in the Chelsea first team was not assured. He was in the starting line-up for the visit of Bolton, who had scooped four points in their previous two visits to the Bridge. When Giannakopoulos put Bolton ahead with a cool finish in a hotly-contested first half, another shock looked on the cards. But Chelsea were never more dangerous than when their pedigree was tested, and Joe cracked in a couple of low drives which troubled the keeper.

Early in the second half, the roof fell in for Bolton. Drogba and Lampard plundered two apiece as a rampant Chelsea pounded the northerners into submission. The talking point of the match, though, was Essien's vicious tackle on Tal Ben Haim. Essien escaped with a yellow and managed to avoid further punishment. Joe's verdict was that Essien was the best athlete he had ever seen in football.

There was no doubt of the impact made by Essien in a very short period. He had brought a great deal of additional bite and power to an already formidable midfield, and it was becoming apparent that Chelsea could, indeed, romp away with the title unless their midfield threat could be nullified. The press were keen to level the playing field, and one suggestion at the time was that every time the Blues were awarded a free-kick, they shouldn't be allowed to take it unless Joe could answer a general knowledge question.

Real Betis visited the Bridge three nights later. Their prized asset was the winger Joaquin, who had terrorised England with his pace in an International the previous autumn. The youngster had been strongly linked with a move to Chelsea and was a quintessential player in the Mourinho mould – fast, with a huge appetite for work and an eye for goal. Mourinho had opted for Wright-Phillips instead, but in the opening minutes Joaquin proudly demonstrated just how much of a talent he was. He was able to surge powerfully past Makelele in a move that ended with the ball being cleared off the line.

Drogba coolly put Chelsea in front from Essien's pass, then Carvalho doubled Chelsea's lead. Joe Cole set the chance up with a powerful run that ended with him being fouled deep in the Betis half. Lampard smashed in the free-kick that the keeper Doblas spilled on the line, and the Portuguese defender scored from point-blank range.

The best goal of the night though was Joe's; Essien again unlocked the Betis defence, racing on to Crespo's clever flick, before sliding a precision pass into the path of Joe. He instantly shimmied one way, then the other, before scoring from 25 yards with a searing drive. It was an exquisite effort; the crowd were delighted to see their hero drill home another fine goal.

Crespo made it four with a tremendous header from a superbly flighted cross from Wright-Phillips. Chelsea were awesome that night, sending out a message across Europe that they were coming for the Champions League trophy and woe betide anyone who stood in their way.

Joe had hit a rich vein of form and had forced himself into the reckoning for the World Cup, also edging in front of Robben for the position on the wing. Robben was still experiencing a dip in form after making such an impressive start for the Blues, and although there was no doubting the voltage that Robben could potentially offer the club, things were still strained between the Dutchman and Mourinho. By contrast, Joe had now integrated himself so fully into Mourinho's system that he had shed his previous maverick image and was now regarded as a complete team player.

The day Chelsea demolished Betis, one of the most famous

players from West London died in hospital in Edinburgh following a car crash. Johnny Haynes, captain of Fulham and England, will always be remembered as the first £100-a-week footballer. Haynes had been described as being a 'technician of unrivalled finesse', renowned for his vision and creativity. In his day, Haynes was known as a playmaker or schemer; Joe Cole is a player very much in Haynes' image.

At his peak, Haynes was the finest passer of a ball ever to have played for England. He played at a time when crowds would go to matches to see individual players rather than teams. Times have changed, and fans now prefer to follow the big corporate teams like Chelsea and Manchester United.

Fast-forward 44 years, and Chelsea were gunning for the record Tottenham had set in 1961 of 11 straight wins. They next visited Everton, rock bottom and scorers of just one Premiership goal all season. It looked like a certain three points, but teams are often motivated to raise their game when Chelsea came to town, so complacency was not an option.

Joe started the game on the flank in the continuing absence of Duff. Wright-Phillips also started, with Mourinho giving him an opportunity to show his quality, having failed to make an impact in his first few games for the club. Eight minutes before the break, Tim Cahill was brought down on the edge of the box and a penalty was awarded, from which James Beattie scored off the bar. Beattie had been a threat to Chelsea throughout the half, Terry having received treatment for an injury to his nose sustained in a clash with him.

In the second half, stung by Mourinho's special brand of displeasure at the break, Chelsea pushed up. Lampard lashed in an equaliser from long range with a shot that dipped over Nigel Martyn's desperate lunge. Drogba appeared to have won it when he netted, but the goal was disallowed for offside against Gudjohnsen, which increased Mourinho's anger. Drogba was onside, but the linesman flagged and the goal was disallowed.

Joe was replaced by Robben after 67 minutes, and then Everton could have pulled off the shock of the season when Terry survived a penalty appeal when he appearing to handle Marcus Bent's shot in the closing minutes. A sullen Mourinho claimed afterwards that he had not seen the incident.

The wind-ups continued after the game, with Beattie intimating that Chelsea could be beaten in a physical battle, and Mourinho, curiously, responding by saying that the only time Beattie had touched the ball in the match was when he took the penalty.

Charlton then came to the Bridge in the Carling Cup as Chelsea started their defence of the first silverware obtained in the Abramovich era. Terry gave Chelsea the lead with a header, but Darren Bent stole an equaliser in first-half stoppage time after a mistake by Huth. Huth's night became worse when he missed a chance to restore the lead and then missed a penalty in the resulting shoot-out. Joe came on for Wright-Phillips on the hour, and it remains a mystery why he did not take one of the penalties. Mourinho blankly insisted to anyone who'd listen that Chelsea had not lost the game because it had been decided on penalties. It was Chelsea's first home defeat since losing to Arsenal in February 2003. The Blues' priorities did not extend to the lesser domestic cup competition, it would appear.

FIRST CHOICE

Blackburn visited the Bridge at the weekend, and Joe was picked ahead of Robben. Joe was carded for a challenge on Lucas Neill early on as the tension from the previous season's mean-spirited encounters spilled over. Drogba and Lampard both found the back of the net within 14 minutes, and it looked at this stage that Chelsea would romp to a comfortable win. Blackburn hit back, though, with two errors by the normally ultra-reliable Cech putting them back in the game. His slight dip in form meant that this was the fifth consecutive League game that Chelsea had conceded. Blackburn, along with Arsenal, had the best Premiership record of wins at Stamford Bridge, five in all, and another shock looked to be on the cards.

Lampard restored the advantage with his second goal and the hundredth of his amazing Chelsea career. It was via another free kick that deceived everyone before bouncing into the net. A number of his goals have seemed to bear an element of good fortune, deflections, and ricochets but, as Jack Nicklaus famously commented, 'The harder I work, the luckier I get.'

Mourinho claimed after the match that Lampard was the best player in the world at that moment in time. In Chelsea's six Premiership home matches, he had score twice in four of them.

Joe clinched it for Chelsea with another deflection, racing through to fire in the fourth. His shot appeared to hit the Blackburn defender Khizanishvili before swerving past Friedel and inside the post. At the time Joe was a reasonable 3-to-1 with the bookmaker Paddy Power to score at any time in the game.

Abramovich was making proclamations that he was going to make Chelsea the most successful club side for the next 100 years. It was estimated that by now he had pumped more than £600 million into the club in clearing the debts, buying new players and paying their wages.

Everything was going really well for Joe at this stage; he was playing for the club with the greatest potential in the world. He had become an integral part of a great team, and he had delivered in every role the manager had delegated to him. He now had Mourinho's trust and confidence, and played with maturity and technical brilliance when given opportunities on the pitch.

Mourinho, though, was behaving more erratically by the day. In the preceding few weeks, he had become involved in an unpleasant spat with Johann Cruyff, arguably one of the greatest players of all time. The trouble dated back to the monumental Barcelona matches the previous season. Cruyff had been bitterly upset at Mourinho's antics in Barcelona and his allegations against his friend Frank Rijkaard. He had allegedly commented that Mourinho's side had done everything 'to make me loathe football'. Chelsea's 4-5-1 formation was at the root of the problem, with Cruyff favouring the more flexible, attack-minded approach of 4-3-3, both as a player and manager.

Mourinho hit back by saying to the *Daily Telegraph* that 'Since 1996, Cruyff only plays golf and criticises... He manipulates and takes advantage of the power he has got for having been such a fantastic player.'

As the season wore on, Mourinho showed that he was

prepared to perpetuate the mind games off the pitch, and seemed to take things highly personally when receiving criticism from sections of the press, and from other high-profile managers as well.

Arsène Wenger said that Chelsea had lost a bit of belief after the disappointments of the Charlton loss and the poor match against Everton. Mourinho responded with a bitter attack on his Arsenal counterpart, calling the Arsenal manager 'a voyeur' and pointing out that Arsenal's start to the Premiership campaign had been less than brilliant, and that he should speak less about Chelsea and concentrate on improving Arsenal's results. They were, after all, trailing the Champions at this stage by 14 points. Mourinho displayed an almost paranoid obsession with Wenger's comments and his attitude to the Blues, by saying, 'He's worried about us, he's always talking about us. It's Chelsea, Chelsea, Chelsea, Chelsea.'

The carping and criticism continued when Chelsea chief executive Peter Kenyon announced the club's new strategy of making Chelsea synonymous with London. How he must have felt when Arsenal swept to the Champions League Final, to lose narrowly to Barça, is not recorded. Abramovich wanted to make his mark, but buying London was not quite as easy as owning estates in West Sussex and properties in France and Russia. Chelsea fans winced when Kenyon used buzzwords like 'marketing tools' and 'global branding'. They were referred to as 'customers' – a far cry from the late Matthew Harding's delightful description of fans as 'emotional shareholders'.

Chelsea's continuing pursuit of global domination moved to another theatre of war on the first day of November when they visited the Estadio Manuel Ruiz de Lopera for the return match with Real Betis. Joe, in a rich vein of form, started the match; Robben was on the other flank. It was a mild evening in southern Spain. Betis had lost all three games in La Liga since their heavy defeat at Stamford Bridge a fortnight before, the last being a 2-0 home defeat to Real Madrid.

Joe started brightly and played a perfect through-ball for Robben early on. The Dutchman was still not at his best and the chance was spurned. Betis then tore into Chelsea, roared on by their fanatical support. Danni, an early substitute for the injured star striker Oliveira, gave Betis the lead midway through the first half. Slack marking by Terry and Gallas gave ample space for the Portuguese striker to control the ball and turn it past Cech.

Almost immediately afterwards, Joe had a great chance to equalise when he pounced on a pass from Gudjohnsen. He looked offside but quickly dispatched a shot that brought a wonderful save from the Betis keeper Doblas. Danni then had a wonderful opportunity to double his goal tally after Cech had failed to hold a shot he would have dealt with easily the previous season.

Joe received another yellow card, and was then replaced at half-time by Wright-Phillips, who was still struggling to justify his enormous fee. He struggled to make any impact as Chelsea tried to claw their way back into the game. Drogba was another second-half sub and missed an easy chance, consigning an out-of-sorts Chelsea to a forgettable defeat. Also worrying was the fact that the result against Betis was their fifth defeat in six European trips. The manager himself conceded that the performance was not acceptable, and Joe admitted that the team was upset by its worst performance throughout Mourinho's 15-month tenure. He told the *Metro*, 'We are hurt but we will come back fighting. To say the least, we did not play well. Things went wrong and I wish I could say what it was. It just did not happen and we are very disappointed. We will look at the game and see where we need to improve but it was a long journey home.'

The recent setbacks could be seen as minor blips in the scheme of things; one defeat in six months, and no Premiership defeats for over a year. Those were records to be proud of for any normal club, but Chelsea were far from normal. The Blues were in a unique position. By virtue of Abramovich's vast wealth, Chelsea was the richest club on earth. Now they had to convince the world they were the best, as well.

The fanbase at Chelsea now comprised a large proportion of the comfortably well-off who could afford to pay in excess of £700 for a season ticket. Fewer and fewer had been around when Nevin and Co. strutted their stuff, devotees of the game and its classier exponents; most now were attracted by the dazzling Premiership circus, and the promise of being part of unprecedented success.

Joe Cole was one of the factors providing a link between the game of yesteryear and today. Having played for West Ham, he was doubly steeped in the culture of a big London club, and understood the heritage of technicians such as Moore, Hurst and Peters. Like Chelsea, Hammers fans had put up with years of suffering and disappointment. They demanded good football, though, even if it did not necessarily produce results. Joe had been seen by Ranieri as the natural replacement for Zola, and was the only player with the range of skills to come close to the iconic Italian.

The late, great Allan Ball, a World Cup winner, was a player with marked similiarities to those of Joe Cole – a tenacious midfielder who scored vital goals. He continued, in the *Guardian*, to explain how he thought the attitude of modern players had changed:

'Getting vast amounts of money takes away the hunger, that little edge. Players of today say, "I go out and play with the same desire…" Nah. It cannot possibly be that way when the comfort zone comes so quickly and so easily.'

Mourinho had changed the team requirements, though, and Joe had become a team player. He was functional, part of the unit that Jose had welded together. He was also fast and combative, and was now as capable of getting back as quickly as he could go forward.

Of the four wide players, Joe was probably the least equipped to deal with the task at the time of his transition. He lacked the wit of Duff, the artistry of Robben and the genuine burning pace of Wright-Phillips. But, due to a combination of loss of form and injury, in the winter of 2005 Joe led the pecking order. Also, and more importantly he had never lost the hunger.

Robben was rumoured still to be unsettled as the winter approached. When he was substituted against Betis, he stormed down the tunnel, but Mourinho sent two of his minions after him to drag him back to the bench to sit out the game. Graham Taylor, commentating on Five Live, said at the time, 'There's a problem between Robben and Chelsea. Sooner or later it's going to come out in the open. Robben is one of those players who needs to be on top of his game to do well.'

The Mourinho-Wenger psychological war games also rumbled on in the background, with neither side backing down and then, in November, Chelsea visited another of their fiercest rivals – Manchester United – at Old Trafford. Sir Alex Ferguson had yet to beat one of Mourinho's teams – Chelsea or Porto – in six attempts. United had only won 4 of their last 30 home games against the Blues, for whom Old Trafford had always been a happy hunting ground. In 1970, they had won the FA Cup in a replay at that ground for the first time in their chequered history. It could so easily be another opportunity for Mourinho to lord it over his illustrious rival.

Joe started in the line-up. The unlikely opening scorer was Darren Fletcher, who had been severely criticised by his captain Roy Keane earlier in the week. He scored in the 31st minute of the first half after Ronaldo had given a master-class of wing play with a sharp turn that flummoxed Ferreira and delivered a wicked centre. The young Scot met the precise cross at the far post and somehow managed to direct his looping header into the top left-hand corner. Petr Cech was deceived by the flight of Ronaldo's cross, and Terry made a half-hearted attempt to clear the danger.

Joe was Chelsea's most threatening forward but the London side could make little impression on the United defence. In the second half, they improved as their 40-game unbeaten run slipped away. Joe had a couple of half-chances but Van der Sar made a string of great saves to deny the Blues.

Joe frequently got into dangerous positions but was unable to take advantage; he was usually so good at making space, but he had precious little in that match. United's two flank players, Ronaldo and Fletcher, stayed glued to their wings and kept dropping back to block any attacking surges by Del Horno and Ferreira. Consequently, Joe had no scope to raid forward and deliver any of his telling crosses. The United defender John O'Shea was detailed to mark him and stuck to his task doggedly. As was so often the case for England, Joe was forced to play inside and down the middle. Chelsea's only attacking option was to press forward down the middle, and try to play through the United defence where they were strongest. Both the United central midfield players, Paul Scholes and Alan Smith, stayed back as Ferguson's plan was to crowd Chelsea out. The midfield fast became a battlefield as it became increasingly packed.

Joe was substituted a quarter-of-an-hour before the end as Mourinho made a last-ditch effort to save the game. In a gamble worthy of Ranieri, Wright-Phillips came on, but was ineffective and never looked capable of making much impact as United won a famous victory. Carlton Cole was similarly thrown on to change the game, but he, too, had little to offer.

Ferguson, at last, had a victory over his rival that he could really savour. It was Mourinho's 50th League match in charge, of which he had won 39, drawn 9 and lost only 2, both in the city of Manchester. It's tempting to speculate on the nature of the conversation between the two managers over the best Portuguese red after the match (the Chelsea boss had complained about Ferguson's 'awful' wine on a previous visit), but one thing's certain – Mourinho would have found the defeat hard to swallow.

It was true that a couple of defeats, although demoralising for the Champions, hardly constituted a crisis. But the question now was whether the team could bounce back and recreate their impressive form of the previous season, or implode on the back of this defeat. The answer would become clear over the coming months.

9

Gold Rush

'This time last year, Joe Cole was a player
with potential – now he is a player.'
Jose Mourinho, 19 November 2005

'GOLD' WAS ONE of the biggest hits of the New Romantic band Spandau Ballet in the 1980s, reaching Number 2 in the charts. It also happened to be one of Joe's favourite tracks. The West Ham crowd used it as a theme song for their hero, substituting 'Cole' for 'Gold' in the chorus –

> '*Joey Cole... Cole!*
> *Always believe in your soul*
> *You got the power to know*
> *You're indestructible*
> *Always believe in... Joey Cole.*'

You could say it was an anthem, and the original version was included on a CD imaginatively titled *Chelsea Players' Top 20*, released in the third week of November 2005. The CD featured the players' and manager's favourite tracks. Jose went for Bryan Adams' 'Run to You', and Arjen Robben won few admirers with 'The Final Countdown' by 1980s rock band Europe. Perhaps it was Lampard who made the most unlikely choice, opting for the slushy 'Stuck on You' by Lionel Richie. Giving him the benefit of the doubt, he could, of course, have been making a cunning comment about being man-marked, but it's unlikely.

In the first Premiership home game in November, Newcastle came to town. The weather that autumn had been unseasonably warm but suddenly it changed and London was hit by a big freeze more which suited the Newcastle fans. Chelsea were facing up to their first crisis under Jose Mourinho – they were top of the league by six points and had suffered one Premiership defeat, but on recent form, standards had slipped considerably.

Newcastle were shorn of their strike force by injury. Veteran Alan Shearer was recovering from a hernia operation and Joe's England team-mate Michael Owen dropped out just before the game. Owen and Joe were buoyant after England's heroic 3-2 win over Argentina in Geneva the previous weekend, with Joe having supplied the perfect cross for Owen to head home the winner in injury time. There was a little controversy over the behaviour of the Argentinian players prior to the match, when it was reported that anti-English songs and insults had been bellowed at full volume on their coach as they travelled to the ground.

Joe was in the starting line-up, and ex-Chelsea players Scott Parker and Celestine Babayaro were on for Newcastle. The men in the black-and-white stripes put up stubborn resistance in the first half as they kept the score goalless. In fact, they could have gone in 1-0 up at half-time had a justifiable penalty been awarded for Terry's reckless tackle on Lee Bowyer.

Within two minutes of the re-start, though, Joe struck. The lumbering defender Titus Bramble lost the ball in midfield to Eidur Gudjohnsen, who instantly fed Joe, who raced through to score. Irish international keeper Shay Given could only watch as the ball whistled through a narrow gap between him and the post.

Hernan Crespo scored a second shortly afterwards, and Damien Duff wrapped it up at the end when his shot looped into the net off Parker.

Joe Cole was named Man of the Match and earned a glowing tribute from Mourinho printed in the *Guardian*. It was now 13 months since Joe had been subject to Mourinho's criticism after the Liverpool game. 'This time last year Joe was a player with great potential – now he is a player. He looks strong physically, strong defensively, he hasn't lost his attacking qualities and that has made him a very good player because he works for the team. Tactically, he understands the game, he plays well for Chelsea and for England and we are all happy.'

For the time being, it looked as though Joe's future was golden.

On the following Wednesday, Chelsea flew to Brussels to play the away leg Champions League game against Anderlecht in the Constant Vanden Stock Stadium. Joe started this match.

Anderlecht were the only team to have failed to score in the Champions League group stage, having built up the unenviable record of 11 straight defeats in the competition. Their domestic form was better, though, lying second to Standard Liege with 29 points from 14 games. In the pre-match build-up, Mourinho insisted that Chelsea should crush Anderlecht, although the Blues had not won away in Europe for a year. The ex-Porto coach pointed out that Chelsea had started slowly in recent defeats, had conceded early goals and allowed their opponents to grow in confidence. He warned his players of allowing this to happen again.

With Mourinho's words ringing in their ears, Chelsea scored twice in the opening 15 minutes to destroy Anderlecht and virtually kill the game off. Lampard set the first up for Crespo with eight minutes on the clock by dispossessing Vanden Borre, marauding down the left and centring with his supposedly weaker foot. Crespo met it first time to blast it high into the net. It was a classy goal and vindicated Mourinho's decision to include him ahead of Drogba. Crespo was delighted to score on his debut in the Champions League that year, having scored twice against Liverpool in the final, but still not getting his hands on the trophy

Ricardo Carvalho, back in favour with Mourinho after his early outburst, scored the second from Lampard's cross. That goal should have opened up the floodgates, but Chelsea cruised along, content to keep control of the game. Joe provided ample support, covering, guarding space and generally making himself available. It was his stop-start runs that were the main threat to the Belgian side throughout the first half.

Having been lucky to escape a yellow card for a reckless

challenge near half-time, Mourinho rested Joe after 63 minutes. The young French prospect Diarra replaced him, with the new signing slotting into the midfield and suggesting that he might be a prospect for the Makelele role at some point in the future.

Essien had a fine match, seamlessly filling in behind Joe, who chose to offer his thoughts on Crespo after the match. He told the *Evening Standard*, 'Crespo showed he is world class against Anderlecht, particularly with his finish. He is so cool in front of goal. That is why you pay fortunes for strikers because it is rare to have such composure.

He has been the same as normal since the England game.

'The singing thing was a lot of fuss about nothing. They do it before their games. The England boys have not really given him any grief. We don't want to say anything because we may have to play against him in the World Cup next year. He is an excellent player and we are happy to have him at Chelsea. He is already in with the banter and I think he has settled really well this time.'

The Chelsea bandwagon rolled into Fratton Park to play 17th-placed Portsmouth soon afterwards. The day before, Milan Mandaric, the club's Serbian chairman, had sacked his manager Alain Perrin who had won just two Premiership matches in the campaign, both away from home. Portsmouth were in desperate trouble. Brian Mears, the former chairman of Chelsea, knew Mandaric well, and commented, 'Mandaric was always touching people... not that he liked them, but because he wanted to see how tough they were before eating them alive.'

JOE COLE

George Best had died the day before, on 25 November 2005, so every Premiership game observed a two-minute silence for the great man before the kick off. It was particularly poignant at Portsmouth, as Best had been a great friend of Mandaric, and was a regular visitor to the south-coast club.

Joe started his sixth consecutive game for Chelsea, and grew in confidence as the game progressed. Crespo struck the first goal after 27 minutes, diverting Ferreira's raking cross-cum-shot past Ashdown. In the second half, Joe started to run the game and the crowd was treated to some surging runs and fantastic control swerved and dummied to provide service to the front men. In one instance, he weaved past three defenders, was dispossessed, and then doggedly won the ball back. As a result, he was targeted for some crunching tackles. One in particular by Andy Griffin incensed Mourinho so much he stormed from his dug-out to rebuke the Pompey defender. The referee Philip Dowd ordered Jose to calm down, and the fans began to barrack Joe for going down too easily.

Joe wrapped it up for Chelsea when he won a penalty after another powerful run was blocked spectacularly by the Serb skipper Dejan Stefanovic, leaving Joe crashing to the ground in the box.

Captain John Terry helped his England colleague to his feet and gave him a pat of encouragement. Joe had toughened up in the last year. The television replays confirmed that Joe had simply been too quick for the Serbian international.

Lampard sent Ashdown the wrong way, and buried his spot kick in the opposite bottom corner. It was his 11th goal of the season in his record 160th consecutive Premiership match, eclipsing David James's record. He would still have some way to go to beat the all-time record of 401 successive League matches played by Harold Bell of Tranmere over a ten-year period in the 1940s–50s.

Mourinho said afterwards that he would not swap Lampard for any player in the world, and shortlisted Ronaldinho, Kaka and Shevchenko as his other dream players. Joe was getting bracketed with Lampard now in the match reports, which commonly observed that the pair had struck up a strong, productive partnership in midfield.

Minutes after Stefanovic's initial foul, Joe went flying in the box again. The referee gave a free kick outside the area, although the television evidence pointed to the contrary. How the Serb avoided a second card was a complete mystery. Lampard fired the free kick into a packed wall and Joe caught the rebound almost perfectly, the shot skimming just over the bar. After the match, Joe joked, 'We knew it would be tough because Portsmouth are fighting for their lives... but I didn't expect them to take mine.'

George Best would have admired the way Joe kept going at the home defence. He had the confidence to keep trying and the courage to risk the fouls and possible injury. The booing continued, which must have pleased Mourinho, with the crowd well aware that Joe's threat was causing the Pompey defence enormous problems. With five minutes left, Mourinho decided to replace Joe with Geremi, saying later, 'He has four bookings already and the next one will see him miss the next game. I thought I would take him off in case he suffered a reaction to some of the treatment. Joe was too powerful for them.'

The game ended 2-0 to the Londoners, and Chelsea were now 11 points clear of nearest rivals Arsenal. The refrain of 'Can we play you every week?' could be heard from the visiting section of the ground; Portsmouth had lost all five Premiership encounters with Chelsea and had failed to score in any of them.

Interviewed afterwards for *Match of the Day*, Joe acknowledged that the spectre of Best had overshadowed the game. The players had watched the montages of some of his classic runs and goals, with the Ron Harris clip being voted everyone's favourite. Joe modestly admitted that he could never emulate the genius of Best but, like him, he wanted to entertain. Mourinho acknowledged his young star's quality, but warned against going over the top. 'Joe Cole is one of the best wingers in the game, but I am going to leave him in peace and not call him the new George Best like you ask.'

The main reason for Joe's resurgence was the toughness and resilience he had added to his game. It was a massive psychological factor. Mourinho had nurtured in him a killer instinct, and now people were sitting up and taking notice.

That week, Joe helped Lampard raise more than £500,000 when he hosted a gala diner in aid of the Teenage Cancer Trust. Mourinho attended along with Jordan, Harry Redknapp (about to rejoin Portsmouth in a sensational turnaround) and the pop band UB40. The tabloids also noted that about 5,000 people living in Britain were worth £5 million or more. Joe was counted among them, but had some way to go to reach David Beckham's alleged income of £47,500 per day.

In the aftermath of the game, the impression persisted that Joe had gone to ground rather too easily. Joe was clearly unhappy with any allegations that he might be prone to diving, and told the *Metro*, 'There are some players in this country who are divers but I am not one of them. I would never dive. It was definitely a penalty. I wasn't trying to get anyone booked or sent off, but they were fouling me so many times that that sooner or later the ref was going to make a decision. It was frustrating for me to be accused of diving because we've not had many dribbling players in this country for a few years.'

Joe had a minor calf strain for the next match against Middlesbrough, so he didn't feature. Terry scored the only goal of the game with a second-half header from close range, and in doing so, went some way to restoring his reputation, which had been savaged for a second time in a month after an exposé in the *Sun*. His first alleged transgression was a romp with a 17-year-old girl in his Bentley. He was then accused of a £5,000-a-week gambling habit, which Mourinho dismissed by saying that £5,000 to Terry was the equivalent of about £50 to the rest of us.

Joe had not quite shaken off his calf injury for the return Champions League match against Liverpool. The game was almost of no consequence, as both teams had qualified for the knockout stages, so the only real question was who would finish first or second in the group, with the winners potentially having an easier tie in the next round. On that basis, Mourinho said that he would rather beat Wigan in the Premiership the following Saturday than win against Liverpool in the group match.

It was the fourth time in 2005 the clubs had clashed in the Champions League and only one goal had been scored. The statistics also indicated that goals would be had to come by – the champions of Europe had had eight successive clean sheets, and the champions of England had four successive clean sheets to their name.

For only the second time that season, Mourinho started with Arjen Robben and Damien Duff. The young Dutch winger had been criticised by Jose, who called on his star winger to put his injury problems behind him and start showing his best form.

The game was a dull affair, with the two sides seeming to bring out the worst in each other. Chelsea had 63 per cent of possession, but were unable to convert it into goals. The worry was that Chelsea, particularly without Joe, were short of true class up front.

The only real talking point of the game was Essien's tackle on Dietmar Hamann. It was a horrific, knee-high lunge with his studs that could have smashed the German's leg to pieces, but the referee did not even book him. Sky TV reran the footage several times and Essien was subsequently banned for two matches. Mourinho was incensed by Sky's actions, and refused to talk to them.

Joe was declared fit for the next home game against Wigan, who had given Chelsea such a battle on the first day of the season. For the second successive week, Terry scored from Lampard's corner. It secured Chelsea's 10th home Premiership victory in succession. They were now 12 points clear of second-placed Liverpool and 17 ahead of Arsenal. The facts suggested that Chelsea were outclassing their opponents on a consistent basis, but the truth was that it was another turgid display. Chelsea had been accused of being a boring team and, for some fans, they were reminiscent of Don Revie's Leeds side from the 1970s – grinding out results, winning at all costs, just a relentless pursuit of honours with apparently little joy on the pitch.

Joe Cole, though, seemed to represent all that was good about Chelsea, and he had another bright game. He almost scored in the first half when he took the ball into the box after a powerful surge from near the halfway line. Mike Pollitt made an excellent block when he looked certain to score. Joe's performance lit up a dull afternoon. Lampard found himself being closed down a lot more and, with his threat nullified, Chelsea had few alternatives. Mourinho described Joe afterwards as Chelsea's most potent attacker, and his development into a crucial element of a Championship-winning side had not gone unnoticed by the England coach. Eriksson had apparently 'pencilled' Joe into his starting line-up for the World Cup Finals, provided that he stayed fit and held his form. Another crucial factor, of course, was that Mourinho would have to retain faith in his qualities, and give him a sufficiently productive run on the pitch.

On the Tuesday after the Wigan match, Chelsea held a pre-Christmas Centenary dinner in honour of the 'Legends'. It was an amazing evening attended by 100 former players, as well as the current squad. The 1955 title-winning side was there, alongside legends like Dixon, the cultured Nevin, 'Butch' Wilkins, Osgood, Harris and Bonetti, and perhaps the greatest former player of all – Gianfranco Zola.

The current side, though, did not dine with their forebears or the lesser mortals. They sat on high, looking down on the rest from a suspended mezzanine level, only to descend and mingle when Mourinho led his class of 2005 down the staircase towards the hushed throng. The dividing lines between the ordinary and the special – the past and the present – were very much in evidence, and this was quite different from the spirit at a club like West Ham, where Joe had mixed freely with the supporters.

After signing a few shirts – even these were carefully rationed, given the proliferation of sales on online auction sites of signed memorabilia – the class of 2005 did not stay long.

Chelsea then won 2-0 against Arsenal with a commanding performance. Joe was once again voted Man of the Match, with the *Sun* voting him the outstanding player on the field and concluding that he was 'a lot more than a show pony these days'.

Arsenal felt aggrieved at losing this vital game against their local rivals. Insults were traded, and aggrieved Gunners pointed out that Arsenal had had 58 per cent of the possession, and a perfectly good goal by Robert van Persie was disallowed for offside against Henry, who had also hit a post.

Robben put Chelsea ahead after 39 minutes, clipping the ball home via the far post after Drogba had sent him clear. Robben had his best game of the season and played with tightly controlled energy throughout the match. It was as if he had something to prove to Mourinho. On the hour, he had a great chance to double Chelsea's lead but instead opted to pass to Joe, when it would have been easier for him to score. The pass was poor and the overworked Campbell scrambled the ball away. Campbell's form was erratic and he was shortly to be involved in more headlines for walking out at half-time in a subsequent match against West Ham.

Joe clinched the game after 73 minutes when he robbed Lauren of the ball. The stand-in left-back for Ashley Cole was the victim of a forearm smash from Essien in the first half and was still a bit groggy. Joe swept forward, skipping past the flat-footed Campbell and hit a low drive wide of Lehmann which again bounced in via the post. Everyone in the ground knew the game was over. Joe ran to the corner and kissed the centenary badge in front of the jubilant Chelsea fans and, in doing so, his gesture showed the fans that he was trying to break down the barriers that seemed to have been built between the players and supporters throughout a period of institutionalisation that surrounded Abramovich's takeover. Over 2,000 Chelsea fans, shoe-horned into the corner of the ground, were more than happy to share their outpouring of emotion with their hero, the firmly established star who'd just out-gunned the Gunners.

It was Chelsea's first League win at Highbury for 15 years and emphasised the widening gap between them and the side that had managed, not so long ago, to go an entire season without losing. Joe Cole's goal reiterated the seismic effect of the oligarch's money, and the fact that Chelsea as a footballing force had been blasted into a different stratosphere. Arsenal were now 20 points adrift of Mourinho's outfit, and showed little promise of narrowing the gap.

Minutes after his goal, Joe almost scored again when he shot from a similar distance and watched as Lehmann, at full stretch, tipped it on to the post. Another goal, his first double for Chelsea, would have been a real bonus.

When the match ended, Mourinho stormed down the tunnel, his head down, without having offered his hand to the vanquished Arsenal manager. No exchanges of post-match pleasantries with Arsène Wenger were made either. Meanwhile, the ecstatic Chelsea players celebrated their impressive victory with the Chelsea fans. It was still early days, but this highly significant victory at Highbury suggested that the Premiership was all but won.

Mourinho's ungracious behaviour drew a storm of criticism in the press. Among the many theories expounded was one that suggested that because he had enjoyed no success as a player, Mourinho was anxious to bask in the reflected glory of his seemingly invincible team. The Chelsea spin doctors were quick to point out that Jose had been upset by Wenger's refusal to acknowledge a Christmas card allegedly sent to him. The card had been designed by a young fan with the proceeds going to the Children's cancer charity CLIC Sargent. The matter seemed ludicrous.

Fulham visited Chelsea on Boxing Day, and Joe started for Chelsea with Wright-Phillips making a rare appearance. Gallas gave Chelsea the lead on three minutes scoring from close range after Huth had headed on Lampard's corner. Joe had forced the corner when his cross, delivered after a couple of stepovers, caused problems to the Fulham defence.

Lampard had recently returned from Zurich were he was voted the second best player in the world at a FIFA awards ceremony. Ronaldinho was named the top player in the world, polling 956 votes; while Frank totalled 306, and said he was looking forward to clashing with the Barça superstar when the teams met again in February. The draw had been made and the prospect was mouth-watering.

The second-best player in the world fired Chelsea even further ahead after 24 minutes when his snap shot took a cruel deflection to beat Fulham keeper Mark Crossley. Fulham looked completely outclassed, and a huge score was on the cards. The Craven Cottage side refused to buckle, though, and two defensive mistakes by Joe enabled the unfancied strugglers to level the match.

Joe fouled a Fulham player on the half hour and could only watch helplessly as the resulting free kick led to the first goal Chelsea had conceded in 718 minutes of play in all competitions. Boa Morte's free kick eluded Terry and was flapped at by Cech, before rolling to McBride who scored from a yard. Neither Cech nor Terry were looking quite as invincible as they had done the previous season. Brian McBride was causing Terry all sorts of problems, and he showed that he could take the knocks as well as dish them out.

At half-time, Wright-Phillips was replaced by Gudjohnsen. The young winger had recently figured in a poll of the worst buys of the season and his form and confidence had taken a severe knock. His tremendous pace and trickery that had mesmerised fans and opponents alike when playing at Man City had just melted away at Chelsea and, with 165 days to go to the World Cup, he looked a long way off making the squad. Joe was now consistently streets ahead of the unfortunate

Londoner in the scheme of things, having played through the early insecurity of warming the bench on a regular basis, and taking the opportunities to make his mark and play his way into the reckoning.

Fulham became the first team to score a second-half goal against Chelsea since the Community Shield match against Arsenal when Helguson scored from the spot after 56 minutes. The same player had been clumsily brought down by Joe when he looked set to score, and Joe was incredibly lucky to still stay on the pitch after committing the foul.

Chelsea were stung by the ferocity of Fulham's fight-back and managed to find a higher gear. Within seconds, Joe was flying down the wing and whipped over a cross that the diving Gudjohnsen headed just over. Lampard then netted from close range but was ruled offside.

Chelsea put all their energy into attack as Drogba was pitched on by Mourinho, in gambling mode, who pulled off Huth. There were now just three at the back, and Chelsea went all out for the win. A quarter-of-an-hour from the end, Joe set up a magical goal for Crespo to win it. The England player burst free on the right and crossed first time into the box. It was a marvellous cross that soared and then dipped. The initial trajectory looked like it had been over-hit. Crespo arrived to turn it into the net with a sublime finish past substitute keeper Tony Warner.

Mourinho agreed that it was a wonderful goal, but then substituted Crespo with Geremi to shore up the depleted midfield and to protect the remaining defenders. In the closing minutes, referee Graham Poll denied Fulham a blatant penalty when Terry made a save Cech would have been proud of from Boa Morte's cross shot. It had been a pulsating match, and a great win for the Blues.

In the post-match press conference, Mourinho once again praised Joe. 'Joe is playing absolutely magnificently every game and I thought it was not very clever to have my best attacking player in midfield. When I came here, nobody knows Cole's position, not even him.'

Joe was on a high, and receiving plenty of well-earned plaudits from his colleagues and observers alike, and he received a further confidence boost from the Special One 48 hours later when he scored Chelsea's winner at Manchester City, putting them 11 points clear of United. It was Joe's seventh goal of the season, his fourteenth in the calendar year.

The hard-earned result at Eastlands gave Mourinho victory over the only side that he had failed to record a win against in his awesome 18-month Premiership journey. It started badly for the Blues when Lampard was ruled out at the last moment with a virus, ending his record run of 164 consecutive Premiership appearances. Gudjohnsen replaced him, with Joe taking on extra responsibility that night and, once again, his performance earning him Man of the Match. The £21 million ex-City winger Wright-Phillips hadn't even made the squad.

City's Joey Barton was their driving force and only Cech's legs kept out an early effort. Stuart Pearce's team pressed Chelsea's midfield throughout the game, denying Makelele any space. These tactics had helped City to deprive Chelsea of four points the previous season and, for long periods, Chelsea struggled to establish control.

JOE COLE

Joe, in the black away strip with grey trimming, was Chelsea's most potent threat as his runs disturbed the City back four. The tricky player nearly scored when he fired in a left-footer that James took two attempts to parry. Ben Thatcher, the ex-Millwall and Tottenham defender, had been detailed to mark Joe, but his ceaseless running caused Thatcher problems throughout the game. Drogba should have been rewarded with a penalty when he clashed with David James, but the referee, Uriah Rennie, waved away the protests and booked him instead for diving.

In the second half, Mourinho brought on Crespo and Robben for Duff and Drogba. Duff accepted his fate; his performance looked very ordinary alongside Joe's exploits. Drogba was furious at being subbed and blanked Mourinho as he came off. As with Wenger after the Arsenal game, no handshakes were offered, giving Mourinho a taste of some of the treatment he would occasionally dish out to opposing managers when results did not go his way.

Robben transformed the game as he set himself up for a chance that James saved brilliantly. Joe had thoroughly exhausted Thatcher, who was booked for a foul on the flying Dutchman. Eleven minutes from time, with the temperature dropping rapidly, Robben galloped down the left and picked out Gudjohnsen, whose snap shot was parried by James. The ball ricocheted off Crespo and fell into the path of Joe prowling in the box. It was the best Christmas present imaginable, and Joe gratefully scored from point-blank range. Joe was mobbed by his team-mates as they celebrated the imminent retention of the Premiership title.

The Portuguese head coach could barely contain his excitement at the result and again singled out Joe. He told the *Times*, 'He was fantastic in every aspect of the game. At the moment, I think Joe is untouchable.'

Joe was at the peak of his form, and attracting the sort of praise and acclaim normally only reserved for superstars. Indeed, that is what he had slowly become. Only Wayne Rooney, in a rich vein of form himself, was attracting more headlines and publicity. Joe was there solely on merit, by dint of his hard work and huge talent. He was not someone who courted publicity, or flaunted his wealth. There were few celebrity trappings or glitz to dazzle the public with as far as Joe was concerned. Perhaps that is one of the secrets of his success – his apparent desire to be a complete anti-celeb.

Joe told the *Telegraph*, 'I think this is the best I have ever played. Playing for the Champions, top of the Premiership, second round of the Champions League and I am playing well for them.

'I love the club, love playing for them and we are all having the time of our lives. Part of it is me, and there are other things like my family. Things are just going really well at the moment and you cannot say it is down to one thing. I have been established for a long time now. I have been a regular for more periods than not over the last 12 months and I have been playing well for the best side in the country. I have always said, as long as I am out there and can show what I can do, winning games with the lads, I am happy.

'I won't get over-excited. I have always taken praise and criticism in the same way... I will remain level-headed.'

10
Footballer's Coming Home

'When I am warming up for the games and the song
"The Liquidator" comes on, it reminds me of when I used to
go and get my steak pie and all that. I am lucky to be
playing for this side.'
Joe Cole, 2006

JOE WAS FULL of optimism for 2006 – there was every
reason to believe that he would build on his successes of the
previous year. Chelsea travelled to West Ham for a lunchtime
fixture against Joe's former team. For West Ham, it was their
Cup Final; they had waited a long time for this day. On the last
occasion the clubs had met, Ranieri was in charge and West
Ham were about to fall through the trap-door of relegation. Di
Canio's goal settled it.

Sadly for Joe, he was forced to miss the game through
suspension. Whether or not he actually would have played is
open to speculation because, a few days earlier, he had been
the subject of some criticism from Mourinho following his
performance in the game against Birmingham.

This was another strange episode in the relationship
between the young England star and his demanding boss.

Chelsea had won 2-0 with two first-half goals from Crespo and Robben. It was another functional performance and Chelsea cruised through the second half as they played their third game in six days. Crespo put Chelsea ahead after 23 minutes and Joe had a part in the goal. Crespo passed to him, and he sent Robben racing down the left flank. The Dutch master cut in and his fierce shot was parried by the Birmingham keeper, but Crespo pounced to score his eighth goal of the season.

Joe then raced through with a clear run at goal. Brilliantly drawing the Birmingham keeper Taylor, he shimmied and was left with an open goal. Joe was staring at an empty net, but instead elected to pass sideways to Crespo to score. Crespo was having an uneven match, and missed this easy chance, along with three others, hesitating just long enough to allow Julian Gray to track back and clear. Mourinho went wild on the touchline, kicking the advertising hoarding in disgust.

Mourinho blamed Joe for failing to kill off Birmingham. The media, taking their cue from the Chelsea coach, similarly laid into Joe. In the early editions, Joe's average score out of 10 for his performance was about 7; by the time they had built up the story, he was down to 5. The thrust of the criticism centred on that favourite phrase when referring to Joe – 'showboating'. What exactly showboating means is open to conjecture. True, Joe's early career may have relied a little too much on the tricks and flicks rather than the team play that Mourinho had developed in him, but this level of criticism seemed unfair in the extreme. It suggested some unjustified deep-seated resentment of the young player.

Robben found himself on the receiving end of Mourinho's temper as well. A few weeks earlier, the Portuguese manager had criticised the Dutch winger saying that it was about time he produced the goods for the team. Mourinho, apparently, did not want any player to get above themselves, or become a more influential personality than him in the club. He was lucky that Abramovich kept a very low profile and did not want to hog the limelight in the way that Bates had done during his tenure at Chelsea. The players Mourinho bought always seemed to be very quiet off the field, almost lacking in any personality. Mourinho favoured players he could mould; no egos, no baggage. With Mourinho, there was enough ego at the Bridge already.

It was significant that Joe was criticised for his performance in the Birmingham match. In the previous home game, when he was directly responsible for both the Fulham goals, no mention was made of him. On several occasions in the Birmingham game, the crowd greeted him with 'olé' when he beat a defender with some classy trick or deceptive feint. Mourinho seemed contemptuous of such displays of virtuosity, his teams being drilled to favour defensive prowess above technical brilliance. Whatever the reason for Mourinho's attitude towards Joe, one thing was clear – no one could take anything for granted as far as the Portuguese coach was concerned, and no amount of past glory would guarantee any player a place in the next game.

Lampard received terrible abuse at Upton Park. He admitted that he never had the relationship with the fans there, and the situation was compounded because Chelsea had always been the most despised enemies of West Ham, with jealousy at its root.

Chelsea's greatest enemies in the 1960s through to the 1990s were Tottenham. This dated back to the famous 'Cockney Cup Final' of 1967, the first time two London sides had contested a Cup Final. In those days, Tottenham were the most powerful side in the land with the financial clout to buy whoever took their fancy; how times have changed. They had on their books perhaps the most famous and arguably greatest player in Chelsea's history – Jimmy Greaves. Another of the club's most famous sons, Terry Venables, was also plying his trade in the white shirt. Chelsea fans, like any up and down the country, hated losing their stars to their rivals. What irked them particularly was the fact that both Greaves and Venables were home-grown players. Blues fans had watched them develop from the youth teams to being fully-fledged internationals.

West Ham fans feel the same when they watch Joe Cole, whose current golden period at Chelsea has its roots in the grounding he received from Upton Park, just as Everton fans must feel a clashing sense of pride and hatred when Rooney visits Goodison wearing the red of Manchester United.

Over the years, Spurs' financial power has dwindled alarmingly, and Chelsea's current pre-eminence has left Tottenham looking very much like poor relations. They are now a much-improved team under the shrewd tutelage of Harry Redknapp, who is an admirer of Joe Cole. Abramovich's money has meant that the gulf between the clubs is still very much in evidence, however.

West Ham v Chelsea as a potentially volatile fixture dates back to the late 1970s and reached its peak in the 1980s when gang hooliganism was at its height. West Ham's hooligan gang in those days was called the ICF – the 'Inter-City Firm' – a group of designer-wearing thugs who took their name from the InterCity trains on which they travelled to away matches. On several occasions in the 1980s, they had actually succeeded in attacking the Chelsea 'Shed' end and capturing it. Joe was just joining West Ham when the ICF were winding down their fabled 'activities'. Increased policing at grounds, all-seater stadiums, CCTV and the waning attraction of organised gang fights all contributed to the decline in trouble. Drugs played an important part in the culture, and such was the impact of Ecstasy, that it was even linked to the decline of violence in football matches.

By the 1990s, 'E' and the rave scene had reached its peak and many of the ex-hooligans were now part of that culture. They had found that there was money to be made in pushing drugs and organising raves, a far better alternative to the risk of being slashed with a Stanley knife rucking at Stamford Bridge. The Chelsea 'Headhunters' would point out that the major difference between them and ICF was that the East Enders' priority was chasing a pound note, whereas Chelsea just loved fighting.

Hooliganism has become another commodity, neatly packaged and sold to the punters. Bookshops have rows of books on the subject – written by and about hooligans – extolling the virtues of administering extreme violence. John King's cult book about the Headhunters, *The Football Factory*, is now available as a DVD, and a DVD of the film *Green Street* was released the day after Chelsea had won at Upton Park. In the film, Elijah Wood, who played Frodo

Baggins in *Lord of the Rings*, played an American student caught up with the West Ham gangs.

Abuse – and outright racism – then replaced violence as the weapon of choice. West Ham, despite the fact that they were one of the first clubs to regularly play black players – the recently honoured Clyde Best being the prime example – had a section of their crowd that was particularly racist. In the 1980s, Chelsea had some promising black youngsters like Keith Dublin, Paul Canoville and Keith Jones, who received shocking verbal abuse from sections of the West Ham crowd.

In March 1995, the black Chelsea striker Mark Stein received monkey chants throughout the match before silencing his tormentors with a wonder goal savagely volleyed in from a corner. Chelsea went on to win 2-1. Football in the UK has come a long way in a few years and, thankfully, events such as those are almost unheard of today, with players such as Henry, Drogba, Emile Heskey, Sol Campbell and Djibril Cissé commanding well-deserved respect. In other European countries, however, and in Italy in particular, the practice of racial taunting still seems to persist from time to time.

Lampard's barracking at West Ham, though, had everything to do with a local boy who'd grown up with the club and returned in a blue shirt. And he had also been universally acknowledged as second only to Ronaldinho in quality. That must have hurt. The Hammers crowd just didn't like him or rate him. It must have been inconceivable to the average West Ham fan that, in a few years, Lampard had progressed from being a target of the boo-boys to being a Premiership medal-winner, and a crucial part of the richest club in the world.

FOOTBALLER'S COMING HOME

David Mellor, the ex-Fulham fan and friend of Ken Bates, wrote that the standard of coaching and the competition at Chelsea had transformed Lampard as a player. Others at Chelsea had not been quite so fulsome in their praise, and even questioned the £11 million that had been paid for him.

Of course, as is invariably the case, Lampard scored the first goal of that tense game. The Ladbrokes kiosk in the ground was offering a rather generous 9-2 against him scoring, which the Chelsea fans devoured. The goal was crashed in from 12 yards after West Ham's Yossi Benayoun's weak headed clearance fell into Lampard's path.

An equally inaccurate clearance from Terry set West Ham up for a shock equaliser. Harewood latched on to the ball and walked it into the net after Cech had kept out his initial shot. Upton Park erupted in a sea of joy. The impossible had happened and the Hammers were level.

For the first time in the game, a furious Mourinho appeared on the touchline, and motioned to Crespo to get warmed up. In seconds, he was brought on for the subdued Duff. Within a minute, he had scored after a gorgeous through ball from Robben. Soon afterwards, he missed two more slightly easier chances. Robben, the best player on the field, blazed over from the near post then Lampard let loose with a thundering volley.

Drogba made the game safe with a strong run after a fine ball from Gudjohnsen, playing almost as well Robben. Mourinho had given him the sobriquet of the 'Blonde Maradona', and he lived up to the image. Lampard was later booked after a clash with Fletcher, but it could so easily have been a seven or eight-goal rout.

In the hectic holiday week, Chelsea had sustained a 100 per cent record. Lampard and Terry flew to Dubai for a couple of days' holiday granted by the boss. Joe's feelings about that sort of privileged treatment is not known.

Terry, always supportive of Joe, flew back to give the team talk before the FA Cup tie against Huddersfield, for which Joe was back from suspension. Huddersfield had a great Cup tradition, having won the Cup at Stamford Bridge in the 1920s when Chelsea staged Internationals and Cup Finals. The Chelsea side showed nine changes from the team that had trounced West Ham. This cup side comprised a collection of fringe players and back-up men, with a few stars thrown in for good measure. Carlton Cole scored the first goal, netting for the first time in years. The England Under-21 striker looked sharp.

Mourinho prowled the touchline; as far as priorities went, the FA Cup came a poor third. He mumbled in the Friday press conference, though, about the great traditions of the FA Cup and how they were going to do everything to get to the final, hopefully at the new Wembley.

Huddersfield, who took 6,500 fans to London, deservedly equalised after 75 minutes through their star player Gary Taylor-Fletcher. Mourinho then played his ace card, sending on Robben, who nimbly set up the ubiquitous Gudjohnsen to fire home the winner near the end and save Chelsea's blushes. At the end of the match, Mourinho did his PR bit and arranged sandwiches and signed shirts for the Huddersfield team.

In the 1970s, Chelsea's greatest successes were in the Cup competitions; they were one of the greatest Cup sides of all time. The bruising 1970 FA Cup Final, with the first replay of modern times, was hailed as a classic. The team's problem was adjusting to the day-to-day, mundane grind of the league. Now the wheel had turned full circle. Chelsea had an incredible record in the Premiership, but their Cup performances distinctly unimpressive.

At that point in the season, Joe had everything to play for. There was another Cup for the taking, and Chelsea were comfortably in the driving seat in the Premiership. Another medal at least was within his grasp. Barcelona were also looming in the next round of the Champions League in what promised to be the 'Match of the Millennium'. And after all the Chelsea business was attended to, there was the impending matter of the World Cup in Germany. It was real *Roy of the Rovers* stuff, and Joe was relishing each and every battle.

First, though, a celebration was on the cards after the Huddersfield victory, and Joe chose to join John Terry for a night on the town. They went off to the swanky Embassy Club in New Bond Street, which, in the 1970s, had been a gay club where the muscle-bound waiters wore boxing shorts and whizzed around on roller skates through dry ice. Freddie Mercury had been a regular visitor.

In 2006, the Embassy attracted quite a different crowd – young, flash, wealthy types, minor celebs… and England footballers.

Terry and Joe met up with a group of West Ham players, which included Bobby Zamora and Rio Ferdinand's brother Anton – East End boys.

Also in attendance was a gaggle of Page Three girls in their regulation diamante Pucci mules and Stella McCartney dresses. Stunning blonde Lauren Pope was among them – the tabloids had run a piece on her and Terry some time back. Former hairdresser Keeley Hazell, a 19-year-old Page Three girl, was also in attendance – West End girls.

It is understood that the group partied, and then Anton, Joe and other 'friends' went to Keeley's semi in downtown Grove Park. What followed next is unclear, but at around 5.30 am on Sunday morning, Joe turned up at the local mini-cab offices wearing just his jeans. The *Sun* stated that he was so badly beaten he was almost unrecognisable. He certainly was not recognised by the early shift at the cab firm, who did not want to provide a car for him, as the Chelsea star was covered in cuts and bruises and dripping with blood. He had lost his shirt, his shoes, and he had no money or a mobile phone. Eventually, a driver agreed to take him, on the strict understanding that his father paid cash when he got home.

The press alleged that another 'guest' had taken exception to Joe and Keeley getting on well and a fight had erupted. Subsequent articles mentioned that Keeley had a soft spot for the 'diminutive' Joe and, when he had disappeared for a while, Anton Ferdinand had gone looking for him. Nothing was said about Terry's whereabouts.

Mourinho could not have been pleased with the headlines Joe had attracted, but he was in the team the following Sunday for the visit to Sunderland. It looked the most likely away victory of all time, as Sunderland were 52 points behind Chelsea in the league.

Sunderland went in front first, though, with another headed goal that emphasised the continuing weakness in the heart of their defence. Joe then set up Crespo's equaliser after 28 minutes when he headed down a cross at the far post for the former Parma striker to smash home.

In the second half, Chelsea besieged the Sunderland goal until they got the winner. They seemed to be playing in bursts, moments of intense pressure followed by periods of relative inactivity. Robben hit the winner with a fierce deflected drive. Delighted with his effort, he hurdled the TV hoardings and ran to the knot of Chelsea fans penned in the corner. It was an act of sheer joy. For that celebration, he was sent off, having earlier received a yellow card. It seemed a harsh decision. Down to ten men, Chelsea dug in and held out for the three points.

Gianluca Vialli theorised at the time that Chelsea were all set to retain their Premiership title not just because they were the best side, but because they had a mentality that not only earns points but also destroys rivals. Their rivals feel beaten from the beginning of the match and, instead of playing in their usual manner, they would change the pattern of their play to find a way to beat Chelsea. Mourinho had created this mentality.

In Sun Tzu's *The Art of War*, a major theme is that every battle is won before it is fought. The Sunderland game is proof of this. Chelsea did not play well – Sunderland even took the lead – but even when Chelsea went down to ten men, they were unable to avoid defeat.

Charlton, their Carling Cup conquerors, visited the Bridge next and came away with another good result – a 1-1 draw. It was a poor lunchtime match played on a cold Sunday. Joe was in the side with Robben suspended following the 'illegal' celebration at Sunderland. Gudjohnsen put Chelsea ahead after 18 minutes after the Charlton keeper Thomas Myhre failed to hold Crespo's header. Joe provided the only other moment of interest in the first half when he deftly chipped a cross into the box with the outside of his foot. Pelé was watching the match as Chelsea's guest and that piece of skill must have caught his eye. After the match he made the memorable quote about him: 'Joe Cole is a very good player. He has the skills of a Brazilian but he needs to learn when to show the skills and when to play the simple game.'

Marcus Bent ruined Chelsea's 100 per cent home record in the Premiership when he equalised on the hour. As at Sunderland, the Chelsea defence was caught out by a lobbed pass. Terry could only watch as Bent back-headed the ball over the stranded Cech. Mourinho brought on Shaun Wright-Phillips for Duff in an attempt to see off the opposition, but the slump in the form of Wright-Phillips continued, with the pacy winger making little impact. Charlton stood firm, and Carvalho was sent off in the closing minutes for a second bookable offence.

The day before Chelsea met Everton in the Cup, the champions of the Premiership reported a loss of £140 million, the highest ever recorded by a football club. A figure of £440 million was quoted as being the investment by Abramovich so far in the club. The annual turnover was reported at £147 million, with transfer fees of £57.5 million. The loss beat Chelsea's own record of £87.8 million set the previous year. The figure was almost treble the worst loss recorded by any other club – a £49.5 million deficit in 2003 by Leeds United.

FOOTBALLER'S COMING HOME

In 2003–4, Peter Kenyon had launched a five-year plan to get Chelsea to break even. The clock was ticking.

The figures included some interesting write-offs. The termination of the kit deal with Umbro to take on a more lucrative one with Adidas cost £25.5 million. There were also the losses relating to Veron and Mutu. Adrian had a figure of £13.8 million against his name, while Veron's was a mere £9 million.

The wage bill for the previous season was a mind-boggling £108.9 million. And throughout all this, Kenyon was trying to tie Joe Cole to a new contract. A figure of £60k a week had been mentioned. Ballack's salary was considerably higher than this when he joined Abramovich's globetrotters a few months later. Kenyon's own salary was reportedly £1.75 million, which made him the highest-paid executive in the game.

Kenyon said in the *Evening Standard*, 'Everyone is different but we are very confident that those contracts we want to extend will be what we want. Joe loves playing for Chelsea and we love him playing for us.' Joe was being very shrewd by putting his contract on hold, if he had a good World Cup his value would soar even more. The signing of Ballack was having repercussions on the wage structure which would push the ante up.

What was obvious to everyone was that the whole enterprise depended on one individual – Roman Abramovich. So far, the Russian billionaire had put his money where his mouth was, and he'd helped to create one of the strongest teams ever assembled. Now, more than ever, Chelsea needed his millions to keep that momentum up, and to take them on to even greater glory.

For the second time in a couple of months, Chelsea came away from Goodison with a draw. The plot was the same, too – Everton scoring first and Lampard equalising. On this occasion, though, Chelsea failed to sell out their ticket allocation for the tie.

Carlo Cudicini, Chelsea's FA Cup keeper, could not keep out James McFadden's first-half goal. Del Horno was blamed for the goal with his failure to cut out Valente's cross. Joe had a quiet game; he was always prepared to demonstrate some increasingly fancy footwork, but he found it hard to create anything, having only one flicked header that went wide.

Chelsea completely dominated the second half but it looked as though they might be slipping out of the only competition that Mourinho was yet to win. In an attempt to save the game, he brought Carlton Cole and Duff on to play with five up front.

Lampard, who was also having a quiet game by his standards, equalised after 73 minutes, racing into the box to hit a fine shot across Nigel Martyn. The former England keeper had defied Chelsea with a string of excellent saves, which were all the more impressive given that Martyn was approaching 40 years old.

Immediately afterwards, Joe was replaced by Huth as Chelsea closed down Everton's options, and forced a replay. With the first leg of the Barcelona game less than three weeks away, a Cup replay was the last thing the Chelsea squad needed, although they were still the bookies' favourites to win the Cup at 13-8.

On the following Wednesday, Chelsea travelled to Villa Park for another Premiership match. Drogba was in Egypt playing and starring in the African Nations Cup, while Michael Essien was still recovering from the injury sustained at Upton Park. Joe set up Chelsea's goal in their third consecutive 1-1 draw. The goal came after 14 minutes when Gallas broke clear on the left and crossed. Joe chested down the ball for Robben to swivel and shoot past Tommy Sorensen. The Dutch winger should have returned the compliment on the half-hour when a great pass from Gudjohnsen put him beyond a static Villa back four. Joe was completely unmarked and in a better position, but Robben opted to shoot and Sorensen saved. An embarrassed Robben avoided Joe's glare as he trotted back upfield. Terry had a shaky match and clearly handled Gareth Barry's shot before the break after the ex-England player deceived him with a neat turn.

Joe was having a real battle with the defender J Lloyd Samuel as Villa refused to crumble under the Blues' initial onslaught. Joe was also struggling a bit with his footing – his excellent balance and an ability almost to defy gravity seemed to have deserted him that night, with his studs giving him little purchase on the greasy surface.

Twenty minutes from time, Duff replaced Joe and, shortly afterwards, the Irishman missed a great chance to seal the game. The three points Chelsea would normally have wrapped up turned into just one when Villa boss O'Leary took a Mourinho-type gamble and pitched on strikers Juan Pablo Angel and Luke Moore with 15 minutes to go. Within two minutes, Moore equalised from close range. Moore was making a name for himself; he had been the first player to breach the citadel of Chelsea's defence earlier in the season. On the following Saturday, he notched a hat-trick against Middlesbrough. Delaney then surged past a lumbering Terry on the right and Glen Johnson missed the low cross.

Manchester United and Liverpool both drew that night as well, so Chelsea's convincing lead remained intact, but the media were beginning to raise doubts over the Champions recent run of form, and their staying power.

Liverpool visited the Bridge on the following Sunday. It was the 9th time that the two giants had collided in 15 months. Benítez's side had yet to beat Chelsea in the Premiership and the Blues completed their second successive double over them with a 2-0 victory.

Another huge build-up by the media had caused major interest in the game. Chelsea's slump of three draws, and the return of the prodigal son Fowler, all added to the mix. Fowler, though, did not even make the bench; he was still in Liverpool trying to regain maximum fitness as he fought to rebuild his career. Almost as a warning to Joe Cole, Fowler's precocious talent was undervalued at Liverpool during Houllier's reign, and his subsequent transfers to Leeds and then Manchester City only served to dampen his flair. Only time will tell if he can regain his form and consistency in front of goal during this latest spell at his home club.

As usual, the game against the European Champions did not disappoint on any level. Liverpool dominated the first half-hour as Chelsea struggled to get a grip in midfield. Peter Couch unsettled the Chelsea defence but, without an in-form Fowler, they could not capitalise on their period of domination. Joe then won a corner in the 34th minute with a strong run; Lampard took it, and Terry headed it on to Gallas, who scored emphatically.

Liverpool had that incredible run of never losing when Ian Rush scored. Chelsea, similarly, had never lost when Gallas had scored. Once again, Liverpool had conceded a crucial goal from a set-piece. John Arne Riise was at fault, ball watching, when he should have been marking Gallas.

Arjen Robben had denied Joe a goal at Villa Park a few nights before when he selfishly chose to shoot when Joe had been better placed. That afternoon, minutes after Gallas's goal, Joe returned the compliment, as he dispossessed Stephen Warnock, dropped his shoulders and burst through to smash a shot into the side netting. Robben was virtually alongside him in the inside channel screaming for Joe to roll the pass sideways for an easy tap-in. Mourinho cursed and waved his arms wildly, obviously annoyed at what he had seen.

It wasn't to be Robben's day as it turned out. Hernan Crespo scored a sweet second goal, but Robben stole the headlines with some seriously suspect play-acting. Nine minutes from the end, the Liverpool goalkeeper, Jose Reina, was sent off after a clash with the Dutchman. The keeper had fouled Gudjohnsen outside the box, and Robben joined the ensuing mêlèe. Reina placed a hand on Robben's jaw, at which he crashed to the turf holding his throat. Reina was automatically banned for the next three games.

An angry Rafael Benítez told the press conference he was on his way to see Robben in hospital. Robben was heavily criticised in the press for his antics, and several past incidents in Holland were dredged up.

Joe had been substituted by Duff, but the winger hobbled off after less than five minutes with a muscle injury. Joe told the *Guardian* afterwards that the match had been a hard-fought affair, and that 'It was like a war at times.'

The pitch had also proved a huge talking point. Barça scouts at the Liverpool match had been horrified at the state of it, branding it a 'potato patch'. It was highly significant that the pitch at the Nou Camp would be relaid before the return match in March. In the replay against Everton, the ball was virtually uncontrollable on some areas of the pitch. It did not stop Chelsea from steam-rollering Everton 4-1, though, to set up a home tie with Colchester United in the 5th round.

Joe was consigned to the bench for the Everton replay, with Shaun Wright-Phillips restored to the starting line-up. Robben gave Chelsea the lead, taking advantage of a chance set up by a superb long ball from Gudjohnsen and Crespo's deft knock-down. Robben had been pilloried in the press for the Reina fracas, and it was heartening to see him earning respect for his skill on the ball, rather than approbation for his antics off it.

Wright-Phillips started brightly, too, and Chelsea were awarded a penalty when he was fouled in the box. It was duly converted by Lampard for the second goal. The quintessential predator Crespo headed the third before half-time and it ceased to be a contest.

David Moyes's well-drilled side pulled a goal back in the second half from the spot. Joe was brought on for the last half-hour and treated the fans to a couple of neat touches, but there was little he could offer on the dreadful pitch.

At the death, Terry restored the three-goal margin with a

shot that threatened to decapitate the stand-in Everton keeper. Chelsea seemed to have recovered their form, and the fans walked into the night dreaming of a Wembley final.

Earlier in the day, Mourinho had been prepared to name the day that he believed Chelsea would clinch their second successive Premiership title. When asked previously when he thought the title would be won, the Portuguese coach demurred, having been worried about the risk of complacency, and particularly the threat to the form of highly skilful players like Joe. The previous season, he had deliberately and accurately named the day to instil confidence in his team. Now, he assured the media, judgement day would be 9th April, when the Blues were home to West Ham.

11

Three Lions on His Chest

'With Joe Cole, technique is definitely one of his strengths.'
Sven-Goran Eriksson

IF YOU WERE asked to name some of the mavericks of English football over the last 50 years, you'd probably come up with players like Matthew Le Tissier, Peter Osgood, Stan Bowles, Tony Currie, Frank Worthington, Alan Hudson, Ray Wilkins, Paul Gascoigne, Paul Merson, Charlie George, Glenn Hoddle… and any number of others. They all also won caps for England as full internationals. In the 1970s, you could also argue that those caps were a great deal more difficult to come by than those dished out by Eriksson, who seemed willing to try out every conceivable combination and would-be superstar throughout his tenure as England boss.

Joe Cole belongs to that list of great entertainers, being one of a handful of English players in the Premiership who might have held his own alongside them. But nothing could be taken for granted, especially where Eriksson is concerned and, for a long time, it looked like Joe was going to end up like the 21st-century version of Charlie George, a child prodigy and wonderful talent, but whose career remained unfulfilled. Despite George's undoubted skill, he won only one cap for England. One joke doing the rounds at Upton Park was: What will Joe do when he wins the World Cup? Turn off his Playstation and go to bed.

Hoddle gave Joe a break by giving him his first taste of the big time when he invited him along to the England base camp at Le Baule in Western Brittany as a guest. This was to watch the preparations for the 1998 World Cup. The World Cup squad included Rio Ferdinand, Graham Le Saux, Paul Ince and captain Tony Adams. Joe was already being compared to Paul Gascoigne, the former golden boy of English football and a surprise omission from the squad. The England team were knocked out of the competition on penalties against Argentina after the infamous sending off of David Beckham. Owen had put England ahead with his wonder strike, but Argentina equalised when Veron engineered a goal for Zenetti.

Joe was 16 at the time and already a schoolboy international of rich promise. Another reason for his inclusion in the set-up at that time was the influence of Glenn Roeder, who was on the England coaching staff. Roeder had a great knowledge of Joe's full range of skills because of the close association he had with West Ham.

Hoddle must have admired Joe's style, not least because he appreciated the maverick quality and blend of skill and professionalism that he so admired in one of his favourite players, Alan Hudson. When Hudson left Chelsea in 1974, he rather surprisingly opted to join the unfashionable Stoke City side managed by Tony Waddington. Waddington was a great admirer of Hudson's talent and restructured the Potteries side to accommodate him. Hudson was the hub of the side and it worked for a long time. With Hudson, Stoke may well have challenged for major honours had the resources been available to have strengthened the side. It is unthinkable now that a side could have been wholly geared around one individual, no matter how talented.

Hoddle made his Tottenham debut away to Stoke in the old First Division and Hudson was playing in the famous red-and-white stripes. The youngster had a fine match and scored the winner with a great volley, not unlike Lampard's blockbusters today. As he left the field, Hudson made a special point of congratulating the budding superstar on his fine performance. Hoddle never forgot that little act of kindness shown to him that day. Throughout his career, Hoddle cited Hudson as the prime example of a brilliant player who was not fully supported by the system. When critics queried Hoddle's scant rewards in terms of caps, he would be at pains to remind them that Hudson only played for his country twice. Perhaps in Joe, he was repaying the debt, recognising that here was a talent to be nurtured, and valued.

When Hoddle left the England job, he was replaced by another legend, Kevin Keegan. Keegan was no tactical coach, by his own admission, and England just managed to scrape into Euro 2000. Joe was on the periphery of the squad that failed to progress out of the group.

Sven-Goran Eriksson was also a big Joe Cole fan. In

October 2000, he agreed a five-year contract to become the first foreign manager of the English national team, with effect from 2001. Eriksson wanted to keep it simple and set up the team to play in his beloved 4-4-2 formation. The first weekend of his tenure, the former Lazio coach took a trip down to Upton Park. The date was Saturday 13th January 2001, and a crowd of 26,014 had turned up to watch 11th-placed West Ham take on Sunderland. The Swede had heard all the hype about the boy wonder Joe Cole, and wanted to see for himself what the fuss was about.

Eriksson stayed until well into the second half, by which time he had seen enough. The Hammers lost 2-0, but already Joe looked a better prospect then Lampard, who had been booed and ridiculed throughout the match by his own fans. Joe's technique was superior and he seemed to react to situations better. Lampard seemed cumbersome and one-dimensional in comparison.

Six weeks later, Joe and Lampard were called up into the squad for the friendly match against Spain to be played at Villa Park. Bad luck struck as Joe was injured in training and was forced to withdraw. Eriksson still had him very much in his plans, though, and his senior debut arrived two months later when he came on as a sub against Mexico in a 4-0 victory at Pride Park on 25 May 2001.

Paul Scholes gave England an early lead, and further goals from Robbie Fowler and a stunning free kick from Beckham meant that England were very much in the driving seat. Joe came on at half-time for Paul Scholes, and he almost got his England career off to a sensational start when, within seconds of the restart, he blasted in a powerful shot that was splendidly turned away by the Mexico keeper Sanchez. A player at the opposite end of his England career, Teddy Sheringham, wrapped things up with the fourth goal.

All in all, Joe had a spirited debut and impressed with his footwork and ability to run past defenders. Michael Carrick, Joe's pal from the Chadwell Heath days, also won his first cap that night. It must have been a marvellous night for Joe's adoptive father George to witness his son's debut for his country. It was the zenith of his career so far. When Joe was adopted, a glittering future as a world class footballer must have seemed nothing short of a ridiculous fantasy.

The next time Joe pulled on a shirt with the three lions on the front, it was for a friendly against Holland in the impressive Amsterdam Arena in February 2002. Wayne Bridge won his first cap that night, and it was the first time that England played in a new 4-3-3 system under the Swede.

The Dutch side was packed with mouthwatering talent – Van Bronckhorst, the de Boer brothers, Overmars, Kluivert, van Nistelrooy, Melchiot, Davids and Hasselbaink. It was a knock-down from van Nistelrooy that set Kluivert up for Holland's 25th-minute goal, the ball going in on off Sol Campbell. On the hour, Vassell equalised for England when he thundered home a wonderful strike from Beckham's corner. Joe came on with Lampard for the last 13 minutes and found time to impress with a surging run redolent of Gazza in his pomp.

Then Joe featured against Italy in a match which was to have a huge influence on his career. The match was played at Elland Road on 27th March. The first half was a dreadful bore with neither side able to create anything. Joe was one of Eriksson's 11 second-half substitutes and, with the score still at 0-0, Joe managed to gain possession from Alessandro Nesta, one of the best centre-backs in the world, now plying his trade at AC Milan. Joe put a lovely ball through for Robbie Fowler to open the scoring for England.

It was a great moment for Joe, but greatness can turn to catastrophe in a heartbeat in football, as Stephen Gerrard knows only too well. During the 2005 Carling Cup Final, when his headed own-goal allowed Chelsea back into the game and, ultimately, to steal the trophy. Having worked so hard for the England cause, Joe dwelled too long on the ball and lost possession inside his own penalty area. He could only watch helplessly as Vincenzo Montella scored. The same player then won the match for Italy from the penalty spot with the last kick of the game.

The press were quick to lay the blame for England's demise on that incident, and suggested that it summed up Joe's career. Eriksson was not quite as scathing, and told the press he hoped Joe would learn from the experience. Joe recalled the incident in an interview: 'I was playing very well. Then I lost the ball on the halfway line and the fella's gone and dribbled past two defenders and put it in the top corner of the net and the next day in the papers everyone was caning me. Italy went on and scored another goal and another player – I'm not saying who he is – lost the ball in exactly the same position and nothing was said. So people do look for it with our type of players. It's just one of them things.'

Joe had an early chance to redeem himself when he was given

a place in the squad for the game against Paraguay to be played at Anfield. Joe, as he had done so often in his rollercoaster career, seized his chance. Gerrard was the dominant figure in the first half and set up Owen for an early goal. Eriksson made six changes at the break, Joe being one of them. Within two minutes he and Fowler created a chance for Danny Murphy to score in off Carlos Gamarra. Murphy linked very well with Joe that night, who forced himself into the World Cup reckoning with a scintillating display of hard running and clever trickery that stupefied the Paraguayan defenders. Once again, comparisons were made with Paul Gascoigne, and Joe was tipped as the surprise package of the competition.

Four years on from his first taste of World Cup competition in 2002, Joe was a fully-fledged and realistic option for Germany 2006. He had made spectacular progress and was one of the most improved players of his generation, playing for potentially the most powerful club in the world in terms of financial backing and trophy potential. And what is more, the England squad prior to the 2006 World Cup included a trio of London-born Chelsea players on whom Eriksson would place a great deal of importance.

In contrast, when Joe left to play in the World Cup in Japan and Korea in 2002, he had a total of less than half an England game on the clock, and there were no other representatives from the blue half of London.

The England party arrived at Awaji Island in central Japan on 25th May after the players and their families had spent a week in Dubai. They also found time to play a friendly in Korea, where they stayed at the luxury Jumeirah Beach Club.

Joe was one of eight subs used in the preparatory friendly against South Korea, in which Owen scored England's goal in a 1-1 draw.

Joe made his full England debut against Cameroon in Kobe in the final friendly before the hostilities commenced. He started the game on the right of midfield. The Barça striker Samuel Eto'o tapped the African Champions ahead after a mistake by Martyn. Vassell, in the best form of his life, levelled for his country but Geremi restored Cameroon's advantage. Geremi was subsequently signed by Chelsea in the initial Abramovich spending spree in the summer of 2003. Robbie Fowler scored for England in injury time to salvage a draw.

England were unimpressive in either of their friendlies but, with so much at stake, it was hardly surprising. Nobody wanted to get injured at this stage. Gerrard was already missing the entire competition through injury, and Beckham was getting through the tournament less than 100 per cent fit.

The time had finally arrived for the opening match against Sweden, to be played in Saitama. It was like a home game for England as the Japanese population was well versed in the English Premier League and, besides Japan, would happily cheer England on to World Cup glory. The Beckham phenomenon was also at its height.

Earlier in the year, Eriksson had announced that England would find it hard to play their normal game because of the heat and humidity, and he was proved absolutely right. The kick-off Japanese time was 6.30 pm, but even then it was 84°F with humidity of 40 per cent.

Alan Smith, the ex-Arsenal striker, was a columnist in the

Active in the Champions League, Joe has seen his share of success as well as failure. A passionate player, here he celebrates with fellow ex-Hammer Frank Lampard as Chelsea outclass Real Betis, but lose in the return leg, and prepares to bring the ball under control and take the game to van Bronckhorst of Barcelona.

© Cleva Media

Above: Joe's boss and mentor at Chelsea, Jose Mourinho, who left the club unexpectedly in September 2007. He has since been appointed manager of Italian giants Inter Milan. © *Cleva Media*

Below: Joe skilfully slots home the only goal of the match to keep England's 2006 World Cup qualifying hopes on track by beating Wales in Cardiff. © *PA Photos*

Above: Joe stakes a further claim to a regular England starting spot with a good performance against Poland in their World Cup qualifier victory in October 2005.   *© Cleva Media*

Below: And again, Joe proves his strength by riding the tackle of Maximilian Rodriguez as England beat Argentina 3-2, increasing his profile in front of England fans.   *© Cleva Media*

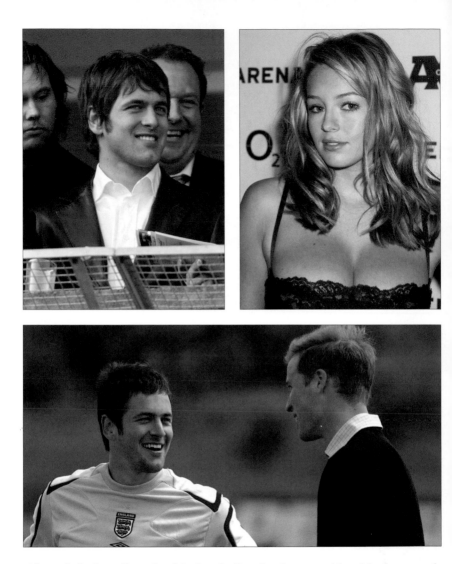

Above left: As a Premiership footballer, Joe has considerable fame and fortune. Here he spends some time and money at the Cheltenham Races.

© *Cleva Media*

Above right: Amid press speculation, Joe was linked with glamour model Keeley Hazell.

© *Rex Features*

Below: The Prince of Stamford Bridge meets the future Prince of Wales during training prior to the 2006 World Cup. William is President of the FA.

© *PA Photos*

Joe's long-term fixture in his love life is fitness trainer Carly Zucker. The couple met back in 2002 and announced their engagement five years later. Carly's profile has skyrocketed after her appearance on *I'm a Celebrity*…in 2008.

Perhaps the pinnacle of his England career to date, Joe scored one of
the goals of the World Cup with a fine looping volley which dipped
into the top-right corner of the Swedish goal. For this moment of
supreme skill and composure, he received widespread acclaim and the
Man of the Match award.   © Cleva Media

In August 2008 Joe thrilled the fans at Wembley when he scored a last gasp equaliser to earn England a 2-2 draw against the Czech Republic.

© *Getty Images*

After the World Cup, Joe suffered an injury to his right leg while on pre-season tour in the US which would keep him out of the start of the 2006-7 season. But Chelsea and England's talented star continues to shine brightly – firmly cemented as a domestic and international talent, Joe is sure to stay at the forefront of the game for years to come. *© Cleva Media*

Guardian at the time and wrote of Joe, 'Is he ever going to really fit the bill for his country on that troublesome left side?'

Joe was on the bench for the game, which England started well with a Sol Campbell header from a Beckham corner. Beckham was clearly unfit, having been rushed back from a broken metatarsal injury. In the first half, England quickly overplayed their hand. Sweden grabbed the initiative in the second half and deservedly equalised through Alexandersson after a slip by Danny Mills. Beckham was substituted for Dyer, and then Joe came on for Vassell after 73 minutes. He was detailed to counter the threat of Freddie Ljungberg, who had been a prolific scorer for club and country at that time. It was the high spot of Joe's career up 'til then, and was a welcome sight for fans of sheer artistry and guile. The game fizzled out, with Sweden finishing the far stronger of the sides. Only Ferdinand kept them in the game, marshalling the defence as if his life depended on it.

The England team were deflated by their failure to open the tournament with a win, but Eriksson tried to raise morale by giving them a day off. Some went shopping, some played golf. Later, they assembled for a meal in the Hard Rock Café, and the team was mobbed by screaming Japanese girls who treated the footballers like pop stars. David Beckham was the primary object of attention, but Joe was given his first taste of 'England mania' Japanese style.

That was the end of Joe's involvement in the 2002 World Cup campaign. The circus moved on to Sapporo, where England beat Argentina, thanks to a Beckham penalty in one of the most memorable games of recent years. The betting shops were offering 10-1 on him scoring the first, or four times that amount if you could couple it with a 1-0 scoreline. It was Ferdinand's best game of the World Cup, and perhaps his best ever. The ex-Hammer threw himself at everything, and looked every inch a £30 million player. The Premiership experience had improved his game and restrained his inclination to error. In the last quarter-of-an-hour Argentina were desperate to break through the England defence, but Joe's ex-team-mate kept them at bay.

In the next game, England played Nigeria; they only now needed a point to qualify out of the 'Group of Death'. It was a terrible game. England ground out the point with a turgid display against a side they should have annihilated. Joe would have had ample opportunity to showcase his talents, but it was Ashley Cole who almost achieved glory status when his cross skimmed along the crossbar.

Back home, the media and the fans began to perpetuate the myth that this England team could win the World Cup. Due to the time difference, the games were shown early in the morning. The pubs were full at 7.30 am as people flocked to see the tournament being played out on the other side of the world, chewing bacon rolls as they supped lager. If ten years previously you had ventured the opinion that virtually the whole country would be getting up at 6.00 am to go down to the pub to watch a football match taking place in Japan, most would have said you were nuts.

Denmark were next on the agenda in the first knock-out stage of the tournament, and Ferdinand scored in the opening moments. The Danish keeper Thomas Sorensen, who had been the main reason for them getting that far, made a mess of the save and the ball trickled over the line. It was a soft goal but it settled the English nerves. Owen scored the second, finally getting off the mark, and Emile Heskey made it 3-0 just on the break.

The fans and the media were always critical of Heskey – much like the treatment Peter Couch receives today – but, like Drogba, he worked extremely hard for the team, and Owen always looked a better player when partnered with him. The fans started to celebrate by doing a massive conga in the main stand.

The second half was an anti-climax. Eriksson ordered the shop to be shut up and England cruised it. At times, Denmark looked a worse side than Nigeria, their best player being the mercurial Chelsea winger Jesper Gronkjaer, who was to change the whole future of his London team with a vital goal in the next 12 months. Gronkjaer outwitted Danny Mills several times, but he received no service.

England moved on to a historic clash with Brazil in the quarter-finals. It would have been interesting to speculate what the score would have been if Joe had been brought on in the second half to weave his magic. He would love to have played against Brazil, and some believed that Eriksson made a mistake in not including him. Of all the squad, Joe had perhaps been the most inspired by the Brazilian style, that element of playing the game for the sheer fun of it. Football played by pure inspiration and magic. It was said that in his early days on the West Ham training ground in Chadwell Heath, he would try to recreate the tricks he had picked up through watching Rivaldo humiliating people. When he had the ball at his feet in that sort of mood, he was almost impossible to defend against.

Pelé's comment that Joe Cole had the skills of a Brazilian was quickly taken up by the media. Joe's mates texted him about the quote and Joe was very pleased. He never keeps any memorabila in his own Esher home because it reminds him of the constant pressure he lives under. The home he shares with his beautiful girlfriend Carly Zucker is a haven where he can switch off from football. Instead his mother Susan was the curator of the Cole legend and its relics and artefacts. Modest Joe was so thrilled that Pelé had even heard of him though he decided to frame the quote.

England's most significant game since the 1966 World Cup Final was played in the Shizuoka Stadium, a state-of-the-art masterpiece. It made Stamford Bridge look like a non-league ground in comparison. Owen put England ahead after a mistake by Brazilian defender Lucio. Ronaldinho then set up the equaliser with a superb step-over to deceive Ashley Cole, followed by a mesmerising dribble.

Brazil then won the game when Ronaldinho's long-range effort sailed over Seaman's head and into the net. At the time, Seaman was slaughtered in the press for his 'error', but having been made more aware of the sheer brilliance of Ronaldinho since that goal, he has proved that anything is possible in his magical world. The goals he conjured up for Barça at Stamford Bridge in the Champions League were proof of that.

Le Saux, arguably the best left-back in the Premiership, never even made the squad and the left side of the team was still problematic. Shortly afterwards, Ronaldinho was sent off for a challenge on Danny Mills. England had 33 minutes to pull the game around, but failed even to trouble the Brazil keeper once. The situation cried out for Joe, the one England player with the trickery to play the Brazilians at their own game. Joe's skills were best suited to exploit England's numerical advantage. When Mourinho raged at Joe after the Liverpool game in October 2004, he was terrified that any irresponsibility by him would cost them dear. 1-2 down against Brazil, there was little to lose by risking Joe. It must have been a huge disappointment being sidelined when he must have felt that he had so much to offer, particularly when the convalescent Kieron Dyer was sent on for Sinclair. England flew back the next day.

There were sections of the press that thought Eriksson should have been sacked after the World Cup exit to Brazil. There was no disgrace losing to arguably the greatest team in the world, but the manner of their defeat and the absence of any real attacking ideas, or a Plan B, did not bode well for the upcoming Euro 2004. Joe wondered where his international future lay. Given less than 20 minutes to show what he could do, he had vindicated his selection with his eagerness and application. A huge advantage was that he could raid forward. However, at that time, Joe was always in danger of becoming a bit-part player when he could so easily have been the star of the show. The trouble with Joe's game at that time was that there was no end product. As always, he responded positively and set about modifying his game and improving his precision in the last third of the field.

Eriksson, even then, knew the future lay with audacious youngsters like Joe, who would become central to his plans for the next World Cup.

Joe's next England game after the Japan experience was a 1-1 home game with Portugal at Villa Park. It was literally a game of two halves as Eriksson made umpteen changes throughout the match. Alan Smith (not the ex-Arsenal player) scored England's goal and Joe came on after 63 minutes.

Then, in May 2003, just after West Ham had been relegated, England flew to Durban to play a friendly against South Africa, to be tied in with the country's launch bid for the 2010 World Cup. The match was played in a carnival atmosphere in front of a crowd of 48,000, and it was Leeds icon and South African captain Lucas Radebe's last match. Nelson Mandela was in attendance that day, and the team got to meet him in person during the visit.

Gareth Southgate headed England ahead inside the first 30 seconds to give them a flying start. Benni McCarthy (who scored the winner against Chelsea for Porto) levelled from the spot after Danny Mills had handled in the box. Heskey hit the winner after Lampard's shot had been blocked. Joe came on after 75 minutes, together with Gareth Barry, who was highly fancied as a long-term prospect.

After their return from South Africa, England had another friendly arranged against Serbia & Montenegro at the Walker Stadium in Leicester. Joe scored his first goal for England, which turned out to be the winner in a 2-1 victory. Terry made his full début against the team ranked 22nd in the world.

Once again, Joe grabbed his chance at a vital moment,

having recently been demoted to the Under-21 squad, whose boss, Peter Taylor, had been keen to give Joe some valuable experience in the side. Joe came on for Lampard and thoroughly enjoyed himself in the last half-hour. Joe was soon entertaining the crowd with his skill on the ball and made some strong runs. A total of 21 changes were made by Eriksson during the match, which disrupted the flow of the game and confused everyone present.

Gerrard had given England the lead, but Jestrovic equalised just on half-time. Eight minutes from time, Joe curled in a perfectly struck free kick to send the fans home happy.

At the end of August, England met Croatia at Portman Road in a friendly. The Russian Revolution had just taken place and Joe was on his way to Stamford Bridge. He linked up very well with Lampard that night. England won 3-1 with Lampard scoring the third, after Beckham and Owen had put England ahead. Joe had replaced Scholes on the hour. Already, Eriksson had been pictured with Abramovich and rumours were spreading that he would be joining Chelsea.

Liechtenstein played England at Old Trafford in another Euro 2004 qualifier in August, in which England cruised to a 2-0 victory. Joe replaced Wayne Rooney (who had scored the second goal) after 69 minutes. Owen scored the first.

Ranieri, now Joe's new manager, was also around this time asking Joe to re-apply his game from an attacking viewpoint, at which Joe was apparently delighted.

Joe's last England game in that watershed year of 2003 was against Denmark again, this time at Old Trafford. The Danes gained revenge for their World Cup defeat with a 3-2 victory in a tremendous match. The evening was a great success for Joe because it was the first time that he actually started an England International. A few months earlier, Joe had told the *Daily Telegraph*, 'I would love to start for England. You miss that when you come off the bench because all the ceremony at the start of a match is a big thing. The national anthem and shaking hands. It's a proud moment for me and all my family.'

Rooney, fired up even more than usual, smashed home a goal after just five minutes. Slack marking by Gary Neville on the left allowed the classy Denmark striker Jorgensen to equalise three minutes later. Straight from the kick-off, Rooney sent Joe scurrying away to score with his left foot. England were back in front with barely ten minutes on the clock. Jorgensen levelled it up when he scored from the spot after a rash challenge on him by Matthew Upson.

Joe went off after 76 minutes and was replaced by Danny Murphy. The edge was slightly taken off Joe's excellent evening when former Newcastle striker Jon Dahl Tomasson grabbed a late winner for Denmark.

In the era of players like Johnny Haynes, England played far fewer Internationals. There were the home championships, World Cup and friendly fixtures against overseas opposition, but today we have the European Championship and the World Cup, as well as a whole series of fixtures against countries from all over the world. It is a lot easier to win a cap today than it was a few decades ago. In the latter stages of 2003 and into 2004, Joe rattled up a collection of appearances in fairly meaningless friendlies, as Eriksson prepared for the 2004 European Championships in Portugal.

In all, Joe played a part in the matches against Portugal, Sweden, Japan and Iceland, but he never made the team for the actual finals.

For a brief while, it looked like his exclusion might derail his hitherto unstoppable rise. He was still on the fringe of Eriksson's team, but was finding it hard to shrug off the 'solid substitute' tag that had dogged his career over the last few years. His domestic situation may well have been a factor, as he had failed to establish a regular place in the new-look Chelsea side under Ranieri – hardly surprising, given the huge roster of world-class stars, and the Tinkerman approach.

England disappointed in Euro 2004, a last-minute loss to France in the group stage showing all too clearly their defensive frailties. England were favoured to do well but were knocked out, once again, on penalties to Portugal, the hosts. The eventual winners were the complete outsiders, Greece, a workmanlike side with a minimum amount of skill, and no flair, although they were highly organised and brilliantly motivated. Football was changing; the scientific, 'leave nothing to chance' era had arrived.

The main problem with England in Portugal was that their midfield seemed only to be able to operate at the same relentless tempo, and lacked any outlet down the flanks. Joe could have provided that.

Stung by his failure to go to the European Championships, Joe was determined to make it to Germany for the World Cup in 2006. He bloomed once more in 2004/05 as he won major honours with Chelsea and cemented a place in the club's first-team line-up.

Alan Smith, writing in the *Telegraph*, said of Joe, 'How would Cole fare in terms of defensive resilience in a formation requiring a bit more responsibility than at the front of Chelsea's 4-3-3?'

England had to qualify for the tournament, though, and Joe was called up for the squad to play the qualifying game against Azerbaijan in the Tofig Bakhramov stadium in Baku. Michael Owen headed the only goal of the game and Joe came on for Rooney towards the end.

Northern Ireland were next to play in the qualifiers at Old Trafford. Joe had his best game so far for England and dominated the match as England won 4-0. The Chelsea star's contribution to the game was massive. Joe was linking up with Rooney to form a spearhead that had the crowd and the press singing their praises. In the third minute, the two greatest prodigies of their generation combined to set up a chance for Joe that just went wide. Joe put England ahead two minutes into the second half with a fine opportunist goal. Then Joe set up the move from which Rooney forced an own goal. Owen also missed a sitter after a great run and pass by Joe. After the match, Eriksson thanked Mourinho for the improvement in Joe Cole.

Lawrie Sanchez, the losing manager that day, spoke highly of Joe to the *Guardian* after the match: 'Joe Cole's in the same category as Wayne Rooney. He's got everything he needs to be a World Class player. He's with a club that's doing well and he's playing for a manager who apparently won't stand for any nonsense. And I'd guess that Mourinho's told him in no uncertain terms what's expected from him.'

THREE LIONS ON HIS CHEST

Then Joe played the full 90 in the return match against Azerbaijan at St James's Park. England won by a comfortable score of 2-0 with goals from Beckham and Gerrard. Joe celebrated victory with the squad by watching the singer Anastacia in concert. Music is a great outlet for him. At this time he was even trying to grow his hair like one of the Gallagher brothers.

England went on a short American tour in May 2005, a few weeks after Chelsea had won the Premiership. Joe played for a hour against the USA at Soldier Field in Chicago in a 2-1 win. Manchester United midfielder Kevin Richardson, one of the country's natural left-footers, scored both goals. Joe laid on the second goal for him with a great pass from the edge of the box.

England then visited the Giants Stadium in New Jersey a few days later to take on Colombia. England won 3-2 with Owen scoring his second hat-trick for England. Joe played until four minutes from time and set up Owen's second goal with an incisive through ball.

In August 2005, England took a heavy beating 1-4 at the hands of Denmark. Eriksson was reeling at the time from heavy criticism for his alleged lack of passion for England. His personal life was also under scrutiny over the scandal caused by his affair with FA Secretary (and later Big Brother star) Faria Alam.

Joe played for the entire match against Denmark, which signalled his and Eriksson's heaviest international defeat. Joe was one of the few players left unaffected by the substitutions and formation changes.

Something had to be done to take the heat off Eriksson. Joe

repaid the confidence shown in him by the Swede when he scored the only goal of the game at the Millennium Stadium against Wales in another qualifying match. It was turning out to be a lucky ground for Joe because the previous season he had won his first major honour there, when Chelsea won the Carling Cup by overcoming Liverpool.

The goal had Chelsea written all over it as Shaun Wright-Phillips set up the chance, with the ball being deflected in off Danny Gabbidon's head. Earlier, he had missed the best chance of the game when he headed wide of an open goal. Wales were rated 83rd in the world and England should have won by a wider margin, but they were edging towards qualification.

Joe told the *Standard* that both he and Shaun Wright-Phillips needed an extended run in both the England and Chelsea sides: 'We need to play, both for ourselves and so that we can be part of two great teams – Chelsea and England.'

A few nights later, England travelled to Windsor Park to play Northern Ireland in the return qualifying game. They suffered a humiliating 1-0 defeat, losing to a 74th-minute goal from David Healy of Leeds. It was England's first defeat in Ireland for 78 years. Joe was dropped from the starting line-up to make room for Owen, becoming the first England player to be dropped after scoring a winning goal in a competitive game since Alan Smith of Arsenal in 1991. Joe was brought on, though, after 54 minutes to replace Shaun Wright-Phillips who had failed to convert several crossing opportunities. Within minutes of his arrival, Joe's twisting and turning was causing problems for the tough Irish defence, but he was not quite able to break through the back line for the rest of his time on the field.

The embarrassing defeat intensified the pressure on Eriksson. At Old Trafford, a 1-0 win over Austria relieved it slightly, but England were generally unconvincing. Lampard scored the goal from the penalty spot. Joe played for 62 minutes before being replaced by Ledley King of Tottenham, whom Eriksson was hoping would become a reliable defensive midfielder. One sour note from that match was that Beckham became the first England player to be sent off twice while playing for his country.

A 2-1 win over Poland won the group for England and a place in the World Cup Finals. Joe played for 86 minutes and had a fine game, setting up England's first goal for Owen. Again, a Chelsea combination of unlocked the Polish defence, when Lampard found Terry, who nodded down to Joe, who then fired low and hard into the box. It might have gone in, but Owen made sure by deflecting it home.

Poland hit back immediately, when Southampton winger Kamil Kosowski went past Terry and crossed at the byline for Frankowski to smash home. Wright-Phillips, who was flying that night, was inexplicably replaced by Crouch.

Lampard scored the goal that took England to Germany. Rooney found Lampard, who passed to Owen; Lampard continued his run and, when Owen returned the ball, he thundered it first time into the net. Eriksson later told the *Guardian*: 'He can be the answer if he carries on like this. He was excellent.'

Joe had one more fine game for England in 2005. In November, they played a friendly against Argentina in Geneva. Played early on a Saturday night, the TV audience was treated to a real thriller. England won 3-2 in a see-saw match that had everything. Two late goals from Owen won it for them, with Joe creating the winner with a wonderful run and cross. It was a cute as his puppy's nose. The words of Di Canio written in his book several years beforehand about Joe were very prophetic: 'He has the opportunity to become one of the top four or five players in the world. Beckham and Owen are outstanding footballers but their style is quintessentially British. There's nothing wrong with that but the Premiership has changed. English football isn't the way it was ten or twenty years ago. Today it can produce a player like Cole and he has a chance of being the symbol of the new English game.'

Based on his recent performances for England, and his current club form, Joe was a crucial part of Eriksson's plans for the finals in Germany, and looked set to show, on the biggest stage of all, just what he can do with a ball at his feet.

12
Back to the Future

'Pop stars... they crave the attention and the fame... they grow
up and they want to be entertainers and singers. But I just wanted
to be a footballer because I just loved football.'
Joe Cole, April 2006

I N THE LATE WINTER of 2005/06, a programme was
broadcast on the BBC called *Life on Mars*, in which a
modern-day cop time-travels back to the 1970s. Chelsea fans
could also be forgiven for thinking that they had slipped
through a space-time continuum, and had ended up in 1973
themselves – Leo Sayer was Number One in the charts, and
Chelsea took a thorough beating at Middlesbrough.

Boro had been known to dish out some hidings to the Blues
in the old days. A team including Peter Osgood, Clive Walker
and Ron Harris were thrashed 2-7 at their old ground
Ayresome Park, and Chelsea lost their place in the old First
Division after losing 1-2 in the play-offs to them.

This time, though, Chelsea were a pedigree outfit, and had
spent over £200 million assembling a world-beating squad. It
was the first time in 83 matches that they had lost by more

than a solitary goal, and it signalled their heaviest defeat under Mourinho's command. Chelsea had been getting away with the odd defensive lapse or midfield confusion for some time, but Middlesbrough exploited the weaknesses that had been apparent for a number of weeks.

The Middlesbrough boss, Steve McClaren, had been under severe pressure as his team struggled in the Premiership. Only a few weeks before, they had gone down 0-7 at Highbury to a rampant Arsenal side, and the fans were naturally very unsettled.

In desperation, the future England manager devised a bold game plan, to attack Chelsea through the centre, and it paid off magnificently. Terry was at fault for all three goals as Boro overwhelmed the Londoners, which was particularly embarrassing for the Blues' captain as he had been smugly telling the press in the week that they wanted to wrap up the Premiership as quickly as possible so they could concentrate on the Treble.

It was a critical time personally for Joe – he was regarded very favourably by fans and colleagues alike, and Chelsea were virtually home and dry in the Premiership. There was also still the possibility of emulating Liverpool's exploits the previous season and lifting the Champions League trophy. Joe knew that high-quality performances at the sharp end of the season would ensure his place in the England squad, and that he'd figure prominently in Eriksson's plans for the World Cup. So much rested on these last few domestic and European games, and his manager's willingness to play him on a regular basis.

In the week prior to the Middlesbrough match, Pelé had told the world that Joe Cole had the skills of a Brazilian, but on the day it was an actual Brazilian – Fabio Rochemback – who fired the home side ahead. Terry's poor clearance was snapped up by him and his low shot easily beat Petr Cech. The giant keeper had signed a new contract that week, but a faint uncertainty had crept into his game. Understandably, the young keeper found it hard to maintain the impossibly high standards of his first golden season in London.

Joe tried to get the team going, but they were unable to strike up any rhythm and it was no surprise when Stewart Downing added a second on half-time. Downing gave Geremi a torrid time all afternoon; he had been a serious contender for Joe's England place, but a bad knee injury had blighted his season. Mendieta had set up the chance for him with a clever decoy run that distracted Chelsea's back four.

Joe was subbed at half-time, to be replaced by his namesake Carlton, but there was little that he could contribute to turn things around for the Blues. Yakubu scored the third late in the game after a sweet dummy to throw off Terry's desperate challenge.

Mourinho said nothing after the game.

Around that time, controversy arose again over the state of the Stamford Bridge pitch. Barça's accusation was that Chelsea had deliberately allowed the surface to deteriorate in an attempt to disrupt the intricate passing game of the Spanish Champions. When Colchester visited the Bridge for the 5th Round FA Cup tie, the playing surface looked like a First World War battlefield. It had rained heavily all day and it did not take long for the surface to become like a quagmire all over the pitch.

For a while it looked as though one of the all-time FA Cup classic shocks was about to be witnessed as Colchester, put together by their shrewd young manager Phil Parkinson for £15,000, rocked the Champions. Chelsea showed nine changes from the defeat at Middlesbrough. Joe was on the bench along with Lampard and Crespo, three aces that Mourinho was saving for the first clash with Barcelona in three days' time. Colchester brought 6,000 fans with them and, as had been the case for Scunthorpe the previous year, the minnows scored first.

Carvalho, still apparently shell-shocked from the hammering at Boro, scored an own goal to give Colchester a shock lead. Glen Johnson started the match at left-back where he seemed even more uncomfortable than he had done on the right. Richard Garcia, the Colchester forward, darted behind Johnson and fired over a low cross. Robert Huth, even less mobile in the mud, failed to clear and the ball and it cannoned in off Carvalho.

Garcia was an old pal of Joe's, having played in the fabled 1999 West Ham Youth side that had butchered Coventry. Garcia had had a handful of first-team games for West Ham before drifting out of the big time.

Colchester led for nearly ten glorious minutes. Mourinho barely concealed his disgust at his team's antics, and sent Crespo and Lampard out of the dugout to limber up on the touchline, offering a stark reminder of their firepower. The Chelsea players were desperate to equalise before the break, and Paulo Ferreira duly equalised with his first goal for the club when Drogba headed on a corner after 37 minutes. An earlier error by Ferreira had allowed Colchester's Mark Yeates to steal in and hit Cudicini's post when the score was 0-0.

At half-time, Mourinho introduced Joe and Lampard who replaced Diarra and Maniche. The Chelsea fans were then treated to 45 minutes of vintage Joe, who ripped the tie out of Colchester's grasp and dumped them out of the Cup. Colchester fought to the end, but they tired badly in the closing stages, and that was when he struck.

Crespo had replaced Duff after 63 minutes; a quarter-of-an-hour later, he unleashed a tremendous shot from outside the box that Colchester's heroic goalkeeper Davison could only parry. Joe raced in and instantly controlled the ball before scoring with a smooth, low shot. The England star made it look easy, but the chance could have been squandered in those terrible conditions and tense atmosphere.

The rain continued to pelt down, and Chelsea hung on. Colchester launched one last attack in a desperate bid to save something from the game. Chelsea eventually cleared and the ball was punted upfield to Joe. Drogba lay injured on the far side of the pitch and the crowd were whistling for Joe to put the ball into touch. That was never his style, though, and he set off on a run past one, two and now three defenders. He weaved his way goalwards, dribbling effortlessly on a dreadful surface, and threw in a high-speed stepover for luck. The crowd were still whistling when he curled a flawless shot past Davison, now rooted to his line. It was a marvellous individual goal of class and persistence, Joe's two finest qualities.

When Barça finally graced the quagmire at Stamford Bridge in the Champions League, all their complaints about the pitch evaporated when they extracted maximum revenge on the side that had so narrowly dismissed them from the competition the previous year. Any hope Chelsea had of winning the match and indeed the tie disappeared when Joe was removed from the action by Mourinho after 38 minutes. He was replaced by Geremi following the controversial dismissal of Asier del Horno a few minutes earlier for a clumsy tackle on the star of the night, the formidably talented Lionel Messi. Geremi replaced Ferreira at right-back who switched to left-back. Mourinho always insisted that incident decided the tie, but the truth was that the gulf in class between the two sides had increased since they had last clashed.

Joe left the field gutted that he had been replaced at such an early stage of the proceedings. During his short spell on the field, he had made eleven accurate passes and one tackle. Joe also appeared to be the only Chelsea player capable of causing any problems to the solid-looking Barça defence.

Chelsea replaced Crespo with Drogba at half-time and came out fighting. After 58 minutes, they surprisingly took the lead. Lampard's free kick, after a foul on Robben, caused mayhem in the Barça goalmouth. Valdes, the Barça keeper, midfielder Motta and Terry all went for the ball on the edge of the six-yard box. The ball flew off Motta's leg and into the net. It was terrible defending, but ten-man Chelsea were not complaining. Joe watching from the bench and wondered whether the Blues could hang on.

Barça replaced the unfortunate Motta with the Swede Henrik Larsson, recently voted the greatest foreign player to wear the green-and-white of Celtic. Immediately, Ronaldinho chipped over a delightful ball that the Swede should have converted, but he headed over.

Twenty minutes from time, Ronaldinho curled over another wonderful free kick and Terry rose above everyone to head into his own net. Like Gerrard's own goal in the Carling Cup Final the previous year, it seemed an extraordinary lapse. Two own goals already, and Terry had been involved in both at either end.

Something then galvanised the Barcelona team, as they moved up a gear. Messi was in spellbinding form, and nearly destroyed the goal when he cannoned a shot against the angle of bar and post. Terry later appeared to shove Messi in the back as he was about to pull the trigger in front of goal, but avoided a penalty decision.

Terry then cleared two shots off the line in the next two minutes, one from Larsson and the other from Ronaldhino. The Catalan giants appeared to have about 15 players on the pitch as they began to tear Chelsea apart. Mourinho took off the disappointing Robben and brought on Wright-Phillips, but it just served to show how far the £21 million youngster was from being at his best. Ten minutes from time, the pulsatingly exciting Samuel Eto'o headed the winner after another high-speed Barça attack set up by Ronaldinho, a move that was another glorious example of classic Barcelona pace and power. Chelsea appeared to have a massive task ahead at the Nou Camp as Mourinho suffered his first defeat at Stamford Bridge.

The team then returned to Premiership action against Portsmouth at the Bridge. The pitch, now resembling mudflats, had been the subject of much debate. It was eventually torn up after the match and re-laid.

Joe played for an hour and was replaced by Eidur Gudjohnsen. The game was scoreless when he departed but, within a few minutes, the Icelandic striker had supplied a perfect ball for Lampard to score. Robben, now being compared to Jürgen Klinsmann in his Tottenham days, sealed it for Chelsea when he scored from another fine pass by Gudjohnsen, who had done enough to win the Sky Man of the Match award. It was Chelsea's 39th unbeaten Premiership home game.

An unused Portsmouth substitute that afternoon was Andres D'Alessandro, once dubbed 'the new Maradona'. Andres had been the rising star of the Under-21 Argentina side that had played England at Craven Cottage six years earlier. In that game, Joe had made his debut under Howard Wilkinson. Few would have bet at that time that Joe would have overtaken the former River Plate superstar. Joe had the determination and the talent to succeed, and at the time was happy to tell anyone who'd listen that he wanted to play for England in the World Cup.

He was now on the verge of turning that dream into a reality and, in preparation for the tournament, Joe departed shortly after the end of the Portsmouth game to catch up with the England squad in readiness for their friendly against Uruguay. This was played at Anfield and a few nights later, Joe was voted Man of the Match as he turned in a thoroughly professional performance. Mourinho's curious decision to withdraw him from the action against Barcelona, and his early withdrawal from the Portsmouth match, meant that Eriksson could employ his talents for the whole of the England game. He revelled in his role, and appreciated Eriksson's decision to keep him on the pitch. It gave him valuable experience, for in his 34 games for Chelsea so far that season, he had only started and finished a game on nine occasions.

Joe was able to test the Uruguayan defence on several occasions with penetrating runs and supremely well-timed crosses and through balls. Omar Pouso shot Uruguay ahead with a spectacular effort that England keeper Paul Robinson was powerless to stop, and then, in reply, Joe cleverly supplied the towering cross for Peter Crouch to head the England equaliser.

Joe then scored the winner in the 94th minute when it looked like the game was heading for a draw, and many of the 40,013 fans were heading for the exits. Shaun Wright-Phillips, on for the disappointing Beckham, had crossed a great ball. It was Joe's fifth goal for his country in 30 appearances. In the match, he had made 48 passes with an 87 per cent completion rate, completed four tackles and conceded two fouls. A fascinating statistic was that Joe had played more minutes on the pitch for England than any other player in 2005. The days of warming the bench seemed to be over.

Joe received terrific press acclaim with the tabloids declaring that he was head and shoulders above any other player on the field.

Joe's big night was marred by the news that Chelsea legend Peter Osgood had died earlier in the day from a heart-attack while attending a family funeral. The 59-year-old was regarded by many as the greatest player to have worn the royal blue. Brian Mears was of the view that Osgood was ahead of a cluster of timeless greats that included Gianfranco Zola, Jimmy Greaves and Charlie Cooke. Perhaps only Joe Cole would be a modern-day star worthy of comparison with the great man. Eriksson had identified Joe Cole as 'the best player on the pitch', and it was fitting that Joe dedicated his goal to the memory of Osgood.

It was an amazing week for Joe, because the following Saturday he scored the winning goal against West Bromwich Albion at the Hawthorns. Joe had come on for Duff after 63 minutes of a dreary, bad-tempered game. West Brom had not beaten Chelsea since 1979 and Chelsea had won 12 of their last 14 meetings. It was another lunchtime kick-off, which did nothing for the atmosphere or spirit of goodwill among the crowd, and tempers were frayed on the pitch, too. His 100th game in charge of the Blues, Mourinho seemed edgy that day, too; the return leg at the Nou Camp was three days away, and Chelsea had a mammoth task ahead of them.

The first half was scoreless, with the Albion just shading it. The real trouble sparked when Mourinho led Chelsea out for the second half four minutes late. This infuriated the West Brom manager Bryan Robson, the iconic ex-England and Manchester United skipper, but Mourinho seemed quite unperturbed at keeping everyone waiting.

Within a few minutes, Drogba put Chelsea ahead with a nonchalant low drive. Then Robben was sent off for the second time in two months after a two-footed challenge on Jonathan Greening. Mourinho sarcastically applauded the linesman. It was Chelsea's fourth red card in 11 matches. This incensed Mourinho and Drogba inflamed the situation when he appeared to feign injury after a challenge by Greening. Drogba was significantly taller and heavier than the Englishman, but he still went to ground as though he'd been hit by Tyson. Robson and Mourinho exchanged a torrent of abuse about the incident, and Terry chased after the referee with a gaggle of blue shirts behind him to complain bitterly about the challenge. The match was descending into chaos.

After 63 minutes, Joe, invigorated by his England success, replaced Duff and, within ten minutes, he scored what transpired to be the winner. It was perhaps the messiest goal he had ever scored; exchanging passes with Drogba in the box, he finished the move with a firm shot that seemed to go through the West Brom keeper. Joe had now scored eleven goals in 2005/6, which eclipsed his previous best of ten the season before. The crowd were also treated to a sublime bit of skill from Joe, when he controlled the ball beautifully and almost scored after delicately curling a shot past the post.

Kanu pulled one back near the end, neatly turning in Robinson's low cross. Chelsea held out, but the game ended bitterly with Mourinho snubbing the customary shake of hands with Robson. The Champions of England were booed off the field by the Black Country crowd.

Joe needed to reproduce another top-quality performance if Chelsea were to progress in the Champions League. His confidence was as high as ever, fuelled by his recent heroics for his country. He told the *Independent*, 'It's a magic game in the Nou Camp, and I can't wait for it. There aren't many weaknesses in our team, and if we can keep 11 on the pitch, we can get a result. We will go for it, because we've got to score two goals and we're capable of doing that.'

On arrival in Spain, Mourinho was severely abused by a crowd of Barça fans, who spat at him and chanted 'translator... translator', a cheeky reference to his first role at the Nou Camp. Mourinho successfully diverted all the flak away from his team, though, as they emerged a few minutes later to mild applause.

Chelsea took no risks that night; they went out of the competition tamely. Mourinho opted for a 4-4-1-1 formation, rather than an attacking 4-4-2 or his usual 4-3-3. Barça played in Mourinho style to deprive Chelsea of a place in the most prestigious competition in Europe. Their game plan was simply to keep the ball, which they did to perfection.

Joe started the game on the left and was carded early on for a foul on Messi, who went off after 25 minutes with a hamstring injury, but Chelsea were unable to establish any superiority. They seemed scared of the Catalan team's awesome firepower.

Joe nearly put Chelsea ahead on the break when Terry headed on Ferreira's free kick and Joe flicked a shot on to the roof of the net. If it had gone in, then perhaps it would have been a different story.

After a dull first half, Chelsea brought on Crespo for Drogba. Almost immediately, Joe set him up for a goal with a fine run and a perfect cross. Crespo's superb strike against Liverpool had been harder to convert, but the ex-Lazio striker stabbed Joe's cross well wide. Chelsea's chance of a historic victory went with that chance.

BACK TO THE FUTURE

The scintillating trickery of Ronaldinho put Barça ahead twelve minutes from time. Just like Joe's piece of brilliance at West Brom, it was the only genuine moment of class in the game. The Brazilian sent the Nou Camp into delirium when he received a pass from Eto'o, swept past Lampard, swerved past Carvalho and shrugged off Terry's challenge. A lightning burst of pace took him clear and he belted home a goal with a drive that Cech was helpless to save. Game over.

Joe was again Chelsea's best player, the only forward who had threatened the Barça defence, but seven minutes from time he was replaced by Robert Huth, whom Mourinho pitched up front in a fruitless attempt to save the tie. The Chelsea coach had done the same thing against Liverpool in the Champions League semi-final the previous spring as the game slipped away. It was an act of desperation; far from being inspirational, replacing his most skilful player with a cumbersome defender was another act of folly. In the last minute, Terry fell over in the box when challenged by van Bronckhorst and Lampard, previously anonymous, rolled in the penalty. It was too little, too late.

High in the plush seating at the Nou Camp, Roman Abramovich's dreams of European glory had evaporated for the third year running. Of the Chelsea opening line-up, picked by Ranieri in their first exit against Monaco in May 2004, only Joe, Lampard, Terry and Gallas remained.

A talking point among the disappointed Chelsea fans was trying to identify a successful buy of Mourinho's. This was despite the fact that the team that had drawn with Barça had cost twice as much as that fielded by the unfortunate Ranieri in Monaco. The side that Mourinho had constructed in his two years in London could apparently go no further.

There were many who believed that the loss to the Catalan side might have spelled the beginning of the end of Mourinho's tenure. Condemned by the media for their baiting of referees, their over-acting and poor sportsmanship, Chelsea were now cast in Mourinho's image – industrious, arrogant, grindingly efficient... and with very little space for the magic of the likes of Joe Cole.

The season seemed over to all intents and purposes. There was still the domestic double to play for, but there was an unmistakable feeling of failure. Chelsea came home from Spain licking their wounds, and Mourinho tried to put a gloss on things, but the general mood of dismay prevailed. It was extraordinary, really, considering Chelsea's history prior to the Abramovich era.

Spurs came to the Bridge on the following Saturday, where Chelsea recorded a vital win in another grim, often dreary game. Essien put Chelsea ahead after 15 minutes with his first goal for the club. Jermaine Jenas equalised for Spurs on half-time, with the Chelsea defence hypnotised. Joe played for 68 minutes before being replaced by an off-form Duff, and the game was eventually won with a last-minute volley from Gallas, still deployed as a full-back.

Joe went to Cheltenham races a few days later with Terry and the lads. The tabloids pictured him in a leather jacket and True Religion jeans, standing with Duff and Lampard. Reports in the tabloids put the squad's losses at a staggering £500,000.

Despite his losses at the races, and the obvious

disappointment of being dumped out of the Champions League, Joe was still winning admirers and impressing the powers-that-be, so much so that a report in the *Telegraph* revealed that he had become the most sought-after player in their fantasy football teams. Already, he was starting to be mentioned as a possible Player of the Year.

The next march for the defending champions was the west London derby – Fulham v Chelsea. The weather had been terrible all week but that Sunday afternoon on the eve of the first day of spring, the sun broke through and London was bathed in warmth. As the fans trudged towards the ground, the talk was of how many Chelsea would rattle in against a Fulham side slowly slipping towards relegation. The history of Chelsea Football Club, though, warns time and again against this sort of complacency. There was also speculation abounding over Mourinho's future, rows with Abramovich and Kenyon and a possible departure to Italy.

Luis Boa Morte gave Fulham a shock lead after 17 minutes when Paulo Ferreira's clearance ricocheted off his shin and past Cech. Chelsea's defence seemed to be the problem; they had only kept 2 clean sheets in their last 16 matches. In an extraordinary decision, Mourinho withdrew Joe and wing partner Wright-Phillips after just 25 minutes. Joe had carelessly lost the ball a few moments earlier to Volz, and Wright-Phillips' attempt at a centre just before that nearly ended up on Hammersmith Broadway rather than the Fulham penalty box. Even so, it was a decision that shocked the Chelsea fans as they watched Drogba and Duff come on.

Joe was furious and could not conceal his disgust by angrily hurling his tracksuit bottoms to the ground. Mourinho refused to return his gaze as Joe glared across at him. Jose later told the *City AM* paper, 'Joe and Shaun did not have a happy game... we were not bringing the wings into attack. I was watching minute after minute and there was no reaction from the team.'

At half-time, Joe had to trudge across the pitch to go to the dressing room. It was a curious arrangement for a Premiership game. The Chelsea fans behind the goal spotted him and gave the substituted star a tremendous ovation, similar to the one he'd been given when he scored his fabulous goal against Colchester. The Chelsea fans now had a special song about Joe:

> *'He's here, he's there*
> *He's every-f-----g-where*
> *Joey Cole, Joey Cole... '*

Mourinho was walking in front of Joe, on his own, and while the fans continued to sing, Mourinho did not even glance at Joe or the fans. Joe raised his hands above his head and clapped them back. Mourinho scowled.

Joe's replacement, Drogba, was involved in more controversy when he put the ball into the net after 58 minutes. It was correctly ruled out for handball. The Chelsea striker had controlled the ball with his right arm as he raced through on the blind side of the officials to direct the ball into the net after a mix-up between the Fulham keeper Mark Crossley and Zat

Knight. Boa Morte led his outraged team-mates over to the linesman who, after an age, awarded Fulham a free-kick for handball. To complete Chelsea's day of misery, Gallas was sent off in the dying seconds. As he left, he goaded the Fulham fans with the gladiatorial thumbs down gesture.

The game ended in more drama as the Fulham fans raced on to the pitch. The last time Fulham Football Club had beaten their neighbours was on Good Friday 1977, before Joe was born. George Best had opened the scoring in a 3-1 win. For some Chelsea fans, their third Premiership defeat of the season was hard to take and some scuffles broke out.

Joe's poor treatment was overlooked in all the excitement. It was the twentieth time Mourinho had taken him off that season. The Chelsea fans were starting to question why he was repeatedly subbed, while other players, who had under-performed, stayed on. Lampard had had a dreadful game, his passing was lamentable and he had failed to create anything. When he was not scoring, he did not look the second-best player in the world.

Four days later, Newcastle came to town in the 6th Round of the Cup. Newcastle now had Glen Roeder as their caretaker manager, who had done so much in furthering Joe's career. He paid him a compliment by specially detailing a midfield player to track him.

Chelsea went through comfortably with a solitary Terry goal scored early in the game. Joe almost doubled Chelsea's lead in the first ten minutes, but the ex-Chelsea defender Babayaro threw himself in front of his goal-bound effort and deflected the ball away. Joe was Chelsea's most dominant player, but the game was dull and uneventful. Without the injured Owen and with the peerless Shearer making his farewell FA Cup appearance, the Geordies lacked any cutting edge. Essien replaced Joe near the end, and a few thousand Chelsea fans took that as their cue to catch an early train home.

Chelsea then moved a step closer to the title with a 2-0 steam-rollering of Manchester City at Stamford Bridge. Joe had an average game and played for 72 minutes before Shaun Wright-Phillips replaced him. Joe had one clear-cut chance to score, but James playing his usual superb game at Stamford Bridge kept it out. Drogba scored both the goals, the aftermath of the second adding to the controversy that raged around the club.

Joe was gradually being absorbed into mainstream culture around this time. A few days after the City game, the *Sun* splashed a photograph of Keeley in a swimsuit across their front page, and printed a photo of Joe next to it. The popular TV show *Footballers' Wives* introduced a boyish character called Callum Watson who was loosely based on Joe; he had a passing resemblance to the way Joe looked when he broke into the West Ham team, and he played with an effortless brattishness that was unmistakable Joe.

Joe was now an iconic figure; he had never chased fame – all he ever wanted to do was play football. Gazza had been one of his boyhood idols, and his heavily documented downfall had been a stark lesson to Joe. The young Chelsea wonderkid-turned-international superstar was and always had been a very private person, now living quietly with his girlfriend Carly in Cobham near the training ground. By now, he was arguably the most popular of Chelsea's players. Their most expensive signing, the £24 million Drogba, had attracted boos from the Matthew Harding Stand when he was named Man of the Match for his performance against Man City. Lampard and Terry had been the big two the previous season, but a sense of complacency had crept into their play. There was also the inescapable feeling that the current team had run their course under Mourinho. There was no question that they were less resilient.

The next game against Birmingham provided further evidence of this. Liverpool had won there the week before 7-0 in the FA Cup and then Manchester United put four past them. Joe was relegated to the bench as Robben returned. Joe came on in the second half after 65 minutes for Duff, and he fashioned out a great chance for Crespo in stoppage time. Joe shook off his marker and chipped a beautiful ball into the path of the Argentinian, but just as he had missed the vital chance that Joe had given him in the Nou Camp, he once again failed to convert a great opportunity. This time, he got his shot on target but the Birmingham goalkeeper Taylor blocked it. The game finished scoreless and with Manchester United winning at Bolton later in the day, so the champions' lead was slashed to a mere seven points with six games left. They had led by 18 points a few weeks earlier.

Joe told the *Metro* that he was confident that Chelsea could hold off Ferguson's side's late charge for the Premiership title. 'We are missing chances but are confident of changing that in the next few games. We need four wins.'

West Ham was the next fixture; Mourinho opted for a 4-4-2 formation which meant Joe being consigned to the bench.

Crespo and Drogba were the twin spearhead with Essien, Makelele, Lampard and Maniche in midfield. Collins headed the claret-and-blues into a shock early lead. Things went from bad to worse when Maniche was sent off for a pugnacious lunge on Scaloni. Things looked bleak for the ten men, but they stormed back and scored twice in three minutes through Drogba and Crespo. West Ham were pitiful, with an eye on their up-coming FA Cup semi-final. They collapsed in the second half and Terry and Gallas added further goals. Joe came on for Drogba in the last minute. There was still time for him to put Robben through to score, but the goal was ruled out for offside.

Chelsea's next match on Easter Saturday was against Bolton at the Reebok Stadium where they had won the title the year before. They won by the same score, 2-0, with goals from Terry and Lampard, but Joe hardly figured. Since the defeat at Fulham, he had been marginalised by Mourinho. The title was almost within their grasp as a shell-shocked Manchester United had been held to a goalless draw the evening before against an already relegated Sunderland.

Chelsea then thrashed Everton 3-0 on Easter Monday. Joe replaced Robben after 62 minutes with the Blues already two up and cruising to a comfortable 28th win of the season.

Mourinho insisted on sticking with his 4-4-2 line-up, but without wingers. Joe was subdued, struggling to maintain his level of form. He appeared to be playing cautiously, with the World Cup looming and a semi-final against Liverpool in a few days. Around that time, he was nominated for the Professional Footballers' Association Player of the Year award.

He was in élite company, the other leading candidates being Thierry Henry, Steven Gerrard and Wayne Rooney. Terry and Lampard were also in the line-up, with Gerrard eventually winning, his exploits in inspiring Liverpool to the previous season's European Champions League victory tipping the voting in his favour. If Joe's momentum had not been slowed by his stuttering appearances in recent weeks, though, he may well have won.

There was some consolation for Joe, though, as he was named alongside Gerrard and Lampard in the midfield of the PFA team of the season. Joe was also voted the best player in his position by his peers, which was a tremendous accolade.

All thoughts of awards, titles and trophies were abandoned, though, with 30 seconds of stoppage time left in the FA Cup semi-final against Liverpool. Chelsea were trailing 1-2 to their arch-rivals, when the ball fell to Joe in the box; he looked offside as he accelerated clear of the Liverpool defence to meet Robben's cute chipped pass. Joe was played on by Steve Finnan, he killed the ball and steadied himself, but as Jose Reina frantically scampered from his line, he fired over the bar from six yards and into the Stretford Road end. John Motson, driven almost hysterical by the excitement, told the watching TV millions, 'Joe Cole... he's missed it!'

Chelsea were out of the Cup and Joe had missed a sitter. For once, he had failed to turn around his ailing team's fortunes. Joe could have thumped the ball, or placed it gently into the yawning goal, but caught between two stools, he missed badly. Could it be that his time spent on the bench in recent weeks had added to a loss of sharpness?

Mourinho, in an interview for the *Guardian*, blamed Joe as one of the reasons for the defeat. 'In big matches, you cannot miss big chances... I don't know why Cole's form dropped, but it's a reality. These kind of players, if they are good, they can win matches for you. If they are not good, they lose the ball and the team loses balance and compactness.'

While delivering his views on the Liverpool defeat, Mourinho employed a monotone delivery and stood rigidly. His tactics had been unorthodox to say the least – kamikaze, even – starting the game without any of his three wingers. Essien had been deployed at the tip of the diamond and Ferreira in midfield. The reborn Liverpool winger Harry Kewell dismantled the hapless Geremi, who was out of his depth at full-back. It was highly reminiscent of Joe's first Chelsea boss, Ranieri. The first half display by Chelsea reflected a side burnt out and devoid of attacking ideas.

Terry had enjoyed good fortune that season – he'd got away with three handballs against Fulham, Villa and Everton – but in the semi-final his luck ran out. After 21 minutes, he raised his boot to Luis Garcia and a bitterly disputed free kick was given by referee Graham Poll. Lampard and Ferreira did not live up to their duties in the wall, and the poorly positioned Carlo Cudicini was beaten low down by John Arne Riise's laser-guided free kick.

Terry then had a goal disallowed for a foul on the same player. Garcia, who had scored the 'phantom' goal in the last semi-final meeting, scored the second with a brilliant chip over Cudicini eight minutes into the second half. The out-of-sorts Chelsea keeper again looked at fault.

BACK TO THE FUTURE

Chelsea without Joe were devoid of any attacking flair or fluidity. Mourinho finally saw sense, and brought on Joe for a weary-looking Crespo. At the same time, Duff replaced the over-run Geremi, and Robben, who could turn a game when he really wanted to, had already been introduced at the break for del Horno.

With three wingers on, Chelsea chased the game. They dominated the rest of the match, mostly played out in Liverpool's half. Joe was Chelsea's best player going forward, and his appearance gave the Chelsea fans stationed in the Stretford End renewed hope. Drogba then pulled a goal back after 71 minutes to set up a frantic finish. And then Joe missed his glorious opportunity to become a Chelsea legend.

At the final whistle, Joe was magnanimous in defeat, despite the double disappointment of his miss and the demise of the double dream. He told the *Daily Mail*, 'I will be haunted by that miss but I won't be the last player it will happen to. A lot of the time, you hear players moaning and being miserable about refereeing decisions, but let's just hold up our hands and congratulate Liverpool on winning the game. We weren't at our best and we are all very down, but we will have to pick ourselves up and give our fans a good party next Saturday by celebrating back-to-back titles.'

Things could hardly get worse for Chelsea, but the groundswell of anti-Blues feeling in the press was stoked by Arsenal storming through to the Champions League final to play Barcelona in Paris. Spurs' great run in the league continued, and they nearly capped a wonderful season as they tried but just failed to hold off the Gunners for the final

Champions League spot. For the first time since the Abramovich caravan had been parked outside Stamford Bridge, the west London side were relegated to the inside pages.

Joe's season was apparently stuttering to a close, but he still had something special to offer in the next match against Manchester United. Chelsea needed a point to take the title, but United refused to surrender, despite conceding an early Gallas goal. Rooney was a constant threat to the defending champions. Joe was back in the side, while Mourinho had been slaughtered in the press after the Liverpool débâcle. For the Manchester United game, he had reverted back to 4-3-3 with Joe and Robben playing wide.

An hour into the game, Joe settled things as he scored the best goal of his career, and one of the best goals ever seen in the Premiership. Collecting Drogba's flick 25 yards from goal, he twisted clear of Rio Ferdinand, and then ghosted past Vidic and Silvestre, dragging the ball deftly under the studs of his boots, and surged through to bear down on goal. Edwin van der Saar rushed out to narrow the angle, but Joe drove a right-footed shot coolly high into the net. It was a crowning moment in his career and kept the title at Stamford Bridge. Few other English players could have scored a goal of such impudence or displayed the composure he had on the ball.

Joe was booked for taking off his shirt as he celebrated with an irrepressible exuberance in front of the ecstatic Chelsea fans. It seemed hardly necessary for him to carve out a third goal for Carvalho.

In the closing minutes, Rooney was stretchered off with an injury that cast huge doubts over his fitness for the World Cup in 41 days' time. Standing in the wings, and in the best form of his life, it could just be that Joe Cole's mercurial skills and experience at the highest level made him the ideal candidate to be cast as saviour of the national team.

And for a lad from north London, who just wanted to play football, life doesn't really get any better.

13
To Be Someone

'Joe is the most improved player in the England set up. I always thought he had the talent but wonder if he'd realise it. His attitude has improved and he does the untidy stuff now as well as the fabulous bursts of skill. He has made the left wing position his own, solving Sven's dilemma.'

Gary Lineker

WITH BACK-TO-BACK Premierships won Joe could concentrate on the World Cup in Germany. After the long years of stultifying mediocrity there was a real belief in the country that England could bring home the FIFA World Cup trophy for the first time in four decades.

First though there was a domestic matter to attend to. Chelsea had signed German captain Michael Ballack on a free transfer from Bayern Munich in a four-year, £90,000 a week deal. Already the papers were talking of Joe being marginalised by Jose Mourinho employing a diamond system that would incorporate Frank Lampard, Claude Makelele, Michael Essien and the former Bayern superstar.

Joe was not deterred by the situation and told the London *Evening Standard*: 'Since I signed, players like Veron, Geremi, Petit, Gronkjaer, Tiago, Robben, Essien, Duff and Maniche have been in the midfield at one time or another and it has been said that, at various times, I would find it a struggle to get in the team. I relish the challenge rather than shy away from it. Competition for places is good for your game. Ballack is a top player and Chelsea need players like him in the squad if we are to continue to progress. I feel I can learn from him and continue to make myself a better player.'

Joe was also the subject of speculation about his England role. He was guaranteed a place in the starting line up but with Wayne Rooney recovering from the metatarsal broken in the Chelsea game the talk was that Joe may play in an advanced central-midfield role.

England had two warm up games before they flew to their luxury hotel in Baden Baden, Germany. In the first game they beat Hungary 3–1 at Old Trafford. It was a happier return for Joe than his last appearance in the Theatre of Dreams against Liverpool. Joe played the full 90 minutes and was named by the *Sun* as the liveliest player in the first half. Desperately unlucky with a glancing header that came back off a post the Chelsea man could have added to his goal tally.

Jamaica were slaughtered 6-0 in the second warm-up game. The nation suspended disbelief as Peter Crouch scored three and introduced his curious robot dance to the world. Joe flickered sporadically but generally he had a quiet game, though he came to life in the last 20 minutes. He made 42 passes as opposed to the total of 26 against Hungary. Jamaica gave a great deal of space away and Joe's best effort was a snap shot that was turned around the post. With a chance to break through on the global stage though, the last thing Joe needed was to pick up a knock. This was his third major tournament for England but this time he knew he would play.

Joe told the *Sun*: 'Four years ago in Japan I was still a kid and just happy to be part of the squad. Then Euro 2004 was a big personal disappointment because I didn't play at all and I didn't want that to happen again. So I knew I had to knuckle down and make sure when the next tournament came around I'd be a part of it. But this time it's new territory to me. I knew I wouldn't be in the starting line up in Japan or Portugal. Now all the indications are that I've got a good chance of playing.'

Play he did in England's opening World Cup Group B match against Paraguay in Frankfurt. It was played on a scalding hot Saturday afternoon with the game kicking off at 3 pm. The country came to a standstill with 12.8 million (86 per cent of the available watching audience) tuning in to Joe and company. It had been an unusually wet spring and a cold early summer in England – then suddenly that day it became extremely warm and people everywhere lit barbeques.

England scrambled to a 1-0 victory courtesy of an own goal by Carlos Gamarra early in the match. Beckham swung in a free kick and the ball flew in off the hapless Carlos. England were minus the recovering Rooney, with Crouch deputising up front. Joe was voted by the *Metro* as England's outstanding performer, earning a 9/10 rating. He ran at defenders, displayed his trickery, tackled back and filled in up front when Michael Owen went off after 56 minutes. The ex-Madrid man had been out for nearly six months with a foot injury and was struggling to regain both fitness and form. Eriksson told the media it was a tactical decision to play Joe just behind Peter Crouch and move him inside from the left flank.

Joe himself went off with just eight minutes remaining to be replaced by Stewart Downing. The little guy had run himself into the ground for his country; he had just run out of gas. The England players had lost between 5 and 10lbs each and had consumed 70 litres of water during the game. The norm was 20 litres. England faded badly in the heat. It was stiflingly hot for Germany at that time of year. This factor took a lot of countries by surprise.

Joe had played at the highest level since he was a teenager and had faced huge mental tests in stadia like the Nou Camp but he said the pressure he felt in Frankfurt was the most he had experienced in football. On the team coach approaching the massive stadium the nerves started to get to him as he saw the huge multitude of England fans congregating.

'I was very, very nervous, the most nervous since I began playing football. It was then, on the coach, that I asked another player how nervous he was. I asked him if he felt more nervous than ever before and this player said "yes". I don't want to say who it was because this was a man who has played at the top, top level of the game. It wasn't shaking nerves but just the tension, wanting to do well, the expectations. It didn't affect me in a negative way, though; in fact I feel I need that to play well.

'Sometimes you have to be clever and slow the game up – there are ways of doing that. I know the fans get frustrated but sometimes you have to keep the ball and get the job done.'

Joe was one of the few players to emerge from the game with

any credit and not be affected by the pressure. He was very dehydrated and didn't manage to sleep until 6 am the next day.

Prince William watched the game. He had visited the squad before they had flown to Germany and had met Joe and the chaps. Joe had described the Prince as a 'nice geezer' at an England Press conference. Prince William is a devout Villa fan.

England's next match was five days later against Trinidad & Tobago in Nuremberg. They were the World Cup's smallest nation but the Soca Warriors pushed England all the way. Two late goals from the Liverpool pair Crouch and Steven Gerrard won the tie and guaranteed England's instant qualification from the group. Joe played for 75 minutes before being replaced by Middlesbrough's Downing again. Once again the match was played in very hot conditions and the first half was played at a funeral pace. Joe did his best to inject some life into proceedings and his gyrations earned an average mark of 7/10 in the papers for his performance. His influence waned as the infernal conditions took their toll but the flicks and tricks were one of the few bright spots in the game. The stats indicated that he made 45 passes with a completion figure of 77 per cent. The most successful move was a dribble and high cross which provided Crouch with a half chance.

Along with Hammers old-boys Rio Ferdinand, Frank Lampard and Michael Carrick, the Trinidad goalkeeper Shaka Hislop was another former West Ham club-mate; wherever Joe went in Germany his West Ham past seemed to be in evidence.

The game was the sort of result that was so often ground out by Mourinho's Chelsea. Joe had to curb his natural tendency to come inside from the left and look to play one-twos.

Eriksson's England set up required him to go down the outside and send crosses over.

News had broken after the Paraguay game that the step-over king had already signed a new improved four-year deal with Chelsea doubling his money to £80,000 a week. Peter Kenyon, the Blues chief executive, told the *Sun*: 'In our two Premiership-winning seasons Joe has been one of our best players. Last summer when contract talks first started he said he wanted to put it on hold for a year because he was confident he would prove he was worth a new deal. Joe has done that. Not only is he important to Chelsea, he is also a first choice for England.'

Joe was now a star, perhaps the third most popular England player after Rooney and Beckham. Joe was very much anti-star dust. At that time he was rejecting the mentality of being a star. The World Cup of 2006 was a particularly happy time for him. For someone who loved football as much as Joe it was paradise to be actually competing at the highest level. Joe was in a continuous process of learning.

Around that time Joe was featured in an advert for Samsung mobile phones. The young superstar was unrecognisable from the podgy, shaven headed West Ham prodigy. Replacing him was the immaculate, Armani-blazered Joe with razor cut hair and movie star smile. It was a makeover that would have won over even Trinny and Susannah.

In his next match against Sweden in Cologne Joe was to take that last huge step from being a 'face' to a household name. England drew 2-2 against Eriksson's home country on the 20 June 2006. Back home it was the first day of Royal Ascot and already the nation was fully succumbing to its quadrennial soccer hysteria. It was a result that clinched their place at the top of the group, thus avoiding a second-round clash against the host nation Germany. It was a tragic night for Michael Owen playing in his 80th game for England. In the very first minute his knee gave way and he sustained cruciate ligament damage. If the night was a tragedy for one former child prodigy it was a total triumph for another. Joe was voted the FIFA Man of the Match and scored one of the finest goals of the competition – certainly of those scored by England. The only strikes approaching it that sweltering summer were Maxi Rodriguez's extra-terrestrial winner for Argentina against Mexico (similar in perfect technique) and Zinedine Zidane's astounding effort against Spain.

The Chelsea star's direct opponent that night was the former Owls and Everton defensive midfielder Niclas Alexandersson, and Joe gave him a pasting all night. In the opening moments he treated the fans to a beautifully executed back heel that brought gasps from the England fans. He never really looked back from that moment as he digged deep into his bag of tricks to perform his extensive repertoire of flicks, step-overs, swerves, back heels and jinking runs.

After 34 minutes Alexandersson headed clear Beckham's cross and the ball fell to Joe 35 yards from goal. Oscar Wilde said class always wins through and in that moment Joe Cole validated the notion of virtuosity that had come to dominate his whole career. The ball bounced and Joe never took his eye off it as it rose at an acute angle. Chesting it down Joe met the ball right-footed and volleyed it enormously high into the night sky. It soared, dipped and dropped, the parabola completely beating the Swedish goalkeeper Andreas Isaksson. It was a magical goal and every England fan in the stadium and millions back home were out of their seats.

Joe's effort was the most spectacular goal scored by an England player since Bobby Charlton in the 1960s. The goal it most resembled was Arie Haan's freakish strike for Holland in the 1978 Finals. The ball was heavier then.

Joe ran to the fans, pointing at his badge amid delirious scenes. It was probably the most exquisite moment of his life – literally a dream come true and the moment he had been working towards. Joe had started at the top like Orson Welles, his career had been like a rollercoaster and it was rare that a player regained such altitude – but Joe had managed it.

England and Joe were cheered off at half-time as they trooped into the dressing room. It would have been nice to say that Joe's goal was the winner – it was good enough to grace the final – but Sweden, a team packed with hard-bitten pros, had other ideas. England had not beaten them since 1968. Six minutes into the second half Markus Allback stepped in front of David Beckham at the near post to head home a corner. It was a real sucker punch. Sweden, encouraged by the cracks appearing in the England defence, pushed up.

Lampard and Terry were having a disappointing World Cup. Terry, without William Gallas to cover his lack of pace and Claude Makelele to shield him, looked distinctly average. Rio Ferdinand, honey to Terry's vinegar, did a fine job of papering over the cracks in the system. When he went off with a groin strain after 56 minutes, Terry became increasingly isolated.

Lampard was not looking the 'second best player in the

world'. He had more attempts at goal than any other player in the competition, without looking like scoring. His partnership with Steven Gerrard, a midfield match which would have appeared to have been made in heaven, just never sparked and failed to live up to expectations.

It was left to Joe to provide the only real menace. The conundrum was that Joe was right footed and played on the right for his club, though England used him so effectively on the left. Terry Venables pointed out that because he was right footed he was always looking to cut inside, and advocated switching wings with Beckham for periods in the game. This tendency to drift inside was very effective against Sweden and it was this move that set up England's second goal.

Steven Gerrard had come on for Rooney after 69 minutes. The resurgent Manchester United striker had wilted in the heat and the Liverpool captain was introduced to shore things up. Rooney, furious at his withdrawal, trashed the bench with his water bottle. With five minutes left, Joe cut inside and then looked up to measure a perfect cross for Stevie to rise majestically and smash home with a bullet header. That second piece of Cole magic should have been enough to seal victory but Sweden equalised in the dying seconds through the old warhorse Henrik Larsson.

Joe received tremendous press coverage for his wonder goal. 'Joe De Cologne' was perhaps the most amusing set up by the *Daily Mirror*. He even got a mention on *EastEnders* – Gary and Minty, both devoted Hammers fans, extolling the virtues of their former player.

Joe told Rob Beasley in the *News of the World*: 'It was right up there with the best goals that I ever scored. I have had so many texts from everyone about it. I have practised that shot for years and had been working on it again before the match. When it works like that it was just brilliant.'

As it was to turn out Joe's goal was probably the best moment of the ill-fated English World Cup campaign.

Joe went on to tell Beasley: 'People were talking about me and yet had never seen me play. It was incredible when I was 18 I was expected to be a world-class player but I hadn't learned the game yet. So I had to make my mistakes in the public eye. It was hard but it was good for me, too, and I wouldn't change a thing about it. I'm older, wiser and stronger now and I'm reaping the benefits for all that. It means now I don't feel any extra pressure playing for England. You know every touch is scrutinised and the expectation levels are so high that I have been dealing with that sort of thing right through my career. So playing in the World Cup and all the pressure is no problem for me.'

England's next game was a second round match against Ecuador, who were ranked 39th in the world. The competition had now reached the sudden death stage but England were fortunate to meet the poorest side still left in the World Cup. With Owen crippled, Eriksson discarded the 4-4-2 formation and opted for Rooney as the lone striker in a 4-5-1 set up. Joe's ex-West Ham teammate, the painstaking technician Michael Carrick, was the holding midfield player. Both had come a long way since the FA Youth Cup Final against Coventry in 1999 in which they had both collaborated, and which now seemed a lifetime ago.

TO BE SOMEONE

Carrick had a fine match but Joe failed to hit the heights of the Sweden match. The boundless freewheeling displayed in the first 45 minutes of the game in Cologne was replaced by a diligent display of hard work up and down the line. Nevertheless, as always he showed some nice touches and effortless close control. Joe's opponent that sweltering early evening was the Aston Villa defender Ulises de la Cruz who marked him extremely tightly and still found time to overlap. Joe's namesake Ashley gave him excellent backup and got stronger as he regained his match fitness. The ultimate complementing of the Cole boys gave England a great deal of strength and invention down what in the past had been the perennial problem left side.

The match was again played out in sweltering heat. Terry miscued an easy header to give Ecuador's Tenorio their only real chance of the game but a brilliant block by Ashley spared Terry's blushes. Lampard's nightmare tournament continued with another lacklustre performance. Only the harlequin Joe was living up to expectations, though his only chance in the game was a first half heading opportunity that was denied him by a nudge in the back.

Beckham scored the only goal of the game with one of his trademark free kicks on the hour. A few years before, the England captain had appeared to be walking on water, but lately he had been treading it as his artistry was dwindling. The goal was his only bright spot in a sterile World Cup. He vomited shortly after his goal.

Thirteen minutes from time the flickering Joe, who seemed to grow more inhibited as the game dragged on, was replaced by Jamie Carragher as Sven bolted the door. Joe was always the 'scapegoat' according to Talksport commentator Rodney Marsh. Marsh could empathise with Joe as he too was another outlaw talent – his England career mashed into a handful of appearances in the 1970s.

It seemed a strange decision to remove Joe from the action when other midfielders were turning in less convincing performances. The problem was the pressure put on the midfield players by the absence of a potent strike force. Joe had to organise the attacks, help Ashley Cole and was expected to finish off the moves. No wonder he was exhausted as he had carried the much-vaunted Lampard in the group stages.

Joe's girlfriend, Carly Zucker, started to attract headlines as the tabloids seized on any opportunity to report the activities of the WAGs (a new buzzword – Wives and Girlfriends – coined by the red-tops.) Shopping trips in the expensive boutiques of Baden Baden and nights out with the girls in the watering holes were all extensively reported as the gossip columns cranked up. By the end of her trip Carly was garnering as much coverage as Girls Aloud singer Cheryl Tweedy, the partner of Ashley Cole. Crowds gathered outside her hotel to catch a glimpse of the 24-year-old brunette going for an early morning run or walkabout in the town.

The presence of the ladies had been criticised as a distraction to the players by pundits like Martin O'Neill, but Joe welcomed it. They had been stuck in hotels for weeks and the chance of meeting his parents and girlfriend was a welcome diversion from the tremendous pressure and weight of expectation that was building daily. Joe badly missed his beloved dogs and was desperate for news on his pets' welfare.

Isolated in the hotel for long, suffocating hours, Joe spent his time playing computer games and listening to his iPod. One of his musical idols, Liam Gallagher, had gone out to watch the tournament and lamented the absence of Joe's team-mate Shaun Wright-Phillips. Now the footballers lived like rock stars holed up in opulent hotels besieged by fans. This was a turnaround because some years before a teenage Joe had banged on the Oasis man's front door when he lived in Islington. Now the stars and celebs flocked to see one of England's brightest stars. Mick Jagger was spotted in the crowd at the quarter-final match against Portugal.

The Portuguese were drilled to perfection by Sven's nemesis Phil Scolari. The game was to be played in Gelsenkirchen, the German Coliseum with a sliding roof. This was a bad omen for Joe because the 2004 Champions League Final had been staged there and Mourinho's slaughter-squad Porto side had triumphed that night. Joe's dream of a passage to a Euro final had perished in the previous round against Monaco.

England slumped out of the World Cup, beaten on penalties by Portugal. It signalled the end of the reign of Sven-Goran Eriksson as coach and David Beckham as captain. The truth was England were not good enough and once again at the vital moment their nerve deserted them.

The game hinged on the dismissal of Rooney after 62 minutes. He had been an accident waiting to happen all of the competition. Scowling and stern, Wayne had made a remarkable recovery from the injury sustained against another Portuguese defender, Paulo Ferreira, in the Chelsea match.

For a while the media led us to believe he could take on the whole of the world and win. But, clearly lacking full fitness and playing in a morale-sapping system, the Manchester United wrecking ball was involved in a confrontation with another Chelsea defender Ricardo Carvalho. Voted the best defender in Euro 2004, used and abused by Mourinho, Ricardo had nullified the threat from Rooney all game. The Portuguese defenders had his number and set a cynical trap which he naively fell for. Rooney, disbelieving, turned his back on the red card and trudged off the pitch.

That was the moment that spelled the end of Joe Cole's World Cup also. He was substituted after 64 minutes for Crouch. Obviously Eriksson needed to bring on a striker but Joe was his most creative player. With the threat from both Lampard and Gerrard snuffed out it seemed an absurd decision. Typical of the idiosyncrasies of Sven was that he had to his credit always shown great faith in Joe, but when he needed him most he curtailed his role. It was Sven rather than Jose who proved to be Joe's Road to Damascus in terms of both increased confidence and match winning performances.

Ten-man England fought heroically and in a jingoistic manner to hold out to extra time. Portugal offered little threat though and there was always the inescapable feeling that England, with a little extra class on the field, could have snatched a mind-boggling victory. Joe could have provided that and England would have progressed.

When the match reached the inevitable penalty shootout the beleaguered Lampard and the battle-weary Gerrard bungled theirs, as did Jamie Carragher, and England were out. In the bierkellers the England fans, heartbroken by a familiar melodrama, could only speculate what the outcome could have been had Joe Cole been entrusted with a penalty.

Jose Mourinho told the *Sun* that Gerrard knew England were out when Lampard missed his kick. 'I saw Gerrard looking up as the sky as if he was thinking, "If our best penalty-kicker didn't score then we're out".'

Mourinho thought Portugal, 'were too hurried. They could have done better but the emotional burden was very heavy. Only those who are there know. Often emotions overwhelm reason, tactical knowledge and the way you want to play.'

The star-spangled squad of Chelsea had 17 players at the World Cup playing for a variety of nations. Joe Cole played as well as anyone. His form in the group matches was outstanding, and if his effectiveness diminished in the knock out stages it was down to the fact that he was intrinsically a right footed midfield player playing wide on the left. The triumphalist superpower that is Chelsea managed by the bossy Mourinho were collectively a better side than the unsophisticated England managed by Sven. Joe played in a proven system under the demanding Mourinho, whereas for England he played in a far less comfortable environment which failed to play to his strengths.

Joe Cole is the future of English football. Once again he was the unsung hero, whereas Lampard complained that he had been singled out for criticism for his performances. Terry, who was particularly disconsolate at the end of the shootout, was linked with the captaincy. Both had disappointing World Cups. On the other hand, the players most often criticised or discarded by the Chelsea coach – Cole, Crespo, Maniche, Robben and Carvalho – had played brilliantly.

The press lamented the faded dreams of the so-called 'golden generation'; Eriksson took the rap as the nation mourned. Joe Cole was rightfully named England's best player in the *Daily Telegraph*'s World Cup ratings.

There may be better players than Joe Cole: better passers, more aggressive ball winners, more crucial innovators. There are players with even defter touches from the outside of their boots. No Englishman, however, embodies the essence of good football and no individual currently burns more brightly than Joe in the Premiership firmament. The future shone brightly and he seemed on the cusp of even greater things.

At the start of the 2006/07 season, Chelsea were odds-on to win their third consecutive title and Joe had unfinished business for England as he told the *Sun*, upon his return from Germany. 'We just didn't get the job done. Now we have to start all over again and look to win the European Championship in 2008'.

In the superb film *Catch Me If You Can*, Christopher Walken tells the story of two mice who fell into a bucket of cream. One of the mice soon gives up the fight and drowns. The other struggles and fights, keeps striving. Eventually the cream turns to butter and the mouse steps free. Joe Cole was the second mouse.

14

Hey Joe

"If you can't pick the brains of Scolari and Capello you
shouldn't be in the game."
Joe Cole, autumn 2008

Let's fast forward two and bit years to a late summer's evening in Barcelona. It's a few months after the Euros of 2008 – a competition conspicuous by the absence of England – and now they are struggling against Andorra. It's a World Cup qualifying match against a team positioned 186th in the rankings. Fabio Capello is the new England coach, but their personnel and drabness of play largely remain the same. Joe had previously failed to start in the last three matches, but had eventually come of the bench to net a last-gasp equaliser against the Czech Republic.

Joe was introduced at half time with the game scoreless. Within six minutes he had scored twice, saving the Italian's blushes and boosting England's chances of qualifying. The first was a typical Cole volley, beautifully executed as he slammed home Joleon Lescott's cushioned turn back. Soon afterwards

315

he clinched the match with a first-time effort past the Andorran keeper after collecting Rooney's pass.

Joe was on for his first ever hat trick but dropped deeper into midfield, immediately incurring the wrath of Capello. If there was the slightest hint of Joe altering his tactical manifesto, he would be targeted by the establishment. What was very clear, however, was that Joe Cole was the most popular player in the England squad; the only player that the fans believed in; the only one capable of bringing any 'joie de vive' to the proceedings.

A few nights later England whipped Croatia 4-1 in Zagreb to smash their proud home record of 35 unbeaten qualifying matches. It buried the bitter memories of their exit from the Euros the previous winter. The match hinged on the dismissal of the Croatian defender Kovac for a brutal elbow to Joe's head on 50 minutes. Bloodied and dazed, Joe was substituted but still he played for his club the following weekend setting up Chelsea's first goal as they crushed Manchester City, the latest members of the billionaire's boys club. Joe was a hero by anybody standards.

'There is no greater indictment of English football - and there are many from which to choose – than its persistent reluctance to make Joe Cole feel indispensable.'
RICHARD WILLIAMS, GUARDIAN

The 2006/7 season was a disastrous season for Joe as he missed the first two months of the campaign with a knee injury sustained on the club's American tour. A stress fracture of the foot in December cost him another four months. The knee ligament injury was against the ML All-Stars at the Toyota Park in Chicago. The England star had only been on the field for a few minutes when he picked up the knock.

Speaking to Sky Sports after the match, a concerned Jose Mourinho lamented the loss of his star: 'That's a real problem. If you tell me there is no problem with Joe Cole and we lose 10-0, then that is better.'

Joe came back for an abortive 10-game return, spending most of them on the bench. The most notable of these was when he scored on a wet night at Blackburn, in a 2-0 victory over Mark Hughes' side in a Carling Cup match. The Islington idol opened the scoring on 52 minutes with a remarkable back heel from Kalou's low cross. Then he was hit by a further problem, injuring his foot in a drawn game against Manchester United. But Joe made a remarkable comeback, defying the agony to return months ahead of schedule.

He told the *Daily Mail*: 'It's a rare injury for footballers and it's normally six to eight months out. I managed to come back in three and half months and managed to play for the last two months of Chelsea's season so I have to be pleased. It's still not right and I have not been able to train properly, but Chelsea needed me and so did England so I came back and did my stuff. It's been frustrating but much worse things happen in life.'

Typical Joe, making light of a serious injury and thinking of others. Such is the pressure on a top player in the modern game, they often have to play in pain with the constant threat of a career-ending injury hanging over them. The increased mental toughness that Joe had acquired in recent years was a key factor in helping him make such a speedy recovery. If he had suffered these injuries in his earlier years, he probably would have doubted that he was capable of getting back on the pitch so quickly.

Joe had been living up to the deafening advance drum rolls all his life, but he was soon back in business and showing the fans that he had lost none of his special talents.

Stats available for the 2005/6 season show that the former West Ham schemer averaged 24 passes and 5 dribbles per game. Chelsea were sorely missing his skills, as a rejuvenated Manchester United left them trailing in the Premier League. The first cracks were starting to appear in the fragile relationship between Abramovich and Mourinho.

Joe certainly did his stuff, firing Chelsea ahead in the first home leg of the semi-final of the Champions league clash with Liverpool. An incisive break from Carvalho, carried on by Drogba, set Joe up to beat Jose Reina from eight yards. It was Chelsea's first goal against Liverpool in a European competition, but it was not enough to stop them crashing out on penalties in the second leg, at Anfield. Joe had a fine game and was often the only forward taking the game to the hosts. The only blemish was his challenge which gave away the set piece that gave Liverpool the decisive goal of the game. That defeat really signalled the end of the Mourinho era at Chelsea. With Abramovich's dream of a Champions League win dying for yet another year, the oligarch finally lost patience with 'the special one'.

The loss of Joe for so long rankled the Portuguese coach. He told the *Mail*: 'Joe was a key player last year. It was the best season of his life and he was crucial from the first minute to the last. This season he has had 5 minutes here and there.'

When the new champions Manchester United faced the Blues in the Cup Final, Sir Alex Ferguson was anxious to land another double for his team. But it was not to be and Chelsea gained a modicum of revenge with a narrow 1-0 victory in extra time, with Joe only playing for 45 minutes before being substituted by Robben. Joe struggled to make any impact against Sir Alex's team and had a disappointing match in what was a poor advertisement for the two finest sides in the land. The only thing of note that Joe did in the game was a lunge on the United defender Wes Brown that narrowly escaped a booking. Nevertheless it was a good ending for Joe and his Cup Winners medal completed his collection of domestic honours; all that was missing from his trophy cabinet was the elusive European Champions League medal.

In the summer Joe scored another fine goal for his country, this time in the 3-0 win in a Euro 2008 qualifier in Estonia. England's campaign had suffered some major setbacks and coach Steve McClaren was obviously delighted to welcome him back.

The season, however, started badly for Joe as he clashed with Mourinho after being named as a substitute in Chelsea's first four Premier games. His position at the club was further undermined by Mourinho's links to the Porto winger, Ricardo Quaresma (a player that was to later join him in Milan). Earlier Mourinho had talked in the press of his 'untouchables', a collection of his favourites who seemed to be integral to his plans and whose place in the team was unchallenged. No need to guess whose names were at the top of the list: Terry and Lampard, followed closely by Makele, Essien, Carvalho, Cole (A), Drogba, Ballack and Cech. But there was no mention of a certain Cole (J).

Mourinho's blind faith in the dynamic duo of Lamps and JT was to prove his undoing. Despite the praise and kudos heaped on the pair, they were unable to bring the Champions League to the Bridge or even help England qualify for the Euros. Perhaps inevitably, Mourinho left Chelsea on a bright day in late September, 2007. Although, in his famous American Express ad he stated, 'my life is about keeping one step ahead.' He later admitted that he should have quit the Bridge after the Cup Final. The *Observer* ran an article stating that Mourinho's relationship with Terry had deteriorated. Joe's views on Mourinho's exit were not recorded.

The fans were, and many still are, devastated by the departure of the man that had brought them back-to-back title (two Carling Cups and an FA Cup). The general consensus was that the only fitting replacement for Mourinho would have to have the looks of George Clooney, the technical knowledge of Wenger, the passion of a Shankly, the strategy of Johan Cruyff, the wit of Bill Hicks, the urbanity of Bryan Ferry, and the ruthlessness of Stalin. Instead of Hugh Grant, the replacement was one Avram Grant, a former Israel national team coach with no managerial experience in England.

Joe blossomed under Grant who, to his credit, did remarkably well in very difficult circumstances. His biggest problem was that he could never win over the fans who believed he wasn't the man to step into José's Armani shoes. To the guys in the Matthew Harding stand he was just Abramovich's stooge, a man completely out of his depth and lacking the charisma required of a Chelsea manager.

Still, in one of his early matches, Chelsea had a fine 2-1 victory in Valencia. Their star striker David Villa gave them an early lead but Joe equalised in the 21st minute from close range. The goal was set up by their new French winger Florent Malouda, another contender for Joe's spot in the team. Joe created the winner for Didier Drogba with what some papers described as 'the pass of the century', a majestic ball, struck with the outside of his right foot. It instantly took four defenders out of the match and fell perfectly for Drogba to run past a defender and rifle home a spectacular goal.

Grant had an understated and relaxed style which Joe responded to instantly... and it showed. Manchester City visited the Bridge late in October and were slaughtered 6-0, with Joe racing through to score number four with a classic finish. The City fullback Javier Garrido was given a torrid time all afternoon by Joe and there is footage of him actually giving up the chase when Joe accelerated towards the goal. This particular incident has passed into City folklore: 'Were you there when Garrido went AWOL against Joe Cole, the game when Chelsea scored six? And it only cost me £48!' That result really made the pundits sit up and take notice. It was a highly significant score line in view of the fact that the Blues had failed to score more than four goals in a Premier game throughout Mourinho's three-year tenure. The Portuguese coach may have had self-possession, even grandeur, but, despite their efficiency, it was never transmitted to his teams.

Chelsea legend Kerry Dixon told the *Guardian*: 'Everybody responds differently to different styles of management and Avram's quiet manner is obviously liked by some of the players. Look at Joe Cole – he's in great form.'

Joe himself was delighted that he had started in nine of the first dozen games of Grant's appointment. The fact that he had a new manager, brimming with new ideas and assisted by new coaches, helped him play a much more expansive game.

The turbulence at Chelsea was almost a parallel to Joe's England career during that period. A hat trick of 3-0 wins at Wembley (over Israel, Russia and Estonia) boosted the technocrat McClaren's hopes of going to the Euros. Joe featured in all of these games, playing his part in the victories as he continued to deliver consistently strong performances, including an athletic scissor kick that was deflected wide for the corner that led to the opening goal against Russia.

He was making the problem left wing position his own. Statistics from the victory over Estonia show that during the match he made nine dribbles, three times more than his nearest challenger, club mate Shaun Wright-Phillips. Shaun had a good run of form around then, after struggling to establish himself at Stamford Bridge following his £21m move from Manchester City.

After scoring the opening goal against Israel, Shaun thanked Joe in the *Daily Mail* for being his inspiration: 'Joe is an idol for everybody and I am a believer that you can learn from every player you work with. To have someone who has been through it all is a plus. Me and Coley are really good friends and chat about all sorts of things. The most important thing is that we enjoy each other's company and there is a tight bond there.'

Joe and his chum headed to Russia for a vital match, with England needing a win to secure qualification. The game was played on a plastic pitch in the cauldron of the Luzhiniki Stadium. Rooney fired England ahead in the first half with a crashing volley, but then let Russia back into the game when he conceded a penalty on the hour. Tottenham striker Pavlyuchenko shot the winner shortly afterwards. For his part, Joe played for 80 minutes before being replaced by Peter Crouch. The limited supply of the ball meant that he had a quiet night, as England put on another car crash of a display.

To his credit, Joe had tried some runs at the Russian defence, but the play was too central. With the debutant left back Lescott struggling against the fast strikers, Joe had to drop deeper to help contain the new Russian star, Arshavin. The temperature dropped and the damp surface of the pitch started to freeze, making it increasingly harder for Joe to impose himself on proceedings.

Before the match, when asked by the media about the problems of the plastic pitch, Joe had a prosaic reply: 'For me, the ball is going to be round and its leather so there's no excuse really.'

The tabloids reported that Joe was seen leaving the stadium in tears, finding it hard to disguise his bitter disappointment at England's loss. He later told the *Telegraph*: 'Football is a harsh game sometimes and especially at this level and four minutes has changed it completely. The only thing you can do now is try and put it into perspective. We are all down as anything. We are all really down.'

Abramovich's wealth had done little to promote the cause of the English national team. Although the squad was packed with Chelsea players, they were, apart from Joe, not really up to the demands of international football at the highest level. The billionaire, however, had certainly boosted the fortunes of Russian football by his investments, which included funding the generous salary of their coach, Gus Hiddink. That night the investment paid off handsomely as Hiddink tactically outwitted McClaren.

England were given a brief stay of execution by Israel's shock 2-1 victory over Russia in Tel Aviv - the Israel striker Tal Ben Haim had been promised a holiday by Joe if his country beat Russia - so England just needed a draw against Croatia to get to the Euros. Joe's gesture was in vain though, because England threw their chance of qualification away by losing to Croatia on a rain drenched evening at Wembley.

Joe played for 80 minutes before being replaced by Darren Bent, at that time England were 2-3 down and heading out of the competition. Three minutes earlier the Croatian sub, Petric, had judiciously shot the winner after sloppy marking by the England defence. For the millions watching on TV, it elicited a sensation that spiders were crawling up their spine. Although Joe had an early, diving header that went just wide, his usual exquisite passing was awry and was unable to provide any real thrust down the flanks. The match stats show that he made 29 passes with a completion rate of 82.8%. A pinpoint cross led to England's equaliser when Defoe was checked going for it.

One of the iconic images of the modern game is that of a lachrymose Steve McClaren, sipping tea on the touchline and sheltering from the downpour under a huge umbrella.

After trailing 2-0 England had clawed their way back to 2-2, which would have been enough to put them through. Terry Venables, McClaren's number two, had pleaded with him to bring on Owen Hargreaves to 'padlock the door' and safeguard the lead.

Joe, who was beginning to tire, would have probably been the player subbed to make way for the pre- Raphaelite hair-styled Hargreaves, arguably the finest midfield holding player in Europe. But Venables' words of wisdom were ignored and England paid the ultimate price... as did McClaren, who was sacked the next morning and replaced by the flinty, brusque Fabio Capello, who had won league titles with Milan, Real Madrid, Roma and Juventus but had not coached at International level.

In an interview on Radio 5, Clarence Seedorf, who had played under the Italian, when asked if Capello would tolerate the WAGs and hangers-on, replied that he would rather use 'lesser' players, who would work harder for the team. Interestingly, he also said that Mourinho had been superb at Porto but had developed a lack of respect for other managers. Joe, it seemed, ticked a lot of Capello's boxes.

Now Joe returned to Premiership action as Chelsea maintained their progress on both domestic and European fronts. Grant's team went unbeaten for 16 games until Arsenal beat them 1-0 at the Emirates, with the former Chelsea star, Gallas, scoring after a mistake by Cech. Amazingly it was to be the only Premier game that Chelsea were to lose under Grant. The problem was that the formidable war machine that was Manchester United were in irresistible form, their star winger, Ronaldo, notching up over 40 goals in the season and voted the 'best player in the world', as United swept aside everything in their path. The league had developed into a three horse race until Chelsea's victory over Arsenal in the spring effectively ruined their chances of the title.

Around that time Mourinho was kicking his Gucci-shod heels in Portugal and was seen driving around in a £2million 612 Scaglietti Ferrari, that had been given to him by Roman Abramovich, five months after his departure from Stamford Bridge. The car was one of 60 made to celebrate Ferrari's 60th birthday and was even engraved 'The Special One'.

Away from football, Joe was keeping busy, enjoying the trappings of a very wealthy young man. Being a great boxing fan, he travelled to Las Vegas to see his favourite fighter, Ricky Hatton, beat the Mexican former lightweight champion Luis Castillo in four rounds. Also present at the fight were Manchester United stars Wayne Rooney and Rio Ferdinand, and the pop star Robbie Williams.

Another singer, Lionel Ritchie, sang at John Terry's wedding reception held at Blenheim Palace. It was said that he was paid £250,000 for his performance, a special request from Terry's bride, Toni Poole. Joe and Carly were amongst the guests who must have thought that they were back in the Shed. Ritchie, however, was upset by his treatment at the hands of some of the multi-millionaires and told the *Sun*, 'I imagine this is what it's like at a working man's club'.

Joe has met so many stars and celebs over the year that he is largely immune to it all, but in the late winter the legend that is Diego Maradona appeared at Cobham, causing quite a stir. Joe told the Metro: 'It made my day. He's one of the few people in the world I really wanted to meet. He's such a legend that you just go a bit silly. His aura was amazing'.

Claude Makele had previously given Joe a signed Zidane shirt – which Joe now has framed at his home and joked that he would now have to pretend he has played against him – but it's unclear whether he managed to get Diego's autograph to add to his collection.

At that time Joe's fame was spreading fast and, according to a gay and lesbian dating website, he had surpassed David Beckham as the biggest icon among gay male soccer fans.

Joe continued to increase his portfolio of properties overseas, including one in Dubai on the Palm Jumeirah. This was one of the largest and most ambitious projects in the world, with an array of amenities including a private beach club and luxury hotel complex built on the artificial archipelago. He also purchased a luxury penthouse apartment in the Hua Hin Country Club near Bangkok, located on the southeast shores of Thailand. Joe selected it because the area was considered to be a golfer's paradise.

He told the *Asia Property Report*, 'I took advice from advisors who look after my property abroad. I am not a good golfer but I do enjoy a round. Firstly you have to invest your money wisely, so you've always got to look at location.' In fact, many Chelsea players were taking advantage of the slump in the housing market by splashing out millions of pounds on luxury homes that were going at reduced prices. As one estate agent said, 'These guys have never heard of boom and bust, just boom and boom.'

Always a boxing fan Joe said that he hoped to get a chance to watch some Thai boxing matches on his trips. Time was at a premium though, with the constant. demands of the game.

The wheels started to come off Chelsea's season when Tottenham and Barnsley knocked them out of the domestic Cups. Chelsea met Tottenham in the Final of the Carling Cup at Wembley. Joe had clinched Chelsea's place in the final when he had scored the only goal of the game up at Goodison to give them a 3-1 win on aggregate over Everton. The strike was superb, Florent Malouda's 50 yard pass (almost a reprise of Joe's 'ball of the century to Drogba in Valencia) was controlled and dispatched in a sublime piece of skill. Joe may have been wearing the day-glo yellow away kit, but through Capello's eyes he would have stood out in a bin bag.

Amazingly, Joe was left out of the opening line up in the Carling Cup Final and, although he came on in extra time, he could not prevent them from losing 1-2. The whole game was surrounded in controversy and, even though Terry eventually started the game, rumours were rife that he had been omitted from the original line up. Concern was growing for his form and fitness, the same concerns that Mourinho had in the final days of his command. Terry and coach Ten Cate (who left soon after) had a heated exchange the day before Spurs victory. The shock defeat intensified the pressure on Avram Grant and Joe demanded talks with him to clear the air. For the second year running he had not started in a Carling Cup final and, at that time, his long term future at Chelsea looked in doubt.

Once again Joe responded in the only way he knew how: in the 4-0 rout of West Ham at Upton Park, he scored the second goal when he met Anelka's cut back, it was a perfect drive past the Irons keeper, Green. Joe refused to celebrate his classy goal out of respect to the West Ham fans, with whom he had enjoyed such a happy relationship with previously. There was certainly still something between, which is remarkable when compared to the vitriol and contempt that was heaped on Lampard. The Chicken Run may not burst into a verse of the Spandau Ballet hit any more, but their respect for their former captain was tangible. The youngster had chosen Upton Park to start his career and the bond would never be broken.

Another way in which Joe had endeared himself to the East Enders was when, in the previous season's clash (in which Chelsea again scored four times), the West Ham programme had run a piece on Joe's remarkable gesture towards his former coach. Peter Brabrook. The ex-Chelsea winger, 69 at the time, faced the prospect of paying a substantial, five-figure sum for a double knee-replacement operation, to repair the damage caused by 18-years of wear and tear from his professional career. Joe had heard about Brabrook's problem and sent him a cheque to cover the cost.

Peter wrote in the programme: 'Joe won't like me mentioning the whole situation to be honest because he's not the sort to shout about things like this. But I wanted people to know what kind of person Joe is. The thing is he had his own worries with injuries. I can't thank him enough. The best thing is he hasn't changed. He was a credit to West Ham. Is a credit to Chelsea and will always be a credit to himself and his family.'

Russell Brand, the controversial comedian and actor, is a staunch West Ham fan. Joe had been to see his stand-up and they have a mutual respect for each other's talents. Brand described Joe, in his *Guardian* column, as 'a man who left the Boleyn with his head held high and his integrity unblemished.' One of Joe's best ever games in a Chelsea shirt was in the epic 4-4 draw at Tottenham in the closing weeks of the season, when he scored twice, a first for him in a Premiership game. Joe was Chelsea's star man that night and when he put them 3-1 up, it appeared to give them an unassailable lead. But Spurs pegged them back to 3-3 with goals from Berbatov and Tom Huddlestone. Determined to cut United's five-point lead, Joe scored Chelsea's fourth with a brilliant solo goal. Robbie Keane, who has since moved to Liverpool, equalised in the dying seconds to deny Chelsea victory and two vital points.

Ultimately, Chelsea dropped too many points, shipped too many goals and generally lacked guidance at crucial times and, for the second year running, finished second to Manchester United. The contest went to the last game of the season, with the destination of the title in doubt until the last minutes. United clinched the title with a win at Wigan, with Chelsea held at home by a late equaliser from Bolton. Joe was understandably disappointed at not regaining the title, but he had the chance of finishing the season in glory as the team had made it through to the final of the Champions League. The game was played at the Luzhniki stadium, where Joe had played against Russia.

The game has since passed into legend as United clinched a remarkable double of domestic and European league titles. Joe had been quiet in the last few weeks of the domestic season and the fans were hoping that he would explode in Moscow. He faced a difficult opponent, in the shape of the United fullback Patrice Evra, and did not have his best game.

Ronaldo put United ahead in the 26th minute with the 42nd goal of his stupendous season, but Lampard got the equaliser with an opportunist goal just on half time. Early in the second half Chelsea took control of the game and Joe had his best phase of the match, showing some neat little touches. The game wore on and turned into a real war of attrition.

Eventually, after 99 minutes and the game in extra time, Joe was replaced by Anelka. Grant was hoping that the former Real Madrid man could win the match with his pace but, ironically, his introduction was to lose Chelsea the match, as he missed a penalty in the shoot-out. The real culprit though was John Terry, whose nerve failed him at the crucial moment when he could have scored the penalty that would have taken the Champions League to London for the first time. He told the world that he slipped when he took the kick, but to many pundits it looked like he might have slipped after the kick was taken. Terry disintegrated into tears as United celebrated. The Russian oligarch had suffered the biggest humiliation of his football career on his native soil.

Inevitably, Grant was sacked a few days later and soon big Phil Scolari was appointed manager. Many believe he should have used that opportunity to 'clean house' and completely revamp the club, but Terry remained and Lampard signed a new deal worth £39m. This came as a surprise to some fans as, for a long time, it looked like Lampard was going to link up with his mentor Mourinho, who was now at Inter-Milan. Lampard was at pains to tell the media that it was, 'never about being greedy, my concern was making the right football decision.'

Only Joe was free from any stigma or scandal. Perhaps the greatest accolade of his Chelsea career came when the fans voted for him, over Michael Ballack and Ricardo Carvalho, as the club's player of the year. Marcel Desailly, the former Chelsea Captain, presented him with the award in the special ceremony at Stamford Bridge. It put him amongst all time Chelsea greats like Peter Osgood, Charlie Cooke and Ruud Gulllit.

But, incredibly, Joe's future seemed in doubt as the tabloids questioned Luiz Felipe Scolari's confidence in him, as Scolari had made every effort to sign fellow Brazilian Robinho from Real Madrid. At one time it looked so likely that Robinho would sign for the Blues that the Megastore even announced that Robinho shirts would be available soon. But it was not to be. There were some new rich kids on the block and, on the final day of the transfer window, Robinho sensationally signed for Manchester City, now the richest club in football. City were about to be taken over by the mega-rich Arabs of the Abu Dhabi monarchy and their hi-jacking of the Chelsea bid smashed the British transfer record.

If the truth be known, Joe had been unperturbed by the speculation about Robinho, who had been substituted by Madrid 19 times in the previous season. After all, in his five years at Chelsea, Joe had already seen off the likes of Damien Duff, Juan Sebastian Veron, Arjen Robben, Jesper Gronkjaer and Shaun Wright-Phillips. In an interview with the *Times*, Joe explained: 'It's a way of life at a big club. You come to

Chelsea and you have to expect competition. I thrive on it. There are always big-name players at this club and I love competing with them. It can only make me a better player.'

He started the Scolari era in the best possible fashion by scoring Chelsea's first goal of the season in the 4-0 thrashing of Cup-winners Portsmouth at Stamford Bridge. To the delight of the fans, Chelsea had started in a determined fashion, stung by last season's failures and determined to recapture the Premiership title.

Joe scored in another 4-0 romp, as a rampant Chelsea launched a fresh assault on Europe, thrashing Bordeaux in their opening Champions League fixture. In the previous campaign, Joe thought that the Chelsea played in too rigid a manner, but under Scolari their football had become more fluid.

This was shown to be the case when Chelsea defeated Aston Villa 2-0 at Stamford Bridge to confirm their place at the top of the table in early October. A useful Villa side, which had racked up some useful results over Chelsea in previous seasons, were comprehensively beaten. At the hub of everything was Joe Cole who was growing stronger with each passing week of the season. Joe opened the scoring and drove his team forward.

At that point of his career Joe seemed to inhabit his persona more completely than ever before. He has gone on record as saying that the class of 2008/9 is the best Chelsea team he has been in, adding that the summer signing, Deco, was the best player he had played with. It is debateable whether Joe would have made statements like this if Mourinho had stayed on at the club.

Two main challenges lay ahead: winning a Champions League medal and taking England to South Africa for the 2010 World Cup. The Champions League has, as any fan will tell you, been tantalisingly close in the past: in 2004 Chelsea were the classiest team of the semi-finalists but Mourinho's Porto lifted the trophy; Mourinho should have won it again in 2005, but the infamous Liverpool game denied them; John 'tears of a clown' Terry blew it in Moscow...

As for the next World Cup, Joe is in a unique position. With his Cockney accent and fierce patriotic streak, he is now the most quintessentially English player, but at the same time, the most South American in style and football intelligence.

Joe is approaching the prime of his career... and at a time when his club and country needed him most. And Chelsea is becoming bigger than ever... no longer because of Abramovich's money or Mourinho's histrionics, but because of a special brand of football of which the finest exponent is the best player of his generation – Joe Cole.